G000066406

SHARED LIVES

Alexander Stephen, shipbuilder
&
James Templeton, carpet maker

MAUREEN BORLAND

First published in 2006 by

Maureen Borland
4 Shanter Place
Kilmarnock KA3 7JB
Tel: 01563 524426
email: jamesborland@freeuk.com

© Maureen Borland 2006

All rights reserved. No part of this publication may be reproduced, stored in a retrieval system, or transmitted, in any form or by any means, without the prior permission in writing of the publisher, nor be otherwise circulated in any form of binding or cover other than that in which it is published without similar condition including this condition being imposed on the subsequent purchaser.

A catalogue entry is available from the British Library.

ISBN
0-9552714-0-1

Cover design by Art Factory, Ayr

Printed, bound and designed by Woolnough Bookbinding Ltd
Irthlingborough, Northants NN9 5SE

Dedicated to three generations of my family:
David and Kevin
Philip and Leigh
Andrew

CONTENTS

ACKNOWLEDGEMENTS

I OWE John Maggs, chairman of Maggs Bros, and his wife, Dr D E Wright, the granddaughter of the Revd Archibald Templeton, a debt of gratitude for giving me the idea for this book.

After some initial genealogical research, I discovered the Templeton connection to Alexander Stephen. Mr & Mrs A M M Stephen, Sir Stephen and Lady Young responded instantly to my suggestion of writing this book, and I could never have completed it without their generous help. They gave me free access to their extensive archives and were delightful hosts when I visited them. David Stephen was the source I turned to when I needed help with yachts and yacht racing.

Many Stephen/Templeton family members contributed in no small measure and I am grateful for all their help. They included, D A S MacLellan; Lady MacLellan; Christopher J C Grant; Heather Aitkenson; Alison Goodbody; Mrs W F Cairns Smith; Lesley Grayburn; John D H Whitcombe and his sisters Mary Burgess and Elizabeth Dixon. I should like especially to thank Lois and Peter Taylor, for their kind hospitality; the day I spent with them was one of the highlights during my research.

I must mention a very dear friend, Jennifer Bradford Knox. She was a diligent researcher at the National Archives at Kew, and without her help I would have been totally lost. Margaret Templeton (no relation); Angus Martin; Donald Macalister Hall; Norma Darbyshire; A D B Sloan; I G Garnham and his daughters Hannah and Kate, and their friend Elinor Cousin; Revd M Wright LTH, Minister of Craigrownie Parish Church, all assisted and I am grateful for their help.

Robert Biggin, Archivist of the Templeton Collection held by Stoddard International plc, Ronald Wilkie, George Grant and the directors of Stoddard, all deserve my very sincerest thanks. I spent many happy hours delving into the Templeton Archives, and I thank Robert Biggin for his endless patience. To the late Alex D Montgomery, Group Export Director, I spent such a delightful morning with him in Crieff. I knew how ill he was, and as we parted he urged me to finish the book before it was too late. Unfortunately I failed him.

In mentioning libraries/archives I can do no more than list them and hope they will know how much I appreciated their help. If I mention the University of Glasgow Archive Services, first, it is because they hold the largest collection of Stephen/Templeton archives. To Lesley Richmond, George Gardener and the rest of the staff of the Archives I am deeply indebted. I should also like to thank the University of Glasgow Library, Special Collections.

The staff of the following libraries and archives all deserve a mention and my thanks; Argyll & Bute Archives; Arbroath Library; Campbeltown Library & Museum; Carnegie Library Ayr; Dick Library, Kilmarnock; Dundee Central Library; East Dunbartonshire Libraries; Girton College, Cambridge; Haddington Local History Library; Malton District Library; Glasgow District Libraries, Mitchell Library; National Archives of Scotland; Columbia University in the City of New York; Newnham College, Cambridge; University of Durham; University of Edinburgh; Watt Library, Greenock;

All the following have also helped in my research and I thank them sincerely. General Register Office for Scotland (Scotlandspeople) a web site that saved me hours and hours of research time. General Register Office, Southport, for English BMDs and for their help in searching Consul Records. Strathclyde Family History Centre. The Royal College of Physicians, Edinburgh. The Royal Infirmary Glasgow. The staff of Templeton House, formerly Thinacre, Ayr.

The Archivists at Merchiston Castle School; Fettes College; Uppingham; Loretto and Carlinfield, all deserve a mention.

I should like to thank Dr Michael Halls and Dr Angela Summerfield for their permission to use the quotations on the back cover. Roderick Brown also deserves my special thanks, he was helpful and generous as always.

I must pay a special vote of thanks to my husband, Dr J C Borland, he was an unpaid research assistant, book collector, computer expert and general 'gofer'.

I apologise to any whose help I have not acknowledged, memory can sometimes let me down. I have attempted to locate all copyright holders but in some cases this has been impossible. I apologise unreservedly to anyone whose copyright I may have infringed.

Maureen Borland. 2006

ILLUSTRATIONS

(1) Alexander Stephen. (*Courtesy* A M M Stephen)

(2) James Templeton. (*Courtesy* Templeton Archives, Stoddard International plc)

(3) Williamina [Mina] Stewart. (*Courtesy* Mrs A Goodbody)

(4) Alexander [Al] Stephen. (*Courtesy* A M M Stephen)

(4) John Stephen [Uncle John]. (*Courtesy* A M M Stephen)

(5) The Golden Wedding of James and Mary Templeton.
    - back row l to r: James Murray T, Maud S, Elsie S, James T, Mary S, Fred S. Al S, Alex S, Alice T; front row l to r: Mary S, Ann T, Mary T, James T, Agnes Jane T, JST; photo on chair Revd Archie; seated on floor Bernard S. (*Courtesy* Mrs L M Taylor)

(5) The Wedding of Alice Templeton to D H L Young (*Courtesy* Mrs L M Taylor)

(6) Frederic J Stephen. (*Courtesy* A M M Stephen)

(6) Sir Alexander Murray Stephen. (*Courtesy* A M M Stephen)

(7) Fearann Coille, Dunoon. (*Crown Copyright* RCAHMS)

(7) Knockderry Castle, Cove. (*Crown Copyright* RCAHMS)

(8) George Scott MacLellan (*Courtesy* Lady MacLellan)

(8) Maud MacLellan (*Courtesy* Lady MacLellan)

(9) Elizabeth Helen Templeton. (*Courtesy* Mrs L M Taylor)

(10) Auchenfail, the Ayrshire home of Alex E and Daisy Stephen. (*Courtesy* Mrs W F Cairns Smith)

(10) Kelly after the fire. (*Courtesy* Mrs W F Cairns Smith)

(11) Mary [Marie] Caroline Ada Templeton. (*Courtesy* Mrs L M Taylor)

(11) Agnes Robson, Mary Templeton, Margaret Frew, daughters of Alex E and Daisy Stephen. (*Courtesy* Mrs W F Cairns Smith)

(12) Frederick Henry Young [FHY]. (*Courtesy* the Executors of the late F H Young. Portrait gifted by the Trustees to Corporation of Glasgow 1967)

(12) Iris Deacon Young. (*Courtesy* the Executors of the late F H Young. Portrait gifted by the Trustees to Corporation of Glasgow 1967)

(13) Agnes R Young, Daisy Stephen, Margaret, baby Patricia. (*Courtesy* Mrs W F Cairns Smith)

(14) Revd Archie and Elizabeth Helen T, Dorothy, Joanna, Isabel, Constance. (*Courtesy* Mrs L M Taylor)

(14) Kenneth Templeton with JS Templeton's casket. (*Courtesy* A S, D A and R K Templeton and Mrs S T Macmillan)

(15) Sir Arthur Young, Duke and Duchess of York, Fred H Young (*Courtesy* Templeton Archives, Stoddard International plc. The photograph was probably taken by a press photographer of the *Daily Record* or *Evening Times*. It has been impossible to say which, therefore, both are entitled to recognition.)

(15) Cecily C MacLellan (*Courtesy* Lady MacLellan)

(16) Eric Aubrey Hawks and Nancy Whitcombe. (*Courtesy* Mrs Mary Burgess)

PART ONE
1795 - 1866

"Life I see is a struggle (and) none know what the soul is - what life is in body (and) spirit till the trials have put them in relation to the stern realities of what is around us ... None can escape the world's heavy cares who live truly (and) grasp such cares boldly ..."

The Diary of James Murray Templeton.
Columbia University, in the City of New York,
Rare Book and Manuscript Library.
Thomas Lake Harris Papers.

In The Beginning

(SAAVEDRA) Miguel de Cervantes, the Spanish writer of *Don Quixote*, said that according to his grandmother 'there are only two families in the world, the *Haves* and the *Have-nots*.' The family of Alexander Stephen, shipbuilder and James Templeton, carpet maker, were among the *Haves*, although it has to be said they did not begin as *Haves*, only by hard work, innovation, imagination and good luck did they prosper.

Alexander Stephen was born on 15 March 1795, at Footdee in Aberdeenshire, the sixth child of William Stephen and Ann Smith. The story starts however when another Alexander, the uncle of William, moved to Burghead in 1750 and began to build and repair small fishing boats. In 1778, at the age of nineteen, William left the family farm of his father, also named William, and joined Alexander as an apprentice shipbuilder. Then at the age of twenty-five William thought he was sufficiently established in his career to contemplate marriage. He was fortunate when he chose Ann Smith as his wife; they were married in February 1784, and the union was blessed with eight sons and four daughters. Little is known of Anne's background except that she brought to the marriage a deep and unquestioning belief in God and God's teachings.

William admitted, later in life that until he was fifteen, in spite of family prayers, he had no interest in religion, and found attendance at family prayers tiresome. However, as a teenager he had an encounter with a wicked woman who opened his eyes to the dangers of sin. Although he did not elaborate on the nature of the sin, it could have been his first sexual encounter. Whatever it was, it had a profound effect on him. He prayed for the first time in his life and went on praying for another fourteen days.

William spent ten years in Burghead before moving to the Aberdeen Yard of John Cochar. In 1793, he felt he was ready to set up his own Yard in Aberdeen. Success did not come easy, orders for ships were slow to appear, nevertheless, the Yard soon established a reputation that it was never to lose. Clients knew that a ship built by a Stephen Yard would be of the finest quality of workmanship.

After initial disappointments, William ran the shipyard in Aberdeen with some success, and this was further enhanced when his sons William and Alexander joined him. William, junior, however, was not satisfied to be an understudy to his father, and he set up his own Yard in Arbroath, a decision that was to cost his father and brother Alexander dearly.

What manner of man was Alexander Stephen? He took the building of ships from sail to steam, and from wood to iron. He saw new routes open up and trade expand, and he was always in the forefront of the latest developments. He was born at a time when sea-faring and sea travel were hazardous, when ships could be wrecked off the rocky coasts of Scotland with a frequency that was horrifying. Alexander was a pioneer, not just a builder of ships, he was also concerned to see that the physical, moral and spiritual welfare of his workers was never neglected.

It was said of him that '[he] was a truly good man, but illiterate, self-centred and in many ways narrow-minded...'[1]

The use of the word illiterate is puzzling in that it usually means cannot read or write, but Alexander could do both with great skill. However, he was not skilled in the social mores. His portrait, painted when he was in his late sixties, shows a man of quiet dignity; he had a strong, almost handsome face, but it was his eyes that held the measure of the man. He looked straight at you and in his expression there was the belief that this was a man you could trust. He was a good man, a man of principle; he was a man of unquestioning Faith in his Maker.

As in so many things he did, Alexander chose as his bride a girl who would give him a loving and stable home life for over half a century. On 23 January 1824, Alexander married the eighteen-year-old Elspeth Murray; she was the daughter of Andrew Murray, a farmer from Longhaven, and Helen Mearns. Elspeth was only two years old when her father died.

It would be surprising if, on the day of her marriage, Elspeth knew that she would become the mother of eighteen children. She had six sons and twelve daughters.

If a Stephen's ship was destroyed at sea, it was a source of deep distress to Alexander. He mourned not just the lost of lives but also the loss of a ship that had been built with such skill and craftsmanship:

> It was characteristic of the man that he was as proud of his workmen, and especially of those whom he had himself trained, as he was of his ships. He had a firm conviction that his "mennie" as he familiarly termed his apprentices, were fit to go anywhere and do anything which a shipwright ought to do; and if a tolerably arduous and salutary course of discipline and training might count for anything the conviction was well grounded.[2]

In 1826, the brig *Unicorn*, launched in 1823 was lost at sea, killing all hands, including Alexander's youngest brother James. He was just twenty-years-old. William, Alexander's father, had his own problems; he was involved in a lawsuit, which regrettably he lost and his creditors took over the Arbroath Yard. William held a bond for the Yard and unable to meet the full amount demanded and no alternative but to file for bankruptcy. This was granted on 1 January 1828.

Faced with financial ruin, William turned to Alexander and another son, John, an Advocate in Edinburgh, for a solution to his problems. John offered his parents a home in Edinburgh, while Alexander set about reviving the family's shipbuilding empire. He took over the ownership of the Arbroath Yard, and within seven years he was able to pay his father's debts, but a further set-back occurred when he lost the lawsuit that had been pending since 1828. Faced with trying to keep both the Aberdeen and Arbroath Yards working, Alexander decided to sell the Aberdeen Yard.

William did not live long after the collapse of the Arbroath Yard and he died before the end of 1829. Two years later Alexander's brother David also died, leaving an ironmongery business in Aberdeen which had failed. Alexander must have wondered if history would repeat itself.

In 1830 Alexander moved his growing family to Arbroath; in the first twelve years of their marriage he and Elspeth had eight children. There was little spare money to buy a property and so initially they rented a house. However in July 1836, after the birth of Mary, their ninth child, Alexander felt sufficiently wealthy to purchase two properties in Ladyloan for the price of two-hundred and ninety-two pounds and ten shillings.

In Campbeltown, on the Kintyre Peninsular, Thomas Templeton, like William Stephen, was building another dynasty. The Templetons had originally come, sometime in the seventeenth century, from Hapland, near the Boswell Estate at Auchinleck, Ayrshire.

Thomas, like the first William Stephen, was a tenant farmer, first at Crossibeg and later at Drumgarve, Campbeltown. He had been born in 1720, the same year as William Stephen. Thomas Templeton, during his very long life -- he lived to be eighty-seven-years-old -- was twice married. In November 1749 he married Janet Armour whose family were immigrants from Ayrshire. During the nine years of their marriage they had seven children; one son, Thomas, died in infancy and a second Thomas was born in 1759. It has not been possible to identify the exact date of Janet Armour's death but it must have been sometime after the birth of her son on 21 March 1759 and Thomas's second marriage to Agnes Colville on 1 July of that year.

It has been claimed, by one of Thomas's direct descendants, that he fathered twenty-one children. It has been possible to identify that he and Agnes Colville had twelve children between May 1760 and October 1783; add those to the seven he had with Janet Armour, and there appears to be only two for which no account can be found.

The migrants from Ayrshire were hardy and enterprising and later they would spread out from the Kintyre peninsular to dominate industry and commerce in the Victorian industrial areas of Scotland:

> These people [the Lowlanders from Ayrshire] formed a community distinct and separate from the original natives who were generally Celtic and Gaelic speaking. What is ... remarkable is the number of their names which came from Norman extraction -- Colville, Galbraith and Montgomery pre-eminently so.[3]

The wild beauty of Kintyre had much in common with the land they had left behind:

> [It] is eminently beautiful with a charm which comes of softness, of round-

ed form, of sequestered peacefulness. The hills are neither high nor rugged but they look out on those that are, on those of Arran to the east across the wide expanse of Kilbrannon Sound, on those of Jura on the west across the Sound of Lorne ... Drumgarve ... stood at the top of Glen Lussa. The stream which flows through its length, the largest in Kintyre, is full of salmon ... it finds its outlet to the eastern shore ... near the Crossibeg ...[4]

Archibald Templeton, the tenth child of Thomas but the fourth child of Agnes Colville, was born on 9 April 1765. Little is known of his early years but life at Crossibeg and Drumgarve must have been harsh in the extreme. Archibald did however make a good marriage when in April 1795 he married Ann Harvey. There are many spellings of the Harvey name in the Parish registers, but there appeared to be strong evidence to suggest that originally it stemmed from the Norman name of Harevei. That, anyway, was the tradition handed down in the family. Ann Harvey was just seventeen when she married Archibald; she was the daughter of James Harvey and Jean McNair -- her mother was Sarah Templeton, her father Nathaniel McNair. James Harvey was a successful merchant; his three sons were, Nathaniel a lawyer and banker, Robert a surgeon, and Archibald a merchant and financier. Nathaniel and Robert remained in Campbeltown but Archibald went to Glasgow. He died childless, and his vast fortune was divided between his many relatives, and for some reason, Ann received a more generous benefaction than others.

Archibald and Ann's eldest son James, was born in June 1802; Thomas in October 1806; Archibald in February 1811, and Nathaniel in November 1812. Some evidence exists to suggest that Ann's first four children, born between 1796 and 1800, did not survive beyond a few months. Certainly it would have been rare in those days for a woman to wait seven years before having her first child.

Archibald and Ann's four daughters were, Agnes born in December 1804; Jean in April 1809; Elizabeth in May 1814 and Ann in June 1817.

James Templeton's education had been rudimentary, yet, the Parish schooling he received in Campbeltown was exceptionally good. The little school could proudly boast that many of its former pupils became men of distinction.

Archibald's brother, John, took over the tenancy of the family farm at Drumgarve when their father died. Archibald was variously described as a manager of a tannery, a grain merchant, a maltster and a sadler.

As his father's various enterprises were unable to employ him, James, now a teenager, went to Glasgow to earn his living. Fortunately, though, his maternal uncle, Archibald Harvey, was well established in Glasgow and could help his young nephew find work in a wholesale drapery company. A diligent employee, James worked his way up to become an assistant and adviser to the owner. Unfortunately, the business was in decline, but as one door closed another opened. Around 1824, at the age of twenty-two, James was offered a position in Mexico, where he worked for the next three years, returning to Scotland in 1827, but he drifted for a few months, unsure and unable to make a firm decision as to the direction he wanted to follow.

Despite his lack of formal education, James was regarded as a man of culture and quiet dignity. He read widely and had a passion for the works of Byron, Walter Scott, Robert Burns and Alfred, Lord Tennyson. He had a love of music, and had a fine tenor voice, although he could not read a note of music. He had a natural instinct for colour and design and this, above all, probably persuaded him that his future career lay in the design and manufacture of Paisley shawls, where his Cousin Matthew Greenlees, also from Kintyre, had already established a business as a shawl manufacturer.

Matthew like James was, one of Thomas Templeton's ninety-nine grandchildren. James and Matthew were only two of the hundred and forty shawl manufacturers in Paisley. Of this number, Matthew became one of the most successful of them. He had a work-force of ninety-eight men and a hundred and sixty women.

To admire a Paisley shawl made in the early 1830s is to understand the sheer beauty of the intricate patterns and the colours. Two of the greatest designers of shawls were local men, Joseph Noel Paton, an artist who was much influenced by the work of William Blake, and Alexander Smith, poet, essayist, novelist and lace designer.

But even with such competition James's business thrived, to the extent that he felt confident he could soon support a wife. He married Mary Stewart on Thursday 1 December 1831, at the City of Glasgow Church. Mary was the daughter of John Stewart, a merchant tailor, and Margaret

Tod, daughter of John, a mason. Six children were born to James and Mary between 1832 and 1843, John Stewart, Anne, Mary, James, Agnes Jane and Archibald.

At the same wedding service, Mary's sister Margaret married Peter Reid, another Campbeltown man. He was the son of Hugh Reid and Janet Langwill.

Mary Templeton, in contrast to her more flamboyant husband, was a gentle, calm soul, full of cheerfulness and optimism. She had all the practical good sense of her generation, but combined this with intellectual qualities that allowed her to share, with her husband, a love of literature, although unlike James she had no musical talent and little interest in the subject. She had no knowledge or interest in art, but she also had no time for those pious individuals who sought to ban dancing, the theatre, and alcoholic drink.

James Templeton was a man of middle height, broad-chested, narrow in flank, spare in flesh. His eyes were grey, and he had a gentle and mild manner:

> He had all the air of a man of purpose and action. This was evident in his walk which in the street quickly carried him beyond every fellow traveller ... His powers of endurance were great and he subjected them to severe strain.[5]

Coincidences abound among the main characters in this tale, and never more so than in 1832, the year of the birth of Alexander, third son of Alexander Stephen and Elspeth Murray, and John Stewart, eldest son of James Templeton and Mary Stewart. A year earlier in Edinburgh, a James Stewart first saw the light of day. The three were destined to form a strong bond of friendship which was further strengthened when they became brothers-in-law.

Alexander Stephen, to differentiate him from his father, is called Al. The Gods were kind to Al, they bestowed on him the gifts of dedication, integrity, compassion and an overwhelming desire to be honourable in all his dealings.

John Stewart Templeton, known as JS, was equally well served by the Gods. He was a man of principle, a deeply religious man, who, nevertheless, could still question his Faith. A harsh critic of his own abilities, he was respected and admired by all who came into contact with him. His circle of friends reads like a *Who's Who* of nineteenth-century commerce and industry.

James Stewart -- no connection to the Glasgow family -- was the son of James Stewart and Jane Dudgeon.

The women of the three families exerted a powerful influence on their sons, and a description of Jane Dudgeon could equally have been written about Elspeth Stephen and Mary Templeton:

> She was the finest specimen of a noble woman ... possessing in their highest development all the features of the great Norse race from which she came ... She was a woman of much refinement, of great ability, and saintly character. To her he [James] owed his innate love and appreciation of all that was beautiful and seemly.[6]

It was not, however, just an accident of their birth or intermarriage which linked the three families; they were joined by the love of ships and the sea, by the love of art and literature and by devotion to the beliefs and principles of the Non-Conformist Church. The families were also linked in that they carried out employment policies that were in the forefront of employer/employee relations.

Expanded Horizons

BETWEEN 1840 and 1843, the Stephen Yard at Arbroath only launched eleven ships, and one of those was a barque for the family, even so Alexander believed that the business would improve. In 1842, his eldest son William entered the business as a carpenter, and a few months later his son James was despatched to Edinburgh to serve his apprenticeship with Miller and Richardson, ironmongers.

Scotland in 1843 was still in the grip of political, economic and religious turmoil. The Chartists were demanding adult male suffrage, secret ballots, annual elections, abolition of property qualification for MPs and the payment of MPs, and finally they wanted all electoral districts to be equal. Looking at the six demands now they seem modest, and except for annual elections, all have been achieved -- but not without a good deal of trouble. The Scottish reformer Robert Owen could well have been speaking today when he advocated wanting to 'establish Socialism without affronting the Capitalists.'[1]

If the Chartists were demanding their rights then the religious leaders in Scotland were also in a militant mood. In May 1843, when the Moderator of the Church of Scotland, David Welsh, and Thomas Chalmers, the undisputed leader of the Evangelical party, led a walk out from the General Assembly, the Free Church of Scotland was born. Alexander joined the Dissenters and for the rest of his life he followed the Free Church Faith, becoming an Elder of the Church:

> The Disruption was a turning-point in Scottish History, for it signalled the end of the parish state. Schooling, poor relief and moral discpline had all been organised through the medium of the parish since the Reformation ...[2]

The end of the parish state saw the introduction of parochial boards and burgh councils.

If some of Alexander's children were being supervised and educated, the younger children were free to roam, and inevitably this included having the shipyard as a playground. Like all forbidden places, the Yard was a magnet for inquiring young minds, but danger lurked round every corner. On the afternoon of Monday 7 June 1841, Alexander's little daughter Elizabeth was killed by a circular saw: she had just celebrated her third birthday.

In the middle years of the nineteenth century many children died as the result of accidents while playing. The seas around Scotland, which give Scotland its beauty, also claimed young lives and in many instances the young victims were never identified. The home and the nursery could also pose unforseen danger. Early in 1843, Ruth, the twelve-week-old, tenth daughter of Alexander and Elspeth, died. She was, according to family stories, slept on by her nanny. But one is left wondering why the nurse took a twelve-week-old baby into her bed, and why she slept so soundly that she was not aware of the child's distress.

Alexander was a kindly father, although he did not believe in indulging his sons. They were expected to work for their privileges. He was also a paternalistic employer, and he treated his men with fairness and compassion, though there was never any doubt that he was the gaffer. An ambitious man, Alexander knew that if he wanted to expand he would need to move from the restrictions of Arbroath.

In May 1843 he sold the Yard to his nephew William, and moved his family to Dundee. It was a risky and dramatic change, but it was in keeping with the dour determination of Alexander to succeed, and if taking risks in difficult times was the price he had to pay then so be it.

The first few years at Dundee were difficult, orders for new ships were slow to come but Alexander never wasted time in doubting the wisdom of the move. He built and equipped new sheds and he built a joinery shop. And if he could not build new ships there were still enough old ships that needed repairing.

The first launch from the Dundee Yard was in 1844, when the brig *Diana*, for A Blives, slid into the water; two further ships were launched that year for Baxter Brothers. A six-week strike in 1846 was just one of the many troubles that beset Alexander in his early years in Dundee, but somehow he always managed to weather the storm. He used the bad times to expand the Yard, believing the good times would return.

In 1838 James Templeton began to manufacture carpets in a cotton mill, rented from Clarke's, at the corner of King Street and Broad Street, Mile End. Templeton carpets were made using a Chenille process developed by Templeton and John Quigley when they were making shawls. Quigley, a reluctant manufacturer, sold his share of the process to Templeton before emigrating to America. Templeton patented the process and before long the first carpets were being produced.

Around 1839-40, James, Mary and their family moved to a flat at 18 Monteith Row, in the Carlton District of Glasgow: a district that he would continue to be associated with for the rest of his life. A picture of life at that time is illustrated in a letter Mary wrote to her husband when he was away on business. Her letter shows that life was a constant struggle to make ends meet, yet there was also humour in her words:

> Mr M'Indoe, our landlord, brought us last night the long promised 8-day clock. I took him into the dining room to give him a glass of wine. The lady who lodges upstairs was with me at the time and, of course, addressed me as Mrs Templeton. "Was it your husband," the landlord asked, "who made the carpets that were in the Exhibition rooms?" I replied that it was. "Templeton," said he, "his name is kent frae Land's End to Johnny Groat's house. There never the like o'yon seen in Glasgow before." So you see, James, although you have not made much money yet, you have made a name.[3]

In 1841, James Templeton made the carpet for St George's Chapel, at Windsor Castle, for the christening of Albert Edward, the eldest son of Queen Victoria and Prince Albert.

In April 1842, in spite of the success of the Royal commission, James was writing to his financial backers, who included, Alex Johnstone MP for Kilmarnock, Peter Reid, his brother-in-law, Andrew and Archibald Galbraith -- all Campbeltown men -- and successful merchants:

> We must try what another year will do [and] if after giving it every trial we do not succeed in increasing it (ie the Sales) it must be abandoned. To me who have sacrificed all my prospects for it my time to have been better employed, and if I do not find them (my partners) ready to procure vigor-

ously I must dispose of my interest so as not to lose time -- or an opportunity of providing for my family.[4]

Problems were mounting in Templeton's factory, the Chenille process that James and Quigley had invented was being copied by three other manufacturers without applying for a licence from the Patent holders. Templeton had no alternative but to take the matter to a Court of Law. The principal offenders were MacFarlane Bros, and the case dragged on for years, leaving James worried and anxious over the final outcome.

However, on a personal level James was delighted when his two younger brothers, Archibald and Nathaniel, joined him in the business. In February 1845, Archibald married Jane Stewart, the third Stewart sister to marry into the carpet business. Shortly after his marriage, Archibald became a director of Templetons and moved to London as their representative. Nathaniel always called himself an assistant carpet manufacturer. He never married.

JS's schooling was spent at the High School, Glasgow, he left at sixteen and spent the next two years in the office of William McKinley, a wholesale drapery merchant. According to his own assessment, his years at McKinley were spent mainly in the pursuit of widening his academic education. He attended, as a private student, lectures at Glasgow University, reading logic, under the expert tutelage of Robert Buchanan, Professor of Logic.

JS identified the year he joined his father in the manufacture of carpets as 1849 when he was seventeen -- a question mark hangs over that date. If his memories of his school and apprenticeship days are accurate, then he left school shortly before his sixteenth birthday and joined his father's business shortly after his eighteenth birthday, in 1850. Whatever the precise date was his involvement with the business, it lasted the rest of his life, and he presided over the enormous expansion of the company.

If business in the shipyard was bad, then at least at home there was time for celebration; on 30 April 1850, Alexander and Elspeth's eldest daughter, Elspeth Murray, married Captain William Storey Croudace. Born in 1821, William was the son of John Croudace, a school master and Ann Storey. According to a record of his career, he obtained his Master Mariner's licence sometime around 1841. His first ship, as Master, was the brig *Coquette*. In 1846 he became Master of the Stephen-built ship, the *William*, built at the Dundee yard for Scott & Munro. From the date of his marriage to Elspeth, he captained the *Amazon*, built by Stephen, for Joseph & F Somes, the London based East Indian traders, who were and would remain one of the Dundee Yard's most loyal clients.

1850 was a notable year in Alexander's life, not only for the marriage of his eldest daughter, but also for his decision to hand over the running of the Dundee Yard to his eldest son William, and to transfer his remaining family to a new yard on the Clyde in Glasgow. On 1 January 1851 he took a twenty-year lease at Kelvinhaugh, and shortly after that date Alexander and Elspeth moved to Glasgow. Their sons Al, John and Andrew stayed on the East coast as they had not completed their studies.

The change of location was not the only matter that occupied Alexander during those dark winter months of 1851. He noted in his day book that he was delighted to approve the marriage of his son William to Jane Skair Henderson. There is some discrepancy about whether she was Jean or Jane -- in 1830, the year of her birth, the names were interchangeable. A thorough search of the records appears to suggest that she preferred the name Jane.

William and Jane were married on 4 February 1851 at Woodwrae, Albermeno, the farm of her parents, Andrew Henderson and Barbara Jarrow. Jane had just celebrated her twenty-first birthday; there is contemporary evidence to show that she had been working for the Stephen's family as governess to the younger children.

The wedding guest list is interesting in that William's father was there, but not his mother Elspeth. Here there is a good deal of circumstantial evidence to suggest that William and his mother were not as close as one would expect of an eldest son. Al, Andrew, John and Ann were there but James was another absent guest.

William and Jane set up home in King Street, the house that Alexander owned before moving to Kelvinhaugh. William and Jane shared the house with Elspeth Croudace who had not yet joined her husband William in

London. The couple's first child, John Stephen, was born in Dundee in October 1851. The remaining children, Blanche, Elspeth Murray, Helen Stephen and Lawrence were all born in England.

If the year began with changes of location and marriages, it ended with the birth of William and Jane's daughter Jane, who sadly died before her fourth birthday. William and Jane had three more daughters, Anne, Alice Murray, Edith Mary, and four sons, Alexander, who died in infancy, Andrew Henderson, William and Frederick Somerville. A rough count of Alexander and Elspeth's grandchildren shows that between 1851 and 1875, they had fifty-three. A further eight were born in the following ten years.

The relationship between Alexander and his sons is best explained in a diary entry of Al's. It also explains that in the autumn of 1853, Alexander had, if only unofficially, decided that James, his second son, would be his successor at the Glasgow Yard.

On Saturday 8 October, Alexander suggested to Al that he should undertake further training as an engineer with Randolph, Elder and Co. Randolph Elder, at that time, made engines for Stephen's ships. Al, however, had other ideas. He told his father that he wanted to study engineering but he wanted to attend classes at Edinburgh University for a year. Al strongly believed that six months at Randolph Elder would teach him very little.

Alexander was amused and he asked James, who was also present during the discussion. "How would it do for you and me to go to college?" To which James replied: "It would keep them out of the coarse [winter] weather."[5]

Alexander then asked Al why he had not spoken of his wishes before, and Al replied, using the same philosophy and logic that would forever characterise his attitude. "I think before I speak, for I was not sure myself what I ought to do."[6]

Al's honest statement silenced his father for a moment, then as if he had in that moment agreed to allow Al to do exactly as he wished, Alexander told him. "You will require to get all the drafts as much as you can before you go."[7]

Rivalry among the six brothers was a reccurring problem. William was his own master in Dundee, while James was understudying at Kelvinhaugh. Al was at Edinburgh University; Andrew was also at Edinburgh studying medicine although he did not get his MB until 1862. John had been educated at Brechin Grammar School, followed by undergraduate years at Edinburgh University where he studied mathematics, natural philosophy, natural history and chemistry. After Edinburgh he joined Randolph Elder for practical shipbuilding experience. Samuel, was the only brother who expressed a wish to sail ships rather than build them, but he, like his brothers, had a good general education including undergraduate training in Edinburgh.

The brothers were given every encouragement and opportunity to make a success of their lives: Alexander was a hard task master, but he was also a fair man both as a father and an employer.

Brothers In Conflict

FIRE was, and is, a constant fear shared by both owners and workers in Glasgow factories. The risk of fire in industrial/commercial premises is still the highest in the country, and Scotland, even now, has the unenviable record of having the highest death toll from fires. In the 1850s, health and safety rules were almost non-existent. Machines and lamps were powered by paraffin, adding to the dangers.

On Christmas Day 1856 -- it was not a public holiday -- the Templeton workers continued as on any other day. In the early morning around six-thirty a *Destructive Conflagration* took place; a worker, identified only as Aitken, was at his loom when he combed his hair only to drop his comb on the floor:

> [Amongst] the woollen waste with which the floor was partially covered. He [Aitken] procured a lamp from his comrade, who was engaged at an adjoining loom, and proceeded to search for the missing article. A spark accidentally ignited some waste, which the workman instantly endeavoured to extinguish by crushing it with his hands; but in this attempt he failed, and before further assistance could be rendered the flame, inconsequence of the oily nature of the waste, quickly spread to the looms and other machinery.[1]

The fire brigade was quickly on the scene, although there were comments made that they took far too long to arrive. As the Carlton Police pointed out:

> The alarm left [them] at seven o'clock, reached the Central Station at about a quarter-past-seven, and the Central engines were in attendance at twenty-five minutes past seven.[2]

The fire spread rapidly and the entire factory and warehouses were destroyed in King and Broad Street. Surprisingly, there was no loss of life, although one elderly lady, Sarah McEwan, who was employed as a sweeper, had to be rescued by a fireman named Dykes. The smoke had caused her to become unconscious but with immediate medical assistance she quickly regained consciousness.

As if the fire was not bad enough, twenty minutes after the fire brigade arrived a gas meter exploded, bringing further destruction to the factory. The damage ran into many thousands of pounds, but fortunately the factory and the warehouse were covered by insurance. Unfortunately, the fate of Aitken is not known, but it would be doubtful if Templeton senior did not quickly dispense with his services, and once the factory was rebuilt and operating again, it would also be a fair assumption that James instructed his workers that they must not in any circumstance comb their hair while operating a loom.

As with many major fires, the adjoining properties were put at risk, including the extensive cotton thread factory of John Clark. The flames spread by a stiff north-easterly breeze further hampered the work of containment; but due to the bravery and hard work of Clark's workers, their building was saved:

> This was accomplished by the workers attaching hose to pipes supplied with water from a number of force pumps worked by steam power with which the works are provided. The workmen turned out into the street, and kept up a powerful pour of water upon the front wall of the mill and occasionally upon the portion of the burning building opposite to them.[3]

The report goes on to describe how the heat was so intense that a wooden screen was erected to protect the amateur fire-fighters, and that on occasions they were given a soaking which allowed them to remain at their awesome task. Praise for the courage and dedication, of both the official and unofficial fire-fighters, was made by James Templeton. There were residents who complained that the destruction of property would have been much less if the supply of water had been better.

The press report showed just how little things have changed since 1856. The reporter, obviously having spoken to members of the Templeton staff who were present, asserts that the insurance claims would be between £300 and £5,000. Within a week a claim had been made to the insurers, and within a month Templeton had negotiated and signed a deal for an empty cotton mill in William Street. Later, the street was renamed Templeton Street and today the road still bears that name.

Templeton immediately made alterations to the building to accommodate the larger machinery used in carpet making. The ground floor housed the winding, fur cutting and cropping machines; on the first floor were the yarn stock and colouring departments; the second floor housed the setting looms; the fourth and attic floors housed the weft looms. In the attic rooms, narrow looms were operated by boys who wove narrow webs for special carpets.

The William Street factory employed approximately three hundred workers, making Templetons, even then, a substantial employer. Templeton senior, like Alexander Stephen, was also interested in not just improving environmental conditions of his employees, but he also had a mission to instruct them in the scriptures: he started a Sunday School for the young male workers.

Mary Templeton also played a significant part in improving the lives of her husband's workforce, and she undoubtedly shared his deep faith in religion. She was a dedicated worker and sponsor to the Glasgow Mission to the Blind, [it changed its name many times until in 1989 it became The Glasgow and West of Scotland Society for the Blind] a charity that would remain one she, her children, grandchildren and great-grandchildren and their Stephen relatives, would support for the rest of their lives. Set up in 1859 by W P Paton, and a distinguished group of west of Scotland citizens, the aim of the Society was to improve the day-to-day lives of blind people living in and around Glasgow. The Mission believed that, with help, encouragement and training, the blind could lead useful and fulfilling lives. They further believed that employers could be found to offer employment to blind persons.

The Mission members visited the blind in their homes, read to them and, where necessary, supplied funds to ward off starvation and poverty. Mary Templeton was among their most dedicated workers, and her charity work also extended to her husband's factory workers:

In the course of her connection with the Church life and with it labours among the poor of the east of Glasgow she initiated classes for factory girls in which she herself taught simple domestic economy ...[4]

Her prepared lessons were later printed in a little book and it was used by girls when they married. Mary was not, however, just interested in her husband's workforce and their families, she had a particular interest in those unfortunate souls who fell foul of the Law:

> The most heroic of her efforts to do good was visiting the prisons and allowing herself to be locked in a cell with some female prisoners to whom she read and whose future life she hoped to influence.[5]

There is something quite terrifying in the idea of a beautiful, well-bred woman spending time locked in a cell, even if the prisoner was only there for some minor misdemeanour. Mary inherited her caring nature from her father and grandfather. John Stewart was a truly good man and had been an Elder in the Relief Church. In old age, when his labour from his tailoring business was over, he could be found in an armchair with a large volume of Scott's Commentary on the Bible on his lap.

Grandfather Stewart had been born with a spirit of enterprise, rather like James Templeton. At an early age he had travelled to London, walking a goodly part of the way. On one dark evening, he bumped into a corpse hanging from a tree -- justice was rough in those days. Executions, from roadside trees, were quite common. The incident was sufficiently frightening for him to lead a blameless life from then on, and to ensure that his children walked in the path of Godliness.

With twelve daughters, Alexander Stephen wondered if he would ever be free from the demands of women as they prepared for their forthcoming nuptials. In November 1854, Anne Fleming, Alexander's second daughter, had married the young solicitor, Duncan Wilkie Paterson. He was the son of William Paterson, a market gardener and Stewart Wilkie. Alexander found that having a solicitor in the family greatly helped when he needed free legal advice.

On Wednesday 22 April 1857, at 64 St Vincent's Crescent, Glasgow,

Helen, Alexander Stephen's fifth child, married the Revd John Logan; it was a good match. John had been born in Irvine, Ayrshire on 4 December 1824, the son of Alexander Logan and Marion Boyd. He had studied at the University and New College Edinburgh, and was ordained at Leslie, Fife in 1855. If there was one shadow in the marriage of Helen to John Logan, it was that, unlike her mother, Helen would remain childless.

Two months later, on Tuesday 25 June 1857, Al married Mary, the twenty-one-year-old daughter of James and Mary Templeton. In a letter to Andrew, written two years later, Al suggested that his marriage to Mary Templeton was not approved of by his father. He does not go into detail as to the reasons for that disapproval, but whatever Alexander's doubts were, Al and his Templeton in-laws became the closest of friends.

Al and Mary honeymooned in Geneva, a city that they fell in love with from the moment of their arrival. They returned to Switzerland many times throughout their long marriage. The couple, on their return, set up house at 7 Sandyford Place.

Alexander was an East Coast man and he never really settled in Glasgow. In 1857/8 he considered handing the Kelvinhaugh yard over to James and Al as equal partners. In keeping with his wishes that the boys should not be handed riches on a plate, he suggested they should repay him, from profits, over a period of years. Alexander had, in November 1856, signed a similar co-partnership with William in Dundee.

In anticipation of his return East, Alexander purchased Corona, near Monifieth, at the mouth of the Tay. It was an impressive house, as befitted a man of considerable means. Corona was a large grey sandstone house, with a grand entrance into an elegant timbered hall and staircase. The drawing room and dining room had marble fireplaces and intricately carved ceilings. Facing south, the floor to ceiling bay windows gave spectacular views over the Tay, giving Alexander the joy of seeing ships sail down to the sea. The house was large enough to accommodate Alexander and Elspeth's seven unmarried daughters, and beautiful enough for them to entertain prospective suitors.

The early years of Al's marriage, coinciding as it did with the early years at Kelvinhaugh, were not easy. Orders were hard to come by and he spent much time searching out prospective owners. He was also frequently called upon to settle disputes that arose between his siblings.

Al's relationship with his brothers was rarely that of an arbitrator and conciliator: he saw issues in black and white, there were never any grey areas. He believed that in any dispute between the brothers, his father always listened to James, and acted on what he said.

Early in 1858 James made it plain that he did not wish to enter into a partnership with his father or Al. It is not certain if he had begun to tire of the business of building ships or whether he simply wanted a more lucrative way of earning a living. Whatever, he considered buying into the Lancefield Forge when Fulton and his partner James Beaumont Neilson decided to dissolve their agreement. Neilson was nearing the end of a very active life; he was renowned as the inventor of the hot blast manufacture of iron -- an improvement that was essential when shipbuilding converted from wood to iron. James would have been in at the beginning, unfortunately nothing came of his attempt to buy Lancefield. Neilson bought out Fulton and continued alone until his death in 1865.

James missed an opportunity when he abandoned Lancefield, but 1858 was the year when everything began to go horribly wrong in his life. He was thirty-years-old, unmarried, and living at home, and from what his younger brother Samuel wrote a few years later, James's home life was not without its problems. The letter is also revealing in that it shows that the brothers had formed their own partnerships, the old adage that two's company and three's a crowd applied. William, of course, was not involved; James and Andrew formed one union; Al and John another, which left Samuel -- James's junior by sixteen years -- the loner. In the letter to his father written from Dunedin, South Island, New Zealand, Samuel lays all the blame for his own misfortunes at the feet of Andrew for bringing among them that 'female witch with the many aliases ... she has been the ruin of Andrew and very nearly myself.'[6]

She is not identified, but, from a letter Al wrote to Andrew in 1859, it is highly probable that she was Chrissy Hogarth, to whom Andrew had just become engaged. It was around this time that Samuel was accused of many crimes including stealing, a claim he vigorously denied. He believed Andrew and his fiancée had told his father lies about his behaviour. It was, though, his disillusionment of Andrew that hurt the most for he had always been told by his mother and sisters that Andrew should be his role model.

Al harboured no such doubts about Andrew's engagement, he wrote to his brother:

> My first thought immediately on receiving yours of yesterday is, that the blessing of our God may be on you and yours. May Chrissy Hogarth and you be happy for ever. I am almost as full of gratitude as you are yourself and I rejoice at the mind, the heart and the compliance you have towards our Heavenly Father in the whole matter. I sincerely pray that Chrissy and you may be blessed together all the days of your life ...[7]

Al goes on to say that he had as yet not met Chrissy, but he hoped to do so in the near future. He called her 'Happy Chrissy' which rather implies that she was a young woman of a charming and happy disposition. Al tells Andrew that he is a little worried that in his recent letters Andrew had hinted that there was something important he wanted to tell him but had so far been unable to voice his concerns. He suggested that Andrew should bring Chrissy to Sandyford Place and they could discuss their forthcoming marriage.

In 1858, however, another young woman entered the lives of the Stephen brothers and one is left to wonder if she were 'the wicked witch of many aliases'. Or was she Chrissy Hogarth under another disguise?

Mary Paterson, or Dundas, was twenty-years-old when she had an illegitimate daughter, Margaret Mary. It is possible that her birth was not recorded: certainly an exhaustive search of all the records has failed to locate it. Nor has a marriage between a Paterson and Dundas been located, which would have explained the two names.

It was said by the family that James was the father of Margaret Mary, but a doubt remains that he has been blamed for something of which he may have been innocent. The possibility must be faced that Margaret's father was either Andrew or Samuel. The events which followed the birth suggest that Alexander was not happy with the behaviour of his sons. Margaret Paterson later gave birth to a son, whom she named Frederick John. Did she deliberately name him after Al's second son?

Sometime in 1858 James went to America. Al gave him a Letter of Credit and prayed it would not be cashed. James was not in America for long, and Al's prayers were not answered. In September 1858, James married at Old Machar, Aberdeen, his cousin Williamina Clark, the widow of the Revd Samuel Grant. She had married Grant on 3 March 1847 but he died in 1853. Williamina, baptised on 30 August 1825, was the daughter of Margaret Stephen, Alexander's sister, and William Clark, a retired ironmonger in Aberdeen.

James and Williamina's marriage was not a success. Williamina came through to Glasgow and with Al's help set up home at Fountain Bank. By the spring of 1859, Williamina had already left James and returned to her parents in Aberdeen, and then began a protracted argument over money. On his marriage James had signed a Promissory Note to William Clark for £450; it was money that belonged to Williamina. It was valid for a year with two repayments to be made at Whitsunday and Martinmas. James, of course, reneged on both dates. There is also a suggestion that James borrowed a further £500 from William Clark.

In a letter to his father Al denied he was responsible for James's debts:

> I was as you know not well acquainted with my brother's proceedings in these matters but understood that this bill was granted by him in fulfilment of some arrangement between Mr Clark and himself regarding a life rent interest the former was to give him, be this as it may. There is no credit with the Firm here on his account, on [the] contrary I will be a very heavy loser by the amounts drawn by him exceeding what would have been his share of profits up to the time he left.[8]

James claimed that Al was withholding his share of the Firm's profits for the time when they were partners, namely from 1 September 1857 until 26 April 1859, a claim that Al rigorously rejected, saying that neither he nor the Firm were liable. With a degree of annoyance he then told his father:

[Nor] do I think it would be a proper proceeding for me to interpose the guarantee of the firm here to this bill, it being a matter with which really neither I nor the firm here have any concern.[9]

Al's anger is apparent when he rebuked his father for suggesting that he should be more tolerant of James's demands. He pointed out that he, more than any other member of the family, had suffered by James's irresponsible actions. In summing up his attitude he again takes his father to task for his generosity to James:

With regards to the sum remitted by you from Dundee I am at a loss how to treat it, but I cannot see in the face of James's large deficiency grounds for coming under any obligation regarding it at present.[10]

It is not clear from the letters whether William favoured their father's generosity towards James, or if he backed Al in his opposition. Whatever, a few days later Al sent the Bill back to Clark. He also informed Clark that the personal items that Williamina had left at Fountain Bank had been packed by a servant and would be sent to Aberdeen shortly.

In a further twist to the sorry tale, Al wrote to Williamina expressing his sheer exasperation:

In regard to the Bill, granted by James to your father I am not aware that you ever before alluded to it and I could not therefore have led you to believe either one thing or another as to the course I intended to pursue. I have never changed any purpose I had and I shall certainly endeavour to act honourably in this as in all other matters.[11]

Al pointed out that he could not know what transactions were agreed between her, her father and James at the time of her marriage. He does accept that the £450 belonged, before her marriage, to her, but that on her marriage she had given James the money and he had given her the Promissory Note. There is a further complication that Al outlines, stating that James had consented to the granting as

an obligation for it as a debt in consideration of your father agreeing to make an alteration in his settlement to the effect of giving [James] a life rent in his property the same as had been given to the Revd Mr Grant.[12]

Once again Al tells his sister-in-law that the matter really is a private one between her, her father and James, and does not involve the Firm. Al absolves both himself and the Yard from any further commitment to her and James:

> I cannot be expected to undertake a new responsibility of that kind on his account, more especially after having done so much already beyond what I ever contemplated.'[13]

It is easy to appreciate the stress of Williamina's failed marriage and the bitterness caused by James's financial dealings had on her family. Margaret Clark, a much loved Stephen aunt, who only a few years before had urged on her nephews to seek a peaceful resolution to family disputes, was appalled at the way her nephews were behaving. Even when her daughter married James she knew that she was dying. She had had breast cancer for eighteen months: she died at 10.30 p.m. on 2 October 1859 at her home in Union Street, Aberdeen.

There is one question that must be asked. Did James know at the time of his marriage that Williamina was dying of phthisis (tuberculosis)? She died on 17 November 1859, having been ill for two-and-a-half years. James was not present at her death; the distress of her father cannot be imagined for he had lost his wife just over six weeks before his daughter's death. He had seen both women die of painful and prolonged illnesses, and his son-in-law was not even concerned enough to travel north to be with the dying women.

James may well have been innocent of fathering Mary Paterson's daughter, but it cannot be denied that when Williamina was dying, he was seducing another woman who was even then carrying his child.

James Washington Stephen was born at Moffat, Dumfriesshire, to James and Eliza Little McCorquadale, on Christmas Day 1859, just forty-two days after Williamina's death. Even then, James's conscience did not particularly bother him. On registering his son's birth on 13 January 1860, he told the Registrar that the baby's mother was Eliza Stephen neéMcCorquadale, thus indicating they were married. In reality, they did not marry until 10 April 1860, at St Cuthbert's, in Edinburgh.

Eliza Little McCorquadale, on her marriage certificate, gave her parents as John McCorquadale, a merchant from Greenock, and Mary Little. An unexplained anomaly is that Eliza was born in 1829, and on her marriage she should have been thirty-one, not as stated, twenty-seven. Lies and deception seemed to be the hall mark of James and Eliza's life! A second son Robert Little was born to the couple on 24 July 1861. The birth was registered as being at 42 Eldon Street, Greenock, and James gave his occupation as shipbuilder.

It is a pity that there is no contemporary portrait of James. He was described by someone who knew him, and who had no reason to exaggerate, as a big handsome man, with thick black hair and a large black beard. Whatever, he was obviously attracted to women and women to him. Perhaps there was a touch of Black Beard the Pirate about this man whom his father regarded as a favourite son, but who was in the eyes of many, including Al, rebarbative.

JS met Mary Stephen, the eighth child of Alexander and Elspeth Murray's eighteen children, when his sister Mary became engaged to Al. Mary Stephen was then only seventeen-years-old. JS's own assessment of the Stephen's family is worth recalling:

> [They] Mary's brothers and sisters] were a happy healthy merry attractive group of young people. Mary was esteemed the prettiest of the sisters. With jet black hair, soft brown eyes, a good figure and regular features she was indeed a lovely creature.[14]

Mary's father was known to comment that his pretty young daughter was always smiling.

A three-year engagement ensued, but in 1858 Mary Stephen suffered from a near fatal attack of pleurisy which left her with an under lying weakness of the lungs. However, by Thursday 14 July 1859 Mary was well enough to marry JS at Corona. The young couple set up home at

4 Clifton Street, close to Park Circus, Glasgow, where JS would have a house for the greater part of his adult life. He was concerned that with an income of between £200 and £300 a year he would not be able to afford to live as he wished. Although he admitted later they lived on £300 per annum for the next eight years. It is, however, worth mentioning that in 1864 his father-in-law, Alexander, was only paying the shipyard carpenters £78 a year. JS's income was, therefore, more than four times that of a skilled craftsman.

JS, from the earliest age, was an ambitious man and he did not enjoy the idea of poverty, but he was to prove in the first few years of marriage that they could live quite well on his meagre allowance. He later wrote of his long engagement to Mary

> our engagement were happy years and I rather like to see young people daring to pledge themselves in this way and to begin domestic life on small means. [15]

He then went on to quote Francis Bacon:

> He that hath wife and children hath given hostages to fortunes; for they are impediments to great enterprises, either of virtue or mischief.[16]

Exactly nine months after JS had married Mary, she gave birth to a son, on Tuesday 10 April 1860. The date has an added significance: on that day the baby's uncle, James Stephen, married his second wife Eliza McCorquadale. Baby James, according to his father, was a large baby and Mary, in spite of her weakened physical condition, insisted on nursing her son. JS was at home on the day of the birth and one can picture him, as indeed so many other Victorian fathers did, pacing outside the bedroom door as midwives, doctors and servants, assisted in the birth.

According to an entry in Al's diary, JS's son was named James Murray, but the birth was registered only in the name of James; he did not use the Murray name until much later. As the diary entry also contains the date of James Murray's death, it would seem that Al added the name later. The diary entry gives no mention of the marriage of James and Eliza.

The Black Sheep

AL may have dismissed the birth of James and Eliza's second son, but six days before the birth of Robert, on 21 July 1861, he was able to celebrate the birth of his own first son, and third child. Alexander Edward, known as Alex, came into a world that was as safe and secure as Robert's was insecure and perilous. Al and Mary's two daughters, Mary Stuart was born in July 1858 and Matilda, known as Maud, in July 1860. A third daughter Elspeth Murray, known as Elsie, was born in May 1867.

JS was distracted with personal worries towards the end of 1862, his second daughter Mary had been born on 8 August, but from the very beginning her health was poor. The birth of Mary had done nothing to improve the health of her mother who had had three pregnancies since her marriage in 1859. Elspeth Alice had been born in July 1861.

JS moved his young family out of Glasgow to a small cottage, Rosebank at Blantyre, in the hope that the country air would improve their health. The change of location did not work; the west of Scotland was still too cold and too wet for Mary's delicate constitution. In late November 1862, JS took Mary, and two-year-old James Murray, and her sisters Marjory and Mary-Ann, to Gibraltar. Here, JS hoped that the warm, dry Mediterranean climate would improve their health. Work commitments made it impossible for him to stay with his wife, son, and her sisters, and so he left them in what appeared to be an idyllic place while he returned to Glasgow.

The New Year, however, brought disturbing news. Al received a telegram from Gibraltar telling him that Marjory was dangerously ill with typhus fever. A few hours later another telegram arrived with the news that Marjory had died on 7 January. According to Al's diary, the delay in letting the family know had been caused by a break in the telegraph connection between Gibraltar and Britain. Marjory had only just celebrated her twenty-second birthday. Al was heartbroken by her death:

> The ways of God are with Himself. How many instances we get as will is in the "Word of God" to teach us to be "Watchful unto Prayer." How very little I thought of such an event to Marjory when on the evening of the Sabbath the 9th November last (which was her birthday) when I wrote the following words, which are quoted before such date "O Lord prepare us all for leaving this world, and when we do so would may be it be to enter into enjoyment of Thyself so that we may inherit the blessings of eternal life and that Jehovah may be our God forever." Amen.[1]

Devastated by the news, Alexander, who was more able to leave his duties than either Al or JS, made immediate plans to travel to Gibraltar to bring Mary, James Murray, and Mary-Ann home. Travel was difficult and by the time Alexander, arrived Mary's condition had worsened. On the evening of 5 February, a month since Marjory died, Mary also died. She had, according to her father, been well enough the day before to take a short coach ride, but the next day she was very weak and scarcely able to speak. She died at five minutes past nine with Alexander and Mary-Ann at her bedside. She died without pain and in peace. The last word she uttered was Jesus.

Thirteen days later Al recorded in his diary:

> Her sorrowful husband ... who has been very kind to her is left with three young children. It is sad to think of such ties being separated forever in this world, Mary was amiable, quiet, gentle, very managing in her own affairs.[2]

Twelve weeks after Mary's death, her baby daughter Mary also died. She had been ill with bronchitis for three months. JS, overburdened by the death of his wife, sent his little daughter into the care of Dr Alexander Paterson and his wife Mary Stuart Dalrymple. Alexander was in practice at Logie, Perthshire, but more importantly he was the elder brother of JS's brother-in-law, Duncan Wilkie Paterson. The Patersons had three children of their own, and JS obviously considered them capable of caring for his little daughter. It is probable that the Patersons also cared for Alice at this difficult time. James Murray was three-years-old at the time of the two deaths and there is no doubt that at such a young age he could not comprehend what was happening in his life. Neverthess he mourned the loss of his mother for the rest of his life.

1863 had begun badly for Al, but on 6 August he was pleased to announce the safe arrival of his fourth child and second son, Frederic John. There is a family story, handed down by subsequent generations, that Mary, unable to spell the name she wished to use, asked a servant if she knew the correct spelling. The final decision was to spell Frederic the French way but without the accents.

Family feuds were to be expected in a family as large as Alexander and Elspeth's, but the animosity among the six brothers reached an even greater intensity in the early years of the 1860s. Shortly before her death, Aunt Margaret had written to William but the letter was obviously meant for all her nephews:

[If] there should arise any dispute or difference among you, the wisest will check it at once, if he be enabled to do it himself shall reap the blessing ...[3]

She then quoted from the Gospel of St Matthew, telling the boys that the peacemakers will be the Children of God. She warns them, however:

Every Kingdom divided against itself is brought to desolation: and every city or house divided against itself shall not stand.[4]

Aunt Margaret concluded her letter by warning that they should not seek riches to the exclusion of all else or they would only increase their troubles. Her warning was timely, family disputes continued to haunt Al and never more so than those that concerned Andrew and Samuel.

Andrew had matriculated in the Faculty of Medicine, at Edinburgh University in 1852/53, but he did not finally graduate with an MD until 1862. Previously he had attended one session at Glasgow University, and five years at Dundee studying Pharmacy and Dispensary. He had spent almost a decade in pursuing his studies, and with his thesis *On the Duality of the Nervous System* completed he was finally ready to accept his first medical appointment. He took up a position as Medical Officer at the Middlesex Hospital in London.

It was about this time that Andrew's engagement to Chrissy Hogarth was ended. As there does not seem to have been a Breach of Promise claim by her, it can only be assumed that if, as Samuel said, she was 'of the many aliases' then Andrew may have discovered her contradictions and lies. On the other hand, she may well have found it impossible to cope with Andrew's irresponsibilities.

Samuel, like Andrew, was unable to settle to a career: he was plagued with ill-health. Of all the brothers, Al appeared to be the one in robust health. In 1863 Samuel and Mary-Ann had both been poorly; Mary-Ann's health had not improved since her return from Gibraltar. Samuel, in an effort to find a career and improve his own health, was sent out to New Zealand. It was from Dunedin, in November 1863, that he wrote to his father telling him that his chest complaint was much improved, and that he believed the New Zealand climate at Otago was the healthiest in the world. He does, though, express his concern over Mary-Ann's health:

> I hope poor Mary-Ann is better, poor thing she has had her troubles and anxieties in this world but I hope it will please God if he takes her away from this world he [sic] will take her to himself [sic] ...[5]

Samuel always believed that it was Andrew and Chrissy who had slandered him and had driven a wedge between him and his father. Before he went to New Zealand there was a family conference to try and determine who was right and who was wrong. Nothing was obviously settled and Samuel went abroad feeling he had been unfairly treated. It was only in letters to his father that he could try to put his side of the story. He was much troubled by the knowledge that he may die before his name had been cleared. Nevertheless, he prayed that Andrew and Chrissy would get the punishment they deserved. Samuel tells his father that he will never again see Andrew, unless the latter became a reformed character. He makes a pitiful plea to his father:

> I could cry like a child just to think of the untruths he has told of me, I don't know whether you will believe me or Andrew, but I trust God will direct you which to believe.[6]

He goes on to admit that he had not been as honest as he should have been, but he now feels more mature and more in control of his life. Samuel was very much the son of a shipbuilder, for in the middle of trying to redeem his reputation he congratulates his father on having twelve ships on the stocks. Even then his congratulations are tinged with anguish, and he objects to his father saying that he had been cut adrift from his position with Cargill & Co:

> Messrs Cargill & Co would at this moment be too glad to have me back again, but it was for my own good that I left them ... Mr Cargill gave me when I left a [reference] ... he mentions that I was truthful, attentive to business, persevered and strictly honest ...[7]

He concludes his long letter with the plea of all young men -- he was nineteen at the time of writing:

> I hope you have made up your mind to advance me the money I asked for two mails ago. [He promises the money will not be spent on foolish speculations, but on] purely bona-fide business transactions.[8]

Also, like numerous young men away from home, he asked for some new clothes to be sent to him, and promises that he will repay the cost when he is again in funds.

Alexander would have had a heart of stone if he had not responded favourably to his youngest son's letter. He adds his own postscript to the letter, declaring that it was one of the most satisfactory he had received from the boy. He tells Al, to whom he sent the letter, that he hoped he would be able to write to Samuel and tell him that he was missed by all the family.

Mary-Ann Stephen was twenty-five-years-old when she announced her engagement to William Wright on Saturday 6 February 1864. Wright, nine years her senior, was born in August 1830, the son of Robert Wright, a soft goods manufacturer, and Agnes Wilkie. He had been married before, his first wife being Annie (Ann) Hall, a daughter of James

Hall and Elizabeth Wyllie, from Fettercairn, Kincardine. The couple had one daughter Annie Hall Wright, born at 14 West Princes Street, Glasgow on 8 February 1860. It has not been possible to locate Annie's death, but it occurred between February 1860 and March 1864. Wright was a tea merchant and it is probable that Annie died abroad.

Mary-Ann and William were married at Corona, on 31 March 1864. There were about forty family and friends present, and the party did not break up until 3 o'clock the next morning.

In ten years, Mary-Ann produced six children: Emily Burlton 1865; Mary Louisa 1867; Alexander Stephen 1868; Elsie Mina 1870; Amelia Sutherland [Amy] 1872, all born in Glasgow; and William Towers born in 1873 at Corona.

The relationship between William Wright and his in-laws was not particularly close, yet in spite of this coolness, when he needed financial help he turned to them for assistance. In June 1868, to help with his business, he obtained a loan of £2000 personally from Alexander, Al and John, and from the Firm. The Bond was not redeemed for ten years, and in returning the loan, he remarked

> it served its purpose well, and that by its use in the early part of my present business has left me independent of any other aid.[9]

If the bond between the two families was not particularly close, it meant that they did not believe the marriage between Mary-Ann and Wright was a union made in heaven. The most often repeated remark made by the family, was 'poor Mary-Ann', indicating that they disapproved of her lifestyle or her husband's demeanour. There is little doubt that Mary-Ann's marriage did not measure up to the happy union of her parents.

The weather was a major influence in the lives of every one connected with the sea. In his diaries, Al made frequent references to the havoc wrought by the tides, gales and rain. Early in January 1866 he wrote: 'Immense number of losses at sea at present owing [to] the very stormy weather ...'[10]

In a series of short essays, James Murray Templeton wrote a graphic account of the sea, this at the time when he was trying to define evil, whether evil was man-made or natural, which he defined as God-made evil:

> While, for instance, the ocean is on the whole subject to man, or subservient to his purpose, yet it possess[es] an unknown energy which may at any moment cause loss of life. This occasional evil -- the horror of shipwreck -- is that which has mainly forced men to evolve the modern ship and means of communication between continents. Had the sea been always calm, always gentle, then the race might have been content with little beyond the dug-out.[11]

Neither the sailor nor the shipbuilder has ever managed to tame the sea; the dangers of 1866 are the same dangers today. The sea continues to claim the lives of those who do not respect its power and its capacity for evil.

Ever since James Stephen had turned his back on the shipbuilding business, he had been in dispute with Al as to what share of the profits from the business he was entitled to receive. Al's contention was that when James pulled-out of the partnership agreement, he was not entitled to a single penny from the profits. The relationship between the brothers had declined since a chance meeting in Glasgow in April 1860. Al had not known that James was back in Glasgow: the date is even more significant as it came just sixteen days after James's marriage to Eliza.

The day after their meeting, Al learned that James was calling on a number of people to elicit their help in his financial dispute with his brothers. Al immediately informed his solicitor Daniel Forbes that James was back in Glasgow trying to bring new arguments into the dispute. According to Al, James's claims were as infamous as before; he was now attempting to involve his father and William in the affair. There was also, in Al's opinion, the unsettled matter of the six-hundred pound Letter of Credit he had given James when he had gone to America. This Letter of Credit had been cashed in America, and had been honoured by a London bank and paid by Al on 10 June 1859.

This date had an important significance in that James's marriage to Williamina Clark was all but over, and in less than five months time she would be dead. Even without paid employment, James was still spending lavishly. Al admitted that he was exceedingly depressed by the whole sorry mess.

Trying to settle the matter consumed a good deal of time and energy during the 1860s. Al's letters to James's solicitor, Robert Smith, became ever more angry. His temper boiled when Smith suggested that James should be entitled to "Goodwill"; this, after Al had repeatedly suggested that the matter should be settled by an arbitrator. In replying to Smith, Al wrote:

> I have perused them with care and I may say that I concur generally in the views expressed by Mr Miller [the arbitrator appointed by Stephen]. Like him I consider the proposition embodied in the memorandum sent him by Mr Pattison to be altogether out of the question. As regards article 1st it is truly obnoxious.... From the outset we have all been agreed that the basis of any arrangement must be a ratification of the Deed of April with the single exception of having James's share and Interest as at that date .... [12]

The April date is again significant. It was the date at which James relinquished his partnership, and accordingly the last date at which he could expect to receive an income from the Firm. The dispute dragged on for months but the time came when Al could tell his father that the matter was over. James's solicitors had finally agreed that James's action was unsound and would probably fail. Al's own Counsel had advised him that if the matter did go before the Court of Session it would be thrown out as there was no basis for James's demands.

James, in spite of his marriage to Eliza MacCorquadale and the birth of his sons, was still without a regular income. He wandered round the west of Scotland, staying with various relatives of Eliza. In 1864, when he and his family were in Moffat, his health began to give cause for much concern. On the evening of 22 February Al received a telegram from his father, saying that he had been informed that James was critically ill. Alexander told Al that it had been at James's own request that his family and friends should be sent for. Alexander asked his son-in-law John Logan if he would go, on behalf of the family, to see just how serious the situation was. Logan left Dundee, early on the morning of the 23rd, but arrived too late. James died at 4.00am that morning. His death was certified by Dr James Munro, who informed the Registrar that his patient had died of disease of the liver and kidney. James was thirty-five-years-old.

Al immediately left Glasgow for Moffat and was met at Beattock Station by Andrew, who had been instrumental in pleading with the family to come to Moffat. The two brothers, one grieving and one still smarting under the onslaught that James had caused him, spoke briefly before Al went to call on Eliza. It must have been a difficult meeting, he had not met Eliza before and she would have known of his animosity towards her husband.

Al then called on Munro and heard the details of James's illness. He felt sorrow and anguish for a life that began with such promise and ended in such pain and degradation. The funeral was held the next day. James was buried in Moffat churchyard close to the crypt wall.

Alexander had lost two daughters and a son in a year, but with James's death he was left with a terrible dilemma of what to do to help Eliza and his grandsons, James and Robert. He could not, in all conscience, bring them fully into the family circle, neither could he abandon them to poverty and the workhouse. He did the only thing he could, he made them a small allowance, sufficient for their needs but not enough to give them any degree of luxury.

Andrew and John Logan were instructed to keep in touch with Eliza and to make sure her sons were not neglected. The sadness of James's life was that his two sons would never share the advantages that Al's children would have as a right. Yet without their grandfather's generosity their young lives would have been destitute and they would, in all probability, have spent their childhood on parish relief. That James and Robert emerged from childhood as two well balanced young men was a tribute to their grandfather and to Al and John. John, in particular was, and would remain, a thoughtful, caring and compassionate uncle.

An African Adventure

THERE are many significant dates in Al Stephen's life. During the early days of January 1866 he made a decision that would alter, forever, his relationship with his brother John. He decided to give John a third share of the Kelvinhaugh yard rather than a quarter share. From his Scribbling Diaries it would appear that the only person he consulted before doing this was his lawyer, Daniel Forbes.

On 3 January, Al and Mary, and their children, Alex and Maud, were at Corona with his parents, the occasion being to announce and celebrate the engagement of his brother John to Elizabeth [Eliza] Wilson. Among the other visitors was the nine-year-old Blanche Croudace, up from London. Again one can only assume that she and her cousin Maud had been invited to discuss their participation in John and Eliza's forthcoming marriage. Eliza's sister Barbara completed the company.

Three years younger than Al, John was destined to play a role that was designed for him, and justified his title of 'Uncle John'. He was a calming and benign influence when problems and disasters threatened either the business of shipbuilding, or the personal and religious lives of the family. John's faith in the Free Church never waived and he never doubted that his God would guide him in all he did.

Towards the end of January, in preparation for his marriage, John took a five-year lease on a terrace house at 5 Fitzroy Place, Glasgow, at seventy pounds per annum rent. The evening before his marriage John gave a small dinner party at his bachelor home at 14 Somerset Place; Al, naturally, was among the guests.

Six years younger than John, Eliza was the seventh child of John Wilson, a silk merchant, and Barbara Harvey. By the time of Eliza's marriage on 8 March, both her parents were dead, but she was able to be married at her home, 15 Queen's Crescent, Glasgow. The Revd Dr Samuel Miller officiated and the witnesses were Eliza's sister Barbara, John Harvey who was probably her uncle (he had been a witness at her baptism), and James Templeton junior. The inclusion of James Templeton provides some proof of the closeness of the two families.

The couple spent their honeymoon in Paris, Geneva and Rome, and they were away for a little under a month. John and Eliza, unlike both their parents, were not to enjoy the delights of a large family. Their first son, John Wilson, was born on 25 September 1867, but died sixteen months later on 8 February 1869. The death certificate stated that the cause of death was uncertain. Four and a half months later, the couple had a little daughter named Elsie Mina, but she died on 16 December 1870.

There were to be other pregnancies but none that would lead to a healthy child being born, making the suffering of John and Eliza almost unbearable. Medical science at that time was not well established and there was little or no understanding of the reasons why so many babies died in the first few months of life. It is possible that the death of Eliza's children was linked to a haemolytic disorder caused by the incompatibility of its rhesus-positive blood with its mother's rhesus-negative blood. This was the fate of many women who had a number of still-born babies. It would be well into the twentieth century before the condition was recognised and before a treatment was established. In the meantime women like Eliza would be left wondering why they could not give birth to healthy children.

John and Eliza were not the only family members grieving the loss of a dear one. Six-year-old James Washington Stephen and his four-year-old brother Robert Little were facing another major tragedy coming after the death of their father two years earlier. About the 1 or 2 February their mother was admitted to the Chalmers Hospital, Edinburgh, with a knee injury.

On Saturday 24 February Al received a telegram from Edinburgh, stating that his sister-in-law was dying. The next day he travelled through to the Chalmers Hospital and was shocked by Eliza's condition. Ten days earlier she had developed pleurisy, a condition that in 1866 was often fatal. Leaving the hospital Al visited his sister Anne and her husband Duncan Paterson, before returning to Glasgow.

At 3.30 pm, on Monday 26 February, Eliza died. She died alone; not a single member of her own or her late husband's family was at her bedside. Only the ward nurse Catherine Hyslop was present. Al received the news from Duncan Paterson and from Mr Cassels, but again there is no mention in his diary that he attended her funeral. Nor is there any mention of her two little boys.

Glasgow in 1866 was an extremely unhealthy place in high summer; Al in common with many newly affluent manufacturers, began to look for a country estate to purchase. It was totally in keeping with his shipping birthright that he should choose to look to the Clyde and its environs. Dunoon attracted him for a number of reasons, its stunning beauty was unsurpassed, and it had a ferry access to the mainland. His Templeton parents-in-law already had a house at Bullwood. Al looked at many properties but when Fearann Coille was put on the market by the agents for the late owner Philip Lucas, Al knew he had found the perfect house. The selling price was £4,500, but with skilful negotiations Al was able to secure the property on 22 March for £4,100. He also bought, by auction, furniture to the value of £356.3.6, which included a billiard table. He was inordinately proud to have secured it in the face of fierce opposition from other bidders.

Al, Mary and Alex spent their first night at Fearann Coille on 3 April; two days later they were joined by his father-in-law, brother-in-law James Templeton and by his fourteen-and-a-half-year-old nephew John Stephen Croudace. John Croudace had joined the Yard as an apprentice draughtsman in January.

Fearann Coille was a substantial estate, comprising a house with nine bedrooms, dining room, drawing room and extensive servant quarters. Within the grounds there was a smaller house, which contained a billiard room, coachman's rooms, laundry, stables, byre and coach-house. The view across the Firth of Clyde was, and indeed still is, spectacular, a haven for sailing. Al commented in his diary that during the summer months he commuted daily from Fearann Coille to Kelvinhaugh, a journey that even now would not be impossible but one that would not be undertaken without a great deal of apprehension and expense.

Dunfillan, James Templeton's Bullwood house, held a very special place in his own heart, and whenever business commitments permitted he and his family would sail across the Clyde to be there. Mary's commitment was as strong as her husband's, and in the grounds of Dunfillan she was able to indulge her love of gardening, something she could not do in Glasgow. They employed a gardener, Roderick McDougall, a Colonsay born man, who James regarded as a trustworthy servant but not a particularly good gardener. However, under Mary's tutelage, she and McDougall produced a garden that was admired by all the visitors to Dunfillan.

The sea has always been a demanding master and accidents at sea were a constant threat to all who did not take the most rudimentary precautions. On 6 July, George Henderson, William's twenty-six-year-old brother-in-law, died while swimming off Carnoustie. At the time of his death, he was employed in the office at the Dundee Yard. And then later that month, Andrew, the eldest son of Andrew and Barbara Henderson, died in Ceylon from cholera.

Mourning after a tragedy was necessary but celebrations also occurred in the extended family. On 7 July, Al and Mary held a small dinner party to celebrate the sixty-fourth birthday of James Templeton.

Al had been distracted in spring of 1866 by a series of strikes at the Kelvinhaugh Yard. These had crippled much of the Clyde Yards and in consequence the companies formed the Clyde Shipbuilders Association in the hope that

> the General Committee be empowered to meet with representatives from the workforce for the purpose of receiving and considering any proposals they have to make.[1]

On 26 May, Al wrote in his diary that in accordance with a decision taken by the Association he had laid off one hundred men. He also mentioned that the apprentices and other tradesmen were still working -- six hundred in all. But, as in all trade disputes, those still working were being threatened by the strikers.

Al had no doubt who the ringleader was:

> An apprentice carpenter David Birnie, who I have had in the drawing office for about 2 years has been joining in some of the demonstrations made by the apprentices in the present strike. I informed him today that if he directly or indirectly took anything more to do in the matter I would send him down to the yard and have taken off him 2/- per week from his pay ... We had been kind to him before by continuing to pay [him] when ill.[2]

Birnie ignored the warning and on 5 June Al sacked him for disobeying his instructions not to encourage the apprentices to strike, and for telling lies. Al was deeply hurt by Birnie's conduct, especially after all he had done to advance Birnie's career prospects. A week later, Al received a letter from Birnie's lawyers threatening proceedings if he did not send them a copy of Birnie's employment conditions. It would be interesting to know what became of Birnie -- did he continue as an agitator for workers' rights and join the fledgling trade union movement? Or did he, like so many other young men at the time, emigrate to the Americas to seek fame and fortune? His dismissal from the Stephen's Yard had the required effect: on 16 June 745 men and boys went back at work. By 23 June the figure had risen to 823, but that was not the end of industrial problems that summer. In August the apprentice carpenters withdrew their labour for a four-day period.

Strikes, though, did not deter Al from enjoying his first summer at Fear-ann Coille. On 27 July he gave a house warming -- which he called a house heating party. The guests inevitably included his in-laws, and their sons, JS, James, and Archie, and their daughters, Anne and Agnes Jane. It was a feature of all the dinners and parties that Al and Mary gave during their long marriage that their Templeton relatives always headed the guest list. This was in marked contrast to Al's brothers, their wives and children, who, with the exception of John, were infrequent visitors to Park Circus or Fearann Coille.

With John marrying in Scotland, the family were rather amazed to receive news that their twenty-seven-year-old sister Hannah had decided to marry William Adams, an accountant from Newcastle, Australia. The marriage took place in Sydney and there was little prospect of any of the family attending. A family story, handed down, says the couple were married on board the Stephen built and owned ship *Earl of Dalhousie*[1st] by the Rev Dr Lang MP. John Dunmore Lang was a Greenock born clergyman and politician who had emigrated to New South Wales in 1823 to establish a Presbyterian Mission. He was a controversial man and much given to speaking his mind, which on four occasions led to him serving a period of imprisonment. He was a member of the Legislative Council from 1859 to 1869.

Alexander had been in London in April when the *Earl of Dalhousie* had left on her maiden voyage, and he must have been there to see Hannah safely on board. On the same day, Samuel joined the *King Lear* as a mid shipman, sailing under Captain Little for a fifteen-month voyage to Bombay and other ports in the Far East.

There are a couple of unanswered questions as to why Hannah was in Australia. Was she going to join Dr Lang as a missionary, and was it a shipboard romance? The couple had only one son, Alexander Stephen Adams, born in 1867. The marriage caused a rift between her and the wider family that was never completely healed. Al, in his many letters and diary entries, never mentioned her or her son, apart from a small Intimation taken from the *Glasgow Herald*, announcing her marriage.

Among the young men to emigrate that year was John Stewart Reid, the twenty-three-year-old son of Robert and Margaret Reid. On 27 October, John called at Park Circus to say good-bye to Al and Mary before embarking for a new life in New Zealand.

Three days later, Al was a member of the congregation at College

Church for the ordination of George Reith. Reith, an Aberdonian, was a lifelong friend of the Stephen/Templeton families, and in moments of crisis both Al and JS would turn to Reith for spiritual and moral support.

1866 saw the launch of *Corona*, a composite barque, from William's Yard at Dundee. The ship sailed under the Stephen flag, and was principally owned jointly by William and his father though William Croudace did own a quarter share. Croudace returned to Dundee from London sometime in September, as skipper of *Corona*.

Croudace's eldest son, John, after working for his grandfather and uncle at Kelvinhaugh, joined his parents in Dundee and completed his apprenticeship at his Uncle William's Yard.

In September, *Corona* was at Portsmouth preparing to board convicts being transported to Fremantle, Western Australia. *Corona's* use as a ship for the transportation of convicts did not last long; a year after her maiden voyage the last convicts were sent to Australia. It was thought at the time that transportation, far from deterring criminals, in fact, encouraged them and that prison at home was a more effective punishment. It was argued by some that transportation was extremely expensive, and simply allowed ship owners to get rich at the expense of the Treasury.

The family's reaction to Hannah's marriage was very muted unlike their reaction when eighteen-year-old Williamina [Mina], Alexander's youngest daughter, announced she wanted to marry James Stewart, a man seventeen years her senior.

It would appear that Alexander was opposed to the marriage of his youngest daughter to the dashing medical missionary. Al, however, disagreed with his father:

> I know Mr Stewart personally very well indeed and admire him as much a
> man as I suppose almost every body does, but then the best of men make a

mistake in this matter, and the question would be, is it so serious an affair, who is to judge of his proposal. As a man it is in his soul and conscience if he is doing right in asking Mina and it is also in Mina's soul and conscience if she accepts him. I do not think it would be our part to object on account of Mr Stewart going to Africa because if we did it would be as if we hindered the cause of Christ in the world.[3]

Al goes on to reassure his father, saying that in his opinion Stewart would make Mina a good husband, and she would make him a good wife. He says that much of the opposition to the marriage was based on the fact that Mina would be separated from her family. He also points out that many good marriages are made when the partners have known each other for only a few weeks and many a bad marriage has come after a lengthy engagement. Al then suggested to his father:

> My idea would be let her take a little time to make up her mind while she lays the matter before the Throne on High and consults with others.[4]

There is, though, another explanation to Alexander's reluctance to bless Mina's marriage to Stewart. It is possible that even in 1866, rumours and gossip had reached Corona that Stewart did not have a blame-free past.

In January 1861, Stewart had travelled to the Zambezi as a missionary, and was met on arrival by David Livingstone. There is an interesting little piece of gossip concerning Stewart's voyage to Africa. Among his fellow passengers was Livingstone's wife, Mary:

> Expedition gossip had it that James Stewart, the good-looking young representative of the Free Church of Scotland ... had an affair with Mrs Livingstone. The idea, on the face of it, was preposterous, for Stewart was a sensitive, handsome man of thirty, while Mary, at forty ... was "a coarse vulgar woman"...[5]

According to contemporary sources, Mary Livingstone was also an extremely fat woman. What is more probable than Stewart having an affair with Mary Livingstone was that as a doctor -- although he did not get his MB or CM until 1866, he had studied medicine at Edinburgh University -- he treated Mary for excessive bouts of drinking and hysteria.

Al had cautioned that Mina and Stewart should have a long engagement, but he was over-ruled and they married on 1 November 1866, at Corona. The date was surely influenced by Stewart's wish to return to Lovedale, the Central African Mission founded by Dr Love of Glasgow. Stewart and Mina would make Africa their home for many years. One of the guests at their wedding was David Livingstone's daughter and a witness was Horace Waller who Stewart had met in Africa. He was a good friend of Livingstone's and a lay superintendent for the Universities Mission.

The slave trade had been abolished by the British in 1807, yet incidents of that abominable trade still continued. Waller was forced to intervene on one occasion and cut through the ropes binding a group of slaves. The Missionaries wanted to preach the word of God to the African tribes, but nothing was as simple or as easy as they expected. Stewart and Waller did not always agree with Livingstone's methods. Livingstone was inclined to take sides between the warring tribes: Waller thought their help should be purely defensive. He did not believe that he should preach with a bible in one hand and a gun in the other.

Stewart and Mina paid Horace Waller a compliment when they named the first of their eight children -- seven daughters and one son -- Williamina [Mina] Waller.

The year 1866, which had brought much happiness with the marriage of Mina and James Stewart but much sadness with the death of the Henderson boys, ended with two glittering social occasions. On 1 December Al and Mary hosted a dinner party to celebrate the thirty-fifth wedding anniversary of James and Mary Templeton and Peter and Margaret Reid. At Christmas, as they had every year since their own marriage -- and would continue to do so for years to come -- Al and Mary hosted a dinner for the family at Park Circus. A typical guest list shows that usually twenty to thirty people sat down to dinner.

PART TWO
1867 - 1883

" We must remember that working perfection does not come by wishing, but by working. None of us possess a magic wand, by waving which he can at once transform all things; but each of us can do some little thing to improve our environment."

The Spirit Progress in our Factories
F H Young.
J T & Co Magazine, February 1920, in the
Templeton Archives at Stoddard International plc.

Happy Days

IT is hard to imagine what Mina Stewart's feelings were when she, her husband of two months, and their travelling companion Jane Waterston -- she was to be the first Principal of the Lovedale School for Girls -- arrived at Lovedale on 2 January 1867. The contrast between Mina's comfortable home of Corona and the stark beauty but appalling poverty of Africa must have filled her with despair. A hint of the harshness of Mina's early days in Africa was given by the Revd John Knox Bokwe -- he was obviously baptised by a Scottish missionary. Bokwe's words speak of the strength of Mina's character and they also show that she brought a few personal items to Africa. Bokwe explained that as an eleven-year-old, he and three companions had heard of the arrival of a new missionary and two ladies so they decided to investigate. It had been raining heavily during the previous week and the road to the main house -- which was only a track anyway -- was muddy, and being small boys, the four companions took great delight in splashing through the puddles:

> A thick pomegranate fence partly hid the front view of the mission-house, and it was not easy ... to gain the object of our visit unless by entering a narrow gateway.[1]

From the house came a haunting sound that Bokwe had never heard before; he stood entranced, and while his companions continued to play in the muddy puddles, he tentatively edged towards the sound. Seated at a strange looking object was a woman, and the sound seemed to be coming from the way she moved her hands over the object. He observed her wipe something from her cheek, and when she saw his slow, hesitant approach, she beckoned him to come forward. It was the beginning of a relationship that would see Bokwe become Stewart's secretary for twenty years, and a friendship that lasted for four decades.

Bowke later recalled that the music being played that day was *Home Sweet Home*, and that while Mina had her piano there was no bedstead in the mission house at this time. Is it any wonder that Mina shed a tear?

The Stephen Yards, like the Templeton carpet factories, were to suffer from devastating fires. On Wednesday 9 October 1867, the Yard at Dundee was destroyed by fire as well as two ships that were being built. Good management by the fire-fighters saved the offices and all the company books, but as Al recorded: 'It is very grievous for my father's sake who is now 72.'[2]

Fortunately the Yard was covered by insurance and immediate plans were made to rebuild; the first ship launched by the new Yard was *Tonbridge*, for J H Luscoombe.

Exhibitions played an important role in Templeton's sales philosophy; the first major exhibition had been the Exhibition of the Industry of all Nations, held in London in 1851. But for the Paris exhibition of 1867, Templeton made a special carpet, it was forty feet long and eighteen foot wide, and showed Christ standing on a pedestal with six Apostles each side of him. The figures were based on Bertel Thorvaldsen's sculpture of *Christ and the Twelve Apostles* in the Church of our Lady in Copenhagen. The weaving of the carpet, however, was not without incident:

> It is said that one of the weavers ... had a grudge against his foreman and deliberately inserted the wrong colour: this was not detected in the weft cloth but when the chenille was set up to produce the complete carpet, it was discovered that the Apostle Peter had bright blue hair.[3]

The error was corrected. The culprit was not sacked but from then on he became known as 'Blue-haired Peter'. It is hard to believe that such an act would go unpunished today.

A second impressive carpet was also made that year for the signing of the Treaty of Peace between Britain and France. The square carpet depicted Queen Victoria and the Emperor Louis Napoleon. Carpets were also made for the King of Denmark and the King of Siam. Abraham Lincoln's wife, Mary Todd, also requested a carpet for the refurbishment of the White House, and not for the first time she was criticised for spending State funds on extravagant furnishings.

Al and Mary Stephen's sixth child, and third son, was born on 26 December 1868. There was some confusion as to what the boy was to be called: he was registered as Charles, but by the time of his baptism his name had been changed to Bernard. The Register of Corrected Entries indicates the change was confirmed on the 27 February 1869.

It was not an auspicious start in the child's life, and he seems to have suffered from the fate of many younger children, constant unfair comparison with his elder and more robust siblings.

The year ended for Al on an optimistic note; he had finally come to the conclusion that if the Yard was to expand they would need to move. The Kelvinhaugh Yard had served them well since Alexander had bought it, but with the end of their twenty year lease it was right to look for larger premises. It is hard, with the distance of time, to believe that in 1868 the area from Govan to Renfrew was one of peaceful tranquillity. Sheep and cows grazed their way through luscious grass; stately houses had access to salmon fishing.

The estate of Linthouse had been for more than fifty years the home of bankers, who daily commuted from their rural paradise to their offices in the City of Glasgow. On the death of Michael Rowand, the last owner, his trustees sold the estate to the Union Bank of Scotland from whom Al purchased it.

Al's last entry in his diary for 1868 said:

> Called on the British Linen [they] offered me as much money as I liked -- even without a sixpence lying in the Bank. I propose to pay the Union Bank on 2 Feb 1869 for Linthouse £29,000 in one cheque.[4]

He had no desire to live in the splendid mansion, and once the contract was signed, work began on converting the house into offices, a storeroom and a model-maker's shop -- Stephen's models were, and remain, exquisite examples of the model-maker's craft. The ground surrounding the house was cleared; workshops, gantries and derricks rose from the bank of the river; tenement houses were built for the workers.

It was not the case that while Linthouse was being developed, work stopped at Kelvinhaugh; twenty-six ships were launched from the Yard in the years 1869 and 70. The last ship to leave Kelvinhaugh on 22 November 1870 was *Alert*, for R M Sloman & Co and the first ship to leave Linthouse on 24 November was *Glendarroch* for William Ross & Co.

The new Yard, like the old, experienced periods of recession -- depression. Al and John, however, were prepared to invest in the lean years so they were ready when the good times returned. In 1871 they financed the building of the engine and boiler shops at Linthouse, and with their policy of always investing in the best, they persuaded Ebenezer Kemp to leave the Dundee firm of Gourlay's and return to the Clyde where he had served his apprenticeship. Al offered him the position of manager of the new engine shop, and it was with some justification that it was later reported of Kemp and Stephen, that they built ships which rivalled the very best that ever sailed the high seas.

Kemp was a welcomed addition to the family of Stephen workers but Al was more tormented by the continuing problems with Andrew. On 8 December Andrew wrote to tell his father that he was to be married. He also informed his father that after three years as Resident Medical Officer at the Middlesex Hospital he had resigned telling his father that he proposed to go into private practice near Westminster Palace.

In view of Andrew's inability to handle his finances it seemed a very risky venture to give up a salaried position and become dependant on private patients. He could, of course, have believed that he would emulate his future father-in-law William Stuart's prosperous medical practice.

Eleanor Sophia Stuart was thirteen years Andrew's junior; they were married at St Mary's Church, Woolwich on 23 December 1868. She was the second daughter of William and Ann Maria Stuart; she had one older sister and two younger sisters, and at least five brothers. Dressed in a gown of satin trimmed with swansdown, Eleanor was attended by her two younger sisters, who were dressed in mauve and swansdown. The guests were a distinguished company of friends of the bride and her parents. Andrew, on the other hand, was only supported by two colleagues from the Middlesex, H A Reeves and Dr Alexander Stevens. It would appear from the guest list printed in the *Kentish Independent* that none of Andrew's family travelled to Woolwich for the grand occasion. Mention was made, though, that Andrew's father was head of an extensive shipbuilding firm in Dundee. There was not a single reference to the Kelvinhaugh or Linthouse side of the business.

On the day of Andrew's marriage, Al noted that he had attended a meeting in Glasgow of the Medical Missionary Society. Andrew's family must have prayed that marriage would give his life direction and purpose. How wrong they were, marriage to Eleanor only increased his paranoia and his extravagances.

It was perhaps unfortunate that Frederick, one of Eleanor's brothers, was a solicitor, as this gave Andrew access to free legal advice in his war of attrition against the family. Shortly after Christmas 1869, he visited Al and later Al gave a summary of the meeting to his father. But like all meetings between the two brothers, Andrew said one thing at the meeting, then, on leaving, changed his mind. He told Al and John that he was ashamed of his previous actions and that he truly wished to make amends and would withdraw all his allegations and law suits against the family. There was an element of blackmail in his contrition, for in return for his good behaviour he wanted the family to allow him to open a credit bank account, using the Company's funds. Al treated this suggestion with scorn as he did Andrew's assurance that he had reformed. Al told his father:

> I told him frankly and fairly without mincing matters what our ideas as to his conduct [should be] and that he had not yet, as far as you and the others were concerned made ample confession, and repentance ...[5]

Al said that Andrew had written his father a letter, which Al assured him was entirely Andrew's own work and that neither he nor John had altered it in anyway. One paragraph in Al's letter is particularly revealing for it shows just how Andrew tried to rationalize his actions:

> ... he [Andrew] puts the settlement made with him in Edinburgh right and
> takes off the impression made in our minds as to what he may have said to
> his sister [Elsie Croudace] which he says he may have said something he
> ought not to have said as he remembers he was getting worried ... that he
> would not be received at Corona.[6]

Andrew knew he was not a welcome visitor at Corona, and he should not
have been surprised that he was being excluded from the family home.
Al told his father of Andrew's wish to set up a credit account, and to
plead his case he had brought up his account books. While Andrew was
in Glasgow he stayed at the Waverley Temperance Hotel, which means
that neither Al nor John offered him a place to stay.

Andrew remained in Glasgow for three or four days, doing all he
could to persuade Al and John to change their minds. His debts were
causing him terrible anguish and like many men who had reached the
end of their tether, Andrew resorted to a form of emotional blackmail.
He told his brothers that apart from his worry over his mounting debts,
he was also extremely distressed by the illness of his wife. Eleanor was
pregnant with her first child; a son, William Alexander, was born in the
autumn of 1869. Andrew and Eleanor would have three sons and three
daughters.

Al was sympathetic to Andrew's anxieties and he expressed his
hope that the invalid would soon recover. He was not, however, as
sympathetic about Andrew's money worries and he made a very relevant
point: 'I would have thought a doctor's practice would not require much
outlay ...'[7]

Al, though, does accept that patients may at times be slow in paying
their bills. It is a complaint that he could equally have made about ship
owners. He again repeated his reasons why he could not grant Andrew's
request:

> I have not myself given a credit account to any one and you know these
> things are generally excluded in business partnerships and I don't think I
> could do such a thing.[8]

He informed his brother that even if such a thing were possible they could not countenance it at present, as the Company was heavily committed to moving to the new Yard at Linthouse which was involving them in heavy expenses. In an honest admission, he said:

> [In] Dundee shipbuilding is about finished and their whalers' have cost them all a good deal of money this year. After the fire Dundee had only completed two ships in 1869.[9]

Al concludes his letter by trying to soften his refusal to help:

> I do not know the form in England that a credit account is joined and I don't know any of your circumstances. If I could help you in any way I would be glad but I really do not see my way to the present proposal.[10]

Andrew viewed the expansion at Linthouse as an example of how rich and successful Al and John had become and he saw no reason why he should not also benefit from their success. Jealousy is a powerful motive between siblings and in Andrew's behaviour there was little that was rational or objective. He had chosen to enter the medical profession and not shipbuilding, and no one had forced that choice on him. It is worth contrasting his behaviour to be recompensed for being a doctor with that of James Stewart. Stewart never sought money for its own sake, or for what it could buy him in personal luxuries. His frequent requests for money were always for the benefit, welfare, and expansion of the Mission at Lovedale, the Gordon Memorial, and later at Livingstonia.

Stewart's boundless enthusiasm and energies were in stark contrast to those of Andrew -- Andrew wanted and he took, Stewart accepted what was laid before him:

> Stewart rode about a thousand miles in very rough country and in districts unknown to him, sleeping at any house, shop or hut that he could find. He spent one night in an outside hide store, and another in a miserable house, where he got for supper "apparently salt beef or salt horse perhaps; but at any rate it was very good" ... He asked to be allowed to sleep on the clay floor of the kitchen under the table, as it was better than the veldt. On another night he came to a German mission-house that was shut up. He managed to get in somehow.[11]

A few years later, on one of his numerous sea journeys, Stewart and a German missionary struck up a conversation — Stewart was a good linguist. The German told a story of when he was absent from his Mission, his house had been broken into:

> "Did the intruder behave himself well and pay for what he took?" Stewart asked.
> "Oh yes," replied the German, "he left money on the table."[12]

Stewart admitted that he had been that intruder. It is hard to imagine that Andrew would have been prepared to face the hardships that Stewart faced. In London, even on modest earnings, he employed a nurse, a cook, a housemaid and a page boy.

A Death at Sea

AL was often depressed by the state of the shipbuilding business but his brother-in-law, JS, was rather more impressed by the changes that were taking place on the Clyde. In a letter to his brother Archie, who was on missionary duties in India, JS tells of the changes Al had been making to the Yard, and there is a hint of envy in his words:

> But what a pigmy my business is compared to Stephen's. His new yard is quite a little Town. Have you been told of his erection of boiler and Engineering works on a large scale in connection with the yard? Not only so, but he has ventured on a novel plan of the erection of an immense travelling crane extending all along the front of the yard parallel with the river. This immense structure -- quite a feature -- capable of lifting a boiler or engine cylinder and dropping it into a destined place in the ship in process of building.[1]

JS went on to say that the wage bill for the three thousand men employed by the Yard must have been in the region of two and a half thousand pounds per week. He told Archie that Al controlled and supervised the whole enterprise with quiet efficiency and dignity.

JS may have envied Al's apparent affluence but he did not act as the poor relation. In the ten years since Mary's death, he occupied a house at 2 Park Quadrant, the northern, or outer road of Park Circus, but in 1873 he moved with Alice and James Murray into 1 Park Circus, within the inner circle. The Park Circus house was a beautiful four storey, yellow sandstone property, designed by Charles Wilson. Joe Fisher, in his book on Glasgow, described the area of Park Circus in fine detail:

> Situated on a piece of ground which rises gently from Charing Cross westward, culminating in the high-standing bluff overlooking Kelvingrove Park, with the University of Glasgow on the opposite height.[2]

There is much about JS's life that one can say with absolute conviction. He adored beautiful things and in furnishing Park Circus he had more than sufficient money to allow his designing talents full rein. In his letter to Archie he apologised for his lapse in not writing as often as he promised, but admited with obvious pleasure that the manufacturer of the Brussels carpet business was improving, after a period when he had regarded himself as only a beginner: 'but now we have crept up into a recognised leading position ...'[3]

Although delighted with the increase in his wealth, there was, as in so many Calvinist Scotsmen, a hint of guilt at his extravagances. He voiced that guilt to Archie

> it will cost me a good deal of money for its furniture, and decoration which you know is rather a hobby of mine to try to make somewhat novel and artistic ...[4]

Al may have differed from JS in his opinion of the success of the Yard. But he would not wait for orders to come to him, like all good businessmen he went looking for them. In January 1874 he travelled to Amsterdam and Hamburg: he was away for eleven days. On 21 April he noted in his diary 'Things for shipbuilding are looking very black -- nothing new for us ...'[5]

In May he travelled to Cologne and Hamburg again and was away this time for ten days. The trips were obviously successful, and in spite of Al's gloomy predictions the Yard was relatively successful. Between 1872 and 1875 they launched nine ships for German owners.

Even when orders were confirmed, contracts signed and payments made, the ship built and successfully launched, the Yard could not assume everything would then be plain sailing. Disputes between builder and customer, although thankfully not that frequent, did occur. Al and John soon found out that going to Law and winning in an Inferior Court was rarely the victory it appeared. If the case went to appeal to a Higher Court then the verdict would all too often cost both the appellants and the petitioners a great deal of time, anxiety and money.

❖❖❖

William, in contrast to Al, was feeling poverty-stricken by the lack of business. It was with a little pique that William told Al that he thought their father was now worth over a hundred thousand pounds. Whatever the brothers lack of orders was costing them their poverty was only relative. The joiners at the Linthouse Yard were given a raise in the hourly rate of a farthing, from seven pence to seven and a quarter pence, but their working week was reduced from fifty-four hours to fifty-one hours, thus giving a wage of roughly one pound ten shillings.

It should be stressed however that Al and his brothers were deeply committed to the welfare of their workers and their families. They did much to improve the living accommodation of the workers, and Al, in particular, was passionate in his determination to improve the schooling for local children.

The Scottish Education Act had become law in 1872, establishing a national system for compulsory education for children between the ages of five and thirteen. At the same time it decreed that local control of schools should be in the hands of school boards, with a committee of between five and fifteen elected members. The members would be responsible for the management, accommodation and attendance, the money for such coming from three sources, government grants, local rates and fees. The fees, however, were modest.

In a letter to the Revd Dr Robert Howie, who in 1872 was appointed Minister of St Mary's Church, Govan, Al expressed his belief that the new Educational Act would benefit them all:

> What a blessing the Education Act of 1872 may yet prove to our district, the more we know of the state of matters the more I am inclined to think that there was the more need of a change in the educational system of this country.[6]

Robert Howie, an Ayrshire born man, was four years younger than Al; he had been ordained in 1860, at the Wynd church, Glasgow, where the Revd Dugald MacColl, was minister. MacColl was an inspiration to Howie, from him he learned the art of raising money to build a new church. Howie's first parish was Trinity Church, Charlotte Street, in the east end of Glasgow, where he raised a considerable sum of money to build the church. When he left Trinity to go to St Mary's he left a church with a strong congregation and debt free. He held his first service at Govan in the Town Hall where he shared the premises with the school children. Howie immediately began to raise money to build a new church and in this he was ably assisted by Al and John.

Al became chairman of the Govan School Board in 1873 and one of his first tasks was to appoint a new master, and as he told Robert Howie he thought they had made a good choice:

> I have not the slightest doubt that he [John Lochore] will be chosen out of the 79 applicants ... and it will give me the greatest pleasure, from all that I have been able to learn of his qualifications, that he should be appointed ...[7]

He then went on to tell Howie that the Govan Board Clerk, John Allan Craigie, had visited Lochore on the 16 October and had reported back that in his opinion Lochore was exactly the man they needed. Al assured Howie that he would not finally commit himself to appointing Lochore until:

> Mr Lochore is to be in Glasgow [on 18 October] and our clerk is to ask him to call on me so I have an opportunity of judging him for myself. You see we don't do things on hearsay in our Board.[8]

The New Year of 1874 was only twelve days old when tragedy again dispirited the Stephen family. William, in Dundee, had launched the *Cyphrenes* in 1872 for the family. On Sunday 11 January, *Cyphrenes* had left Gravesend on her maiden voyage to Australia, carrying cargo and thirty-seven passengers. Samuel had been appointed her Master and his young wife was among the passengers. Samuel had married the eighteen-year-old Euphemia Mary Marsley [known as Massie] Baxter, on Christmas Eve 1872. She was the fifth child of John Baxter, a textile mill owner, of Ashbank House, Blairgowrie, and his wife Frances Hay Gardiner. Samuel had two reasons to be happy, he had command of his own ship and his wife was six months pregnant.

In the early evening of 12 January, Al received a telegram from

William to say that *Cyphrenes* had put into Portland Roads. William told him that Samuel was missing and that according to information he had, Massie had last seen her husband at eight o'clock that morning.

Al made immediate arrangements to travel to London but before he left another telegram arrived from his sister Janet to say, that according to further information they had received, Samuel had fallen overboard. A report in a newspaper a few days later gave a fuller picture of what had happened. The wind that day was gale force and it must be asked why Samuel thought it wise to walk on deck in the teeth of such extremes of winter weather:

> ... when off St Alban's Head the captain left his cabin apparently for the purpose of taking a walk on deck, and to smoke, leaving his wife ... He did not return, and his wife became alarmed, more especially when she heard the chief officer call for him all over the ship, but without success.[9]

As Al hurried to London, Massie had already contacted her sister Helen and her husband who were much closer and would reach her quicker than Al. Helen and James Alexander Luke, a Colonial Broker, had married in 1870 and once again the web of interconnecting marriages was spun. James's younger brother, David Smith Luke married in September 1872, Helen Stephen Croudace, Samuel's niece.

There is a suggestion in Al's diaries that in January 1874 he paid seven hundred pounds with an additional hundred and fifty pounds of interest, from his own account, to Daniel Forbes. The money was to repay a loan made to Andrew in December 1869. It was not the first time that Al had paid the debts of his brothers and it would not be the last such payment. Andrew's financial problems continued to dominate the family for the rest of that year.

The timing of this repayment may have made Al feel slightly guilty at his brother's financial plight. On 9 January, he was able to say, with some pride, that he had been involved in the shipbuilding business for twenty-five years. And during that quarter of a century he had seen the business grow to become one of the best on the Clyde, with a reputation for quality and for delivering vessels on time and on budget.

In mid Jauary Al was in Amsterdam and Hamburg on business for nine days, but when he returned to Scotland on the 24 he was immediately plunged into Andrew's problems once again. Andrew had written to his father begging him to end their feud. His plea fell on deaf ears, for Forbes had already recommended that they should ignore Andrew's requests to be allowed back into the family fold.

Elsewhere there was little joy in the hearts of Alexander and Elspeth as they sat down to dinner on 4 February to celebrate their golden wedding. They had very little reason to feel either happy or contented with the battles that were raging around them. Whatever presents they received from their other children, nothing could have compensated them for the distress they had suffered that January with the death of Samuel.

On 6 April, at her Blairgowrie home, Massie gave birth to Samuel's daughter and named her Mabel Alexandria. Four days earlier, Elspeth was grieving the loss of another of her daughters, and even the birth of a granddaughter could not have compensated her for the death of Mary-Ann who died at five minutes past six on the morning of Thursday 2 April 1874, at her home in Kew Terrace. She had been ill for thirteen days with congestion of the brain brought on by typhoid fever. She was thirty-six-years old and it was only eleven years since she had been in Gibraltar when her sisters Mary and Marjory died. Her last words echoed much of the teachings of her devout family: "My own precious God is all to me now."[10]

Al had the very unpleasant task of travelling to Corona to tell his parents of the death of their daughter. Mary-Ann's funeral was held on 6 April and her remains were taken to be buried at the Southern Necropolis, that *City of the Dead* that dominates the sky-line to the east of the Merchant City of Glasgow.

James Stewart was home from Lovedale in the early months of 1874

and on 18 April he attended the funeral service of David Livingstone in Westminster Abbey. As Stewart later recalled, it had been a sad occasion for him and three old friends, Horace Waller, Sir John Kirk and Edward D Young. Stewart had openly expressed opposition to Livingstone and his desire to create a Mission at Blantyre; shortly after Livingstone's funeral Stewart admitted:

> When I came home, I had no intention of proposing this scheme [the scheme was the establishment of a Mission, which became known as Livingstonia] than of proposing a mission to the North Pole. It seemed, however, to be thrust upon me, almost to be waiting for me. I feel in one way more at rest and more quiet since I have taken up this burden.[11]

Stewart may have thought he was right in taking up a new burden, but Mina had other ideas. She now had three daughters under the age of six and the thought that James would again be away from Lovedale for long periods caused her much misgivings. James told Mina:

> I am not volunteering for this service. If some of my friends I now see were to hear me doing so, they would pull my coat-tails and say: "Remember the little woman at Lovedale." Ah! I did remember her, and the little ones playing about the door, or crawling over the floor ... But I would say this for the little woman or little lady at Lovedale, I never yet found her shrink from duty ... Lovedale will always be our headquarters and our home ...[12]

It was, in most people's opinion, essential that a monument to Livingstone should be erected as soon as possible -- it almost seems that by dying he became a national hero overnight. Stewart saw no sense in erecting a marble monument in Westminster Abbey: he knew that Livingstone would have wanted his memorial to be a living entity in his beloved Nyasaland.

Stewart was not given to instant decisions, he would have to consult others; ideas were one thing but the money to carry out those plans was an entirely different matter. On a summer evening a few months after Livingstone's funeral, at John Stephen's country house at Shieldhall, Stewart made his plans known to a small group of influential men. Encouraged by their commitment, in May the following year, he told a meeting of the General Assembly the outcome of those discussions. It was late in the evening when he rose to speak. The assembled delegates were tired and perhaps even bored at the end of a long day's debating. Stewart, sensing their apathy, threw away his prepared speech and spoke with dignity and with obeisance:

> I would humbly suggest, as the truest memorial of Livingstone, the establishment of this Church, or several Churches together, of an institution at once industrial and educational, to teach the truths of the Gospel and the arts of civilised life to the natives of the country, and which shall be placed in a carefully selected and commanding spot in Central Africa, where from its position and capabilities it might grow ... and become a great centre of commerce, civilisation and Christianity. And this I would call *Livingstonia*.[13]

Livingstonia was built on the shores of Lake Nyassa, and was ready for occupation by 1880, due in no small part to Stewart's enthusiasm and money raised by the Free Church of Scotland and the Stephen/ Templeton family.

In 1874, whether in response to JS's having moved into an elegant new house, Al decided that he should also move, for he and his family had been living 15 Park Circus for some considerable time. On 10 February they looked at a house at 17 Park Circus Terrace which was on offer at £11,000. They made an offer on it but did not expect it to be accepted. They were right, it wasn't. Two weeks later they looked at a house at 6 Park Gardens, costing £13,500, but again regrettably it had just been sold. It would appear that house buying in the 1870s was as stressful as it became a hundred and thirty odd years later. They finally settled on 12 Park Terrace.

In July 1874, Andrew sent his mother a number of hand bills, making the sort of allegations against his father and sisters that were they made to-day, would have police, social workers and media descending on Corona *en masse* even though what they alleged was absolute rubbish. There is in James Murray Templeton's diary, a pencil sketch of Alexander drawn at the time of his seventy-fifth birthday. It is the text to the drawing though that raises a smile. Someone, presumably Alexander, had written: 'You wouldn't believe it I am 75y (What an old ... a different hand added the word **sinner**, followed by two exclamation marks).'

Andrew, in an attempt to cause his father, Al, and John, even more embarrassment, distributed the same hand bills around Govan. It can only be a matter of speculation what the workers felt at the end of a long day's shift reading that their guv'nor was guilty of such crimes. It is also fair to assume that many of the hand bills were torn from their hoard-ings and tossed into the gutter, where they belonged.

Faced with doing something or nothing, on the advice of Daniel Forbes the family decided to ignore Andrew's irrational and senseless behaviour. If they thought silence would have an effect on Andrew they were sadly mistaken. He needed a solution to his debt problems and he knew only his father and brothers had the means to bail him out. Find-ing that indirect action had no effect, Andrew, Eleanor and one of their children paid an uninvited call at Corona. They were escorted from the property.

In September 1874, Al and Mary were on a short holiday touring the Highlands and perhaps for once hoping that someone else would solve Andrew's problems. Their holiday was not a great success. It rained and rained without ceasing, as all those who have visited Pitlochry and Brae-mar in that late summer can testify.

John, though, was trying to help Andrew with his problems; he went to South Kensington where in the company of William, James Stewart and Duncan Paterson he met Andrew. On their return to Scotland they went to Corona where they reported that very little progress had been made. Andrew had confessed that he had mortgaged his home at 58 Queen's Gate Terrace, and had sold his furniture, but was renting it back at an astronomical rate of interest.

John told them that Andrew kept a staff of six, and that he seemed unable, or unwilling, to admit that his profligate life-style could not continue. Andrew believed that he was being denied his rightful inheritance and that his father and brothers were deliberately cheating him as they had cheated James. There was, John believed, little chance of a speedy resolution of the matter. He told them that Andrew should be allowed to come to Corona at the end of October. He thought Andrew should be given one last chance to end his feud with the family.

Al had other problems to contend with, in September and again in November, he went to Swansea and Liverpool to try to secure orders for the Yard. Without new orders, none of them would have a healthy or wealthy future. The Yard actually only completed eight ships in 1874. The visits were successful, and in 1876 the Yard launched three barques for Welsh owners: *Picton Castle* for Simpson Brothers; *Lord Clyde* for Gilbert Tulloch and *Llewellyn* for Captain John Rosser.

The relationship between employers and employees during the industrialisation era of the nineteenth century has frequently been portrayed as one of exploitation and dominance of the employer over the employee. While this may have been true in many industries, there is much contemporary evidence to suggest that it was not true in the case of Alexander Stephen and Sons. The difference in wages of the workers and the owners was, however, extreme: while Al could confidently look for a house costing £11,000, a draughtsman at the Yard, earning less than £3 a week would have had difficulty paying the rent and feeding his family.

Strikes were a fact of life, and in early December the carpenters and joiners downed tools when the Company announced that there would be a reduction of one penny an hour in wages. Negotiations between management and workers rarely produced a settlement without the obligatory strike, but in the end compromise was reached and work again commenced.

It was well known that JS held an affection both for Ayrshire, the land of his ancestors, and for Kintyre, the birthplace of his father. It is then not surprising that he became a member of The Kintyre Club. Founded in 1825, the object of the Club was

> to raise a fund for giving of charitable relief to indigent natives of the district of Kintyre, or their children who reside in and about Glasgow; and to encourage learning and industry, by offering rewards, in bursaries, books or medals ...[14]

Their first President was Alex W Johnston, Member of Parliament for Kilmarnock from 1841 until his death in 1844. A Kintyre man and one of the original financial backers of James Templeton, Johnston was also a manufacturer and merchant in Glasgow before becoming an M.P. One of the early members of the Club was Archibald Templeton who joined in 1829; his sons, James, Archibald and Nathaniel became members in the 1840s. JS was enrolled as a teenager in 1846. His brothers, James and Archie were enrolled in 1854 and 1856 respectively. JS's son James Murray, according to the records of the Club, was enrolled in 1860 -- the year of his birth. Was JS trying to instil in his son the notion that duty to those less fortunate should be the main focus in his life?

Honorary or free membership was awarded to men, not from the Kintyre Peninsular, but men of standing in the community in which they lived. Al and John Stephen, both noted for philanthropy and charitable giving, were active supporters of the Club.

Peter Reid was President four times 1829, 1853, 1854 and 1862. Dr John Pirie, married to a niece of JS's grandmother, Ann Harvey, served as President in 1870 and 1871. After Robert Harvey's death in January 1867, Pirie left Kintyre for Glasgow where he became the physician and surgeon to both the Stephen/Templeton families. JS was President in 1874 and his brother James in 1879.

Lady members were enrolled as associates after 1882. All the Templeton women, including Elizabeth Mary, Thomas's orphaned daughter, who was then teaching in Watford, became members.

It was incumbent on the directors to arrange a dinner or other social occasion, at least once a year, providing such an event was not financed out of the Club's resources. On Friday evening 18 December 1874, JS and Al both attended the annual dinner at McRae's Hotel, Bath Street.

End of an Era

There were two significant deaths in the early months of 1875. The first was of sixteen months old William Towers Wright, son of the late Mary-Ann. He died of Scarlatina on 25 March at 19 Kew Terrace. Scarlatina is an acute infectious disease and would have meant that little William's sisters, Emily, Mary, Elsie, Amelia, and five-year-old brother Alex would have been placed in quarantine, and kept strictly away from the dying boy.

The second death was of Alexander Stephen who died on 24 April at Corona at the age of eighty. Al received a telegram from John, who had travelled through the day before to say their father was, according to Dr Ritchie, unlikely to see another dawn. William arrived from Dundee but there was little he could do. Elspeth sat with Alexander throughout the night as his condition continued to worsen. Janet arrived on Saturday morning, having travelled overnight from London, but she arrived just too late: her father died at 11 o'clock.

Al left Glasgow on the 1.50 p.m. train which took a little under four hours to reach Corona where to his distress he found that John had not overstated the situation. John told him that on the Saturday morning their father had risen as usual, bathed and dressed but had had difficulty in doing up his buttons. He went to seek help from Elspeth but he collapsed just as he reached her; with some difficulty she managed to get him to a chair. The servants were called and Alexander was helped into his wife's room. Finlay, the coachman, was despatched to Broughty Ferry to fetch Dr Ritchie.

Alexander, according to John, desperately tried to take something from his pocket but he was unable to do so, nor was he able to make his wishes known to his wife or son. It was later discovered that he wished to sign a cheque.

The funeral of Alexander was held on 28 April. The Revd John Lyon, who conducted the service, had been at West Ferry Church for a little over thirty years. Unlike Alexander, he had been a west coast man, having been born in Bute in 1806 but spent the greater part of his life in the

East. Alexander had been a staunch supporter and office-bearer to Lyon and the two had become firm friends. Al noted that the last time his father had been at church was three or four weeks before his death. He had been in the shipyard for a time on the Tuesday when all commented on how well and hearty he looked. In accordance with his wishes Alexander was laid to rest in the Monifieth Cemetery, in a lair just behind his beloved Corona.

What manner of man were his family, workmen and friends mourning that day? According to a contemporary source:

> Those who had the opportunities of knowing the man knew that beneath the brusque manner and strong, shrewd sense which distinguished him there lay a deep fund of generous and kindly emotion. [He] had a strong faith in himself, and the thoroughness with which he attended to every detail of his business was, unquestionably, one of the chief secrets of his success.[1]

It was Al who expressed the sadness that the family felt at his father's passing:

> I am in sorrow that he has gone but have some comfort in the knowledge of his gain. It is so sudden a call that it is … now [that] thoughts … [of my] … love of my father.[2]

The last morning that Alexander had attended a service at his Church, the Revd Lyon had preached from a Psalm. 'As for me, "I will behold they face in righteousness. I shall be satisfied when I awake with they likeness."'[3]

Alexander had every reason to be satisfied with his life, and all that he had achieved.

After the interment, the family mourners returned to Corona, and later they assembled in the drawing room, with its stunning view of the Tay, for the ritual reading of Alexander's Will. It was a custom then, and one that continued in rural Scotland until well into the middle of the twentieth century, that women did not attend the church service or the interment. It is highly probable that Alexander's daughters, daughters-in-law and granddaughters followed that tradition.

Serene and dignified in her bereavement, Elspeth would, for the first time since her husband's death, have been able to survey her remaining children. It is doubtful if her youngest daughter Mina Stewart was at the funeral. In 1875 she gave birth, at Lovedale, to her fourth daughter Leonara Nyasa. Elspeth had endured the early deaths of five of her twelve daughters and the premature deaths of two of her six sons. Now looking at her remaining brood she must have wondered at how different in character they were.

William had at a very early age been given the opportunity to run the Dundee Yard, but his father's constant presence must have dampened the young man's enthusiasms. William had a preference for building and running whalers and sealers, and in this he was among the best. He combined the business of building ships with owning a large whaling fleet. He opened a factory to cure and treat seal skins, and he built a storage facility for the oil obtained from whales. It was said of him that he had the largest stock of seal skins, oil and whalebones in the whole of Scotland.

Elspeth could not help but compare him to his two younger brothers. Al and John were the bulwarks in family's disputes. They shared the same principles of duty, service and unshakeable faith in their God. The reputation of the Kelvinhaugh and Linthouse Yards had been built with their hard work and loyalty to the men who worked for them. As she looked at Al and John she must have known that the future of the family was safe in their hands. Al's sons, Alex and Fred, would, in the fullness of time, take over the duties of their father and Uncle.

And what of Andrew? Poor, deluded Andrew, so talented and yet such a flawed character. It had been his choice to study medicine, and after his graduation in 1862 the family had hoped that he had finally found a path to happiness and contentment. Regrettably, it caused him and the family nothing but heartache. He did not share Al and John's work ethic, all he wanted was a life of riches and privilege. He had never been able to achieve his heart's desire.

Alexander's Will was read to the family by his friend and solicitor, John William Thomson. It is not hard to guess that there were one or two surprises for those assembled that day. Alexander had not disposed of his substantial fortune in a way that would allow the beneficiaries access to large sums of money. He had formed a number of Trust Funds; each of his daughters would receive a twice yearly legacy of interest on the invested capital. They would become financially independent, but not so independent that their wealth would outrank their husband's earnings.

A Special Trust was established with Al and John as the main Trustees and it was this fund that raised a few hackles. In his desire to be fair to all his descendants, Alexander had left instructions that his grandsons, James and Robert, the sons of James and Eliza, should be helped. Since their mother's death in 1866, the boys had been boarded with James Kiellar, a schoolmaster at North Queensferry and his wife Ann Macfarlane. In a letter to Kiellar, Al enclosed a small sum for the boys' board, and outlined the provisions under his late father's Settlement:

> ... since my late Father died we have only a limited sum that we can devote on behalf of the boys. We are very glad to learn that the boys are doing well, and as to Robert the sooner he joins the engineering trade the better.[4]

The letter proves beyond doubt that after James and Eliza died the family were concerned to ensure that their sons were taken care of. Kiellar and his wife were obviously extremely good foster parents; they had two daughters, Margaret and Jane, so the boys grew up in a loving and hard-working family. In 1876 Ann Kiellar became a certificated teacher, and by then she was sixty-six-years-old. Three years later, Jane then aged thirty-two was appointed an assistant teacher; both mother and daughter taught at Kiellar's school.

When Ann died in 1879, Kiellar retired at Christmas 1880 and went to live in Edinburgh with his second daughter Margaret, the wife of John Hay Paterson. Kiellar died five years later leaving a gulf in the lives of not just his daughters and his grandchildren, but also in the lives of James and Robert.

Two other grandchildren that Alexander remembered were James Murray and Alice Templeton. Samuel's young wife, Massie, was perhaps the most disappointed by the terms of her late father-in-law's Will. If she had expected to receive a substantial legacy, it was left to Al to set out the facts for her. On 30 July he wrote:

> I have only this week received from Mr Thomson of Dundee a copy of
> my late Father's settlement, but as we have also received no funds ... at
> our disposal under the settlement, and it will be sometime ere this can be.
> Meantime I am sorry that I cannot do anything in this matter. I return the
> papers you sent me as you wished. I hope your child is well?[5]

Al's commitment to the Govan School Board was rewarded when in
September 1875 he was at the opening of a new school at Lambhill,
twelve months after the Board first proposed and passed the plans for the
building. The school had separate entrances for boys, girls, and infants. A
large playground was provided with covered sheds and a drinking fountain. The school rooms were light and airy, but, amazingly in these days
of small classes, each classroom could accommodate two hundred children. In all, the school could take thirteen hundred pupils.

In his opening speech, Al made particular reference to the fact that
in May 1873, when they had taken a local census of children without
education, they found the number to be in excess of four thousand. Immediately, the Govan School Board proposed to open a series of temporary schools while they set about raising the finance to build five more
schools in the area.

It was not sufficient for Al to ensure the children had good buildings,
he also insisted all teachers should be certificated and that all children
should take an annual examination set by the Government Inspector. Al
added a rider which has some resonance to today's educational crisis:

> As a Board they had been very fortunate in getting earnest, faithful teach-
> ers. The best way to get good men, and to keep them, was to pay them
> well: and it was the unanimous wish of the Board that the teachers should
> be well paid.[6]

Al went on to give a warning to truant children and feckless parents:

> They had hitherto been exercising the compulsory powers very leniently,

but now that they had provided accommodation it would be their duty to see that no children were growing up in ignorance.[7]

He had, in 1873, approved the appointment of John Lochore to the staff of the Govan Schools and had been delighted by the progress the young man had achieved in the two years since he had moved to Govan. In the 1881 census Lochore gave his occupation as school teacher -- Head Master, which rather confirms Al's assessment.

Education was not just a priority for his workers' children but also for his own family. When it came to choosing the right school, he was equally objective; in September his eldest daughter Mary went away to Dr John Hill's School, in Clapham, London. Bernard, until he was eight, had been taught at home by governesses, but in October 1875 he became a pupil at the Albany Academy, in Sauchiehall Street, run by James Naismith McRaith. Alex and Fred, and their cousin James Murray had all been pupils of McRaith.

The early months of 1876 were again busy for Al as he attempted, with John's help, to sort out the vexed problems of Alexander's Trust Settlement. Massie Stephen continued to demand more financial help and Al was forced to write and tell her that her settlement had additional complications. There is in his letters a formal attitude that does not speak highly of his closeness to his sister-in-law. He sent her a small cheque, the amount of which Massie immediately disputed, and Al was honest in answering her questions:

> The sum I sent [about £1,000 at today's value] was intended to be simply a payment on account of interest [and] the reason for this is that Mr Thomson not having settled the Legacy duty with the Stamp Office officials, there is some doubt whether they will exact only one per cent or a larger per centage in consequences of your not being a blood relation of Alex[ander] Stephen.[8]

A few weeks later Al wrote again to Massie, apologising for the delay in answering her last letter, saying that he had been away from home.

He admitted that he had still not heard from Thomson about the Stamp Duty, but in the interim he sent her another small cheque. He also expressed his concern to hear that Mabel was ill and hoped she would be better shortly.

Problems caused by the settling of Alexander's Estate continued throughout 1876, and from comments made by Al, it would appear that things were anything but plain sailing. In October he noted:

> D W Paterson [his brother-in-law] called [and] saw John as to proceedings of my father's Trustees [and] Mr Thomson said he was to bring their doings under review of the Court of Sessions [and] also that he was to have the books of [Alexander Stephen and Sons, Dundee] examined by an Edinburgh Accountant.[9]

The settling of Estates, especially one as complicated as Alexander's was always going to upset someone; expectations among his large family were never likely to be satisfied. In appointing seven non-family executors, Alexander may have thought he was minimising the problems, but it soon became apparent that he had only sown the seeds of conflict.

There is some evidence to suggest that Duncan Wilkie Paterson was also having difficulty in meeting his commitments to his growing family on just the fees he received as Solicitor to the Supreme Court. According to contemporary sources, he was a speculator. It was reported that he was heavily involved with the English civil engineer, Henry Hughes, who wanted to build an underground railway in Dundee. Hughes later blamed Paterson for the collapse of the project and for the subsequent loss of his engineering company.

Paterson, nevertheless, was able to send his daughters Mary Stuart and Jemima Lindsay to Highgate Ladies College, in London. In the fullness of time, his sons, James Cowan and Duncan Wilkie junior would go to Loretto. Such expenditure was crippling even in the late 1870s and early 1880s. His eldest son, Alexander Stephen, had also been expensively educated including his training for the Bar, before being elected to the Faculty of Advocates in 1882. Two years later he married Eleanor Hughes, the eldest daughter of Henry, a union which angered both the Paterson and Hughes families.

There was not the same measure of closeness between the Glasgow and Dundee Stephen cousins as there was between the Glasgow families. Al never missed an opportunity of recording in his diary the happenings of William and his family. This was certainly true when his niece Alice married Alexander Gordon Thomson, the grandson of the Dumfries architect James Thomson. Alex's father, William Gordon Thomson, had moved to Dundee with his mother Mary Gordon and his three brothers shortly after James Thomson's death in 1832.

Alice Stephen married Alex Gordon Thomson on 23 August 1876, at Helenslea and as a wedding present, William Gordon Thomson had built for them a magnificent red-sandstone town house set in two acres off Fairfield Road, West Ferry. The house was designed by the French architect Hippolyte Blanc who is remembered for his remodelling of Edinburgh Castle in the 1880s. In designing Red Court, as the house became known, Blanc created a house in a French Renaissance style but using red sandstone, shipped from Thomson's birth county of Dumfriesshire. In such a house it is difficult to pick out one feature among so many, but surely the best is the staircase with its Pre-Raphaelite stained-glass window, based on a painting by Edward Burne-Jones with a quotation from Shelley: 'Music, when soft voices die, / Vibrates in the memory ...'[10]

Alice's marriage was not the only one to take place in Dundee in 1876; Margaret, Alexander's second youngest daughter, married Robert Mudie. In marrying into the Mudie family, Margaret was forging a link with the son of one of her father's oldest friends, Robert Aitken Mudie. Mudie senior was also one of the Trustees of Alexander's Deed of Settlement. The Mudies were a long established East Coast family with interests in shipping and coal. Al and Mary travelled to Corona for the ceremony. Margaret and Robert, would make their home at Corona but the marriage was not blessed with children.

The close personal and working relationship between the families is a recurring theme, and after the death of Alexander, Al took over the role as Head of the Clan. It was a role he was spiritually and emotionally good at, although he was less autocratic than his father. There was much that bound the two men together, for both were extremely good employers — liberal in their views, tolerant of other's failings and always trusting in the goodness of their God. They respected the men in the Yards as much as they respected their household servants.

In November 1876, Al noted in his diary 'Mrs Charlotte Scott, who has been nurse to my family since May 1860, left tonight for London. In leaving our service I note she has been loved by the children all along.'[11]

At Elderslie House, Largs, on 28 June 1877, after fourteen years as a widower, JS married again. Emily Jane Fraser Campbell was twenty-two years younger than JS. He left no record of how his teenage children, James Murray and Alice, viewed the prospect of having a step-mother a little older than they were.

As was common in many wealthy middle-class families, there was little physical or emotional contact between parents and children. JS could provide James Murray and Alice with beautiful surroundings, servants and educational benefits, but he could not give them the closeness of a father's love. James Murray craved maternal love more than most and he looked to Alice to fill that void. He constantly compared his life to that of his Stephen cousins, and in his Aunt Mary he saw the mother he never had.

The relationship between Alice and James Murray was never as close as he wanted, nor as close as he perceived that between Mary, Maud, Elsie and their brothers. Alice was always more of her father's daughter than James Murray was his son. She was practical, with a strong sense of duty, her belief in God followed closely her father's belief. She had no understanding of James Murray's continual questioning of his Faith. In art, literature and music she was conservative, and had no sympathy for James Murray's ideas on mysticism. There is one very telling comment, made when James Murray was in London, which perhaps best explains what he wanted from his sister:

> Would that once in her life she would fling her arms round my neck or something of that sort, instead of her impassioned manner.[12]

The need to feel love and to be understood was a recurring theme in James Murray's life, and it is doubtful if he ever found the happiness that he so desperately sought.

It is difficult to believe that James Murray saw in his father's new wife the mother he wanted. Emily was the daughter of William Campbell, who had been a physician and Inspector of Hospitals in Bombay, and his wife Emelia Beach. The couple had seven children, all but one born in India; their son William was born in Largs in October 1858, which tends to suggest, that Emily had been born in India but it has been impossible to verify the exact date and location.

Of his father-in-law and his new wife JS wrote:

> He [William Campbell] was born in Largs where his father had been also a doctor -- "the doctor" in his way. This father-in-law when I first knew him had retired from his profession, and, having invested his savings in a coffee estate in Ceylon, was a comparatively wealthy man, the owner of the property of Burnside, Largs. ... My wife, when I married her ... was a bright clever rather pretty young lady of the fair hair and blue eye type, happy and kindly in disposition. She seemed very healthy too ...[13]

In just one short month, Jane Skair Stephen, William's wife, had had the pleasure of seeing her eldest daughter marry, but she had also mourned the death of her mother, Barbara Jarrow. Jane died on 28 March 1877 at the age of forty-seven and according to her death certificate the cause of her death was 'change of life'. She died shortly before the birth of her first grandchild, William Murray Gordon Thomson. A daughter, Jean Maud Henderson, was born in 1880 to Alice and Alex Gordon Thomson.

Two years after the death of Alexander, Al and John were still trying to placate the family as to their entitlement under the terms of their late Father's Trust Settlement. Expectations from various family members remained high and needed to be squashed, and in a series of letters Al set out the terms under which they would receive their legacies. Massie's demands for a larger share of her father-in-law's Estate never ceased. Al's replies to her became ever more formal:

> I have your note of yesterday. At the last November term we under took [to pay] the money at interest payable at the normal times of Whitsunday and Martinmas, so that we will have no interest from then till May term comes. We will arrange to send the money as soon as it comes in at the time of Whitsunday and Martinmas.[14]

Throughout much of 1876/77, Al was corresponding with James Kiellar about the welfare of James and Robert. James was approaching eighteen and Robert was two years younger, but were still in the care of Kiellar. In March, Al had written to Kiellar voicing his concern over the cost of the boys' board telling Kiellar that under the terms of their late grandfather's Settlement, the amount the boys had in capital was only £500 which when invested would yield an income for each of them of £20. He then went on:

> We would wish to consult you what in your opinion is the best to be done for their welfare. We will have to build on the principal sum in order to pay at present and our wish is that we would propose their remaining with you with a hope that you could see your way to reduce this Board money. But kindly think over the matter and give me your ideas.[15]

In November, Al was again in touch with Kiellar. In his letter Al mentions that both James and Robert had obtained work at Scott Engineering in Kirkcaldy, but he was concerned that the works were about to close. Al suggested to Kiellar that on the boys' behalf he should try and get them into the Douglas Works, which had a high reputation. When he had no reply from Kiellar, Al wrote again telling him that he had personally been making enquiries in Edinburgh and Kirkcaldy on behalf of James and Robert and that:

> My brother-in-law the Revd John Logan, thinks he can be in Kirkcaldy to make suitable arrangements for their learning their trade. Mr Logan proposes to come and see you with the boys, but I suggested if you could spare the time that you with the boys might be able to meet Revd Logan in Kirk-

caldy, but I have asked Revd Logan to write you on the subject ... I do hope good places will be got for the boys.[16]

There was a stark contrast between Al's concern for the welfare of James and Robert and his total and absolute disregard for Margaret Mary Dundas. But it was not only Al who refused to acknowledge the child. In his Deed of Settlement, Alexander had originally made a substantial bequest to Margaret Paterson or Dundas and her children, Margaret Mary and Frederick John. The ink could hardly have been dry on the Deed before Alexander added a codicil withdrawing the bequest. The reason for his change of mind is not clear, but with the exception of John, no one else in the family took any interest in Margaret Paterson or her children.

Money Worries

CONTRASTS are often invidious. To contrast the lives of the Stephen/ Templeton children with the lives of the children of their workers would show that they shared nothing other than living in the same city. The average wage for a shipyard worker was between £1 and £2 for a fifty hour week, women and children earned even less. In 1878 the Stephen/Templeton children were the recipients of generous rewards as is illustrated in a letter written to JS by Al:

> Under powers of my late Father's Deed of Settlement ... on behalf of James [and] Alice Templeton, (the sum of one thousand being placed in our hands for each of them). I enclose cheque for £237.9.2. interest in our hands to this date.[1]

The money was to be divided equally. In 1878 James Murray was eighteen, and it was becoming obvious to those who knew him that his interests lay more in the world of art and literature than in the world of carpet making. He had begun to see the natural beauty that was all round him as he enjoyed holidays in Dunoon and Cove. On one occasion, while on holiday at Aberfoyle, he wrote an evocative diary entry:

> After a fortnight of rain, wind and storm with the cold of early Spring, we have tonight the first ... coming peace and true weather of the season. Sitting at the door at ease all nature around me appears breathing repose. The trees ...have their outlines softened against the pale sky in the dimness of our long twilight ... All nature in harmony and seems to feel as I do the contrast and dawning hope.[2]

A few days later he recollected that they had a visit from an elderly female relative. He does not name her but it would not be hard to believe it was one of his great-aunts from Campbeltown for he speaks of her as being old. His Campbeltown aunts, Agnes, Elizabeth and Ann were in their late sixties and seventies, and would have seemed ancient to an impressionable young man. James Murray admits that the visit had been a disappointment. He makes the rather obvious comment that not all family members are alike in character. There was though much to admire even in those members one did not particularly like, or whose opinions and views one did not share:

> How much greater power have sketches to recall scenes than words ... And this makes one more eager to gain some knowledge of painting [and] sketching that I in future may carry away with me in my travels a more certain memory of the places visited ...[3]

Contrasts again intruded at the end of May. Al sighed off the Company's books for the year and noted rather pleasingly that the Yard had, in spite of all the set backs, made a healthy profit. His share of the profit, he was delighted to admit, was nine and a half thousand pounds. His pleasure was marred by the news from Corona that his mother was 'not being quite well from weakness of the heart ... but [in] no immediate danger according to her doctor.'[4]

Al travelled to Corona where John was awaiting him. Later in the evening of 4 June, Al was allowed into his mother's room:

> ... she was conscious ... breathing with difficulty --- [she] was kind to all around her. Said little at night, she told John to take a walk in the garden at 11.30, she died peacefully without pain and conscious to the last. She found peace and glory and trust in her Saviour -- a woman Beloved, without guile and a good Christian.[5]

Her death was confirmed by Dr William Grant as having taken place at 11.35 pm. If Elspeth expected her death would end the family feuds, she would have been sadly disappointed. Al, as was his nature, took charge of all the funeral arrangements; he recorded that the day after his mother's death was the first time he had seen her Will. It must have surprised him that he and John were not appointed her executors, but his sisters, Janet, Elspeth Croudace and Margaret Mudie were. Her Will had been made just ten months earlier, obviously without consulting her sons. In

1878, it was rare for women to have any control over money. It was not until the 1884 legislation was passed that allowed married women the same rights over property as unmarried women. Elspeth was obviously ahead of her time.

There were however more immediate problems for Al to solve. It was usual for invitations to funerals to be issued in the name of the eldest son, assuming the spouse was also dead. Unfortunately, William had already arranged to go down to Terrington, Yorkshire, to marry his second wife, Elizabeth Margaret Henderson, a cousin of Jane's. Fourteen years William's junior, Elizabeth was the daughter of John Henderson and Elizabeth Freer, of Slingsby.

Al was not willing to have the invitations go out in William's name when he would not be there to greet the mourners. His sisters were of the opinion that the name on the invitation was not important. Al would not concede, and as in so many other family disputes, he turned to Daniel Forbes for advice. The invitations went out in Al's name.

He then took the unilateral decision not to inform Andrew of their mother's death until after the funeral. Elspeth's funeral duly took place on 10 June, the service being conducted by the Revd John Lyon. She was interred at Barnhill, reposing beside her late husband.

Al returned to Park Circus on the evening of 6 June and from there he wrote a short letter to Andrew, and although he signed it 'your affectionate brother' there is little in the way of warmth in his stark words. It is very unlikely the letter reached Andrew in time for him to journey north for the funeral:

> I have just returned from Corona where I was telegraphed for on Monday in consequence of our Mother's sudden illness. You will be grieved to learn that she died on Tuesday night at half past eleven. Her end was peaceful.[6]

Al and his remaining siblings hoped that with Elspeth's death, their feud with Andrew would end. It did not end immediately. Andrew still had very pressing financial problems that made a peace settlement difficult for him to contemplate, unless of course his brothers reversed their decision and agreed to pay his debts. Three days after Elspeth's funeral, Eleanor, had a meeting with Al, John, James Stewart and Napier in Daniel Forbes's office. They told her that if in future she or Andrew wished to communicate with the family it would have to be through Forbes.

Eleanor must have relayed the information to Andrew who was staying again at the Waverley Temperance Hotel. His reaction was predictable. He wrote the most intemperate letter to Al: 'Your time has at last come when you must answer to your own conscience and to the public for your past life as bearing on me.'[7]

He then went on to describe Al's perceived sins, raking over old ground, repeating that the family had robbed James of his rightful inheritance. He accused Al of trying to have him committed to a lunatic asylum, and then again repeated his monstrous allegations against his late father and his sisters. His letter is such that if Al had for one moment, entertained the idea of bailing him out, he must have dismissed the idea when he read: 'You with my father and his family were parties to utterly the foulest slanders on my character.'[8]

As if that was not bad enough, he then accused his mother and sisters of writing his father's Will which disinherited him. His letter ends with a threat:

> Before you and they cheat me out of my just rights you shall break before public opprobrium of your fellow man and I trust God will see fit to make you in your heart truly repentant for all you have done wrongfully to me and mine.[9]

Conciliation and contrition should have been Andrew's weapons but he did not understand either concept. He followed up his abusive letters to Al by distributing handbills again around the Govan area making his false allegations. Al and John sent some of the Yard workers to retrieve the offending bills.

On the same day that Andrew wrote to Al, he also wrote to Forbes. His letter was a strange mixture of threat and bluster and there was no suggestion that he was prepared to compromise:

> I beg to say that I shall not withdraw anything until I learn I am to receive my full share of my father's estate. I cannot wait longer than two o'clock for your answer.[10]

At a further meeting, this time without Andrew or Eleanor, which took place on 14 June, Al was joined by James Stewart, Duncan Paterson and John Logan, and by David Osborne, a solicitor from Cupar, Fife. It was that meeting which approved a solution to Andrew's debt problems. On 1 August, Andrew signed a Minute of Agreement whereby he would receive £7,000 from members of the family. He would be given £3,000 immediately to pay his debts, the balance would be invested and then he would receive £300 a year. There were three conditions, the £300 would be safe from his creditors and he would destroy all defamatory material in his possession, and he would withdraw all his law suits and stop his smear campaigns.

The death of JS's mother-in-law, Elspeth Stephen was not the only cause for sorrow that summer. JS had taken his young wife Emily to Crawford Park, Dunblane, hoping that the peace and beauty of the Perthshire countryside would bring about an improvement in her health. He was delighted when Emily announced that she was pregnant, and he thought that for once the Gods were smiling on him. He was forty-five and dearly wanted a second son to relieve James Murray of the burden of being his heir-apparent.

JS's joy was short lived, early in 1878 Emily became extremely ill and the male child she was carrying was still-born. On the afternoon of 19 September, Emily died of chronic desquamative nephritis and anasarca. She was twenty-four and had been married to JS for only one year and three months. His grief was overwhelming and he questioned the very existence of God; he had recalled that at the time of his marriage Emily had appeared to be in good health. Alice and James Murray must have wondered if their father would ever find the happiness that he so desperately sought.

The year had begun so well for JS, with the retirement of his father and Peter Reid. The merging of the factories under his and his brother James's control had promised so much. Now he wondered if he had the strength to go on, but whatever his personal grief he had the welfare and the survival of his workforce to consider. It was said of JS that he was a man of self-esteem and ambition: never were those qualities more needed than in those bleak days of autumn 1878.

When the history of the twenty-first century comes to be written, much attention will be given to the collapse of financial institutions and the dot-com companies. These were, for the investors caught up in them, major scandals and caused untold harm. But as was evident, skulduggery by bankers, accountants and financial directors was not invented in the twenty-first century.

In October 1878, Glasgow and, indeed, the whole of Scotland, heard the alarming news that the City Bank of Glasgow had ceased trading. The bank had been founded in 1839 and the majority of its investors were small merchants and manufacturers. It opened branches right across the city, one attraction for customers was that they opened in the evening to receive deposits. Less than twenty years after its inception rumours were circulating as to the viability of the bank, but these were squashed by the bank's directors.

At the AGM held in June, the directors reported that the bank now had one hundred and thirty-three branches and that deposits had risen to £8,000,000. They proposed to pay a healthy dividend to all shareholders.

Not a word was said about the perilous nature of the bank's financial status, but the rumours persisted. It was said that the bank had approached their competitors for assistance. This time the rumours proved to be accurate, on 1 October the bank closed its doors and suspended all business.

Al was horrified by the news and made an early appointment to see the manager of his and the Yard's Bank, but the meeting did little to lighten his gloom. Syme? reported that the prospects for the shareholders of the City of Glasgow Bank were bleak. Al's gloom was reflected throughout the city; the Stock Market all but closed, and business in the rest of the city was at a virtual standstill for the rest of that day.

The eight directors were arrested and sent for trial at the High Court in Edinburgh; the indictments have echoes in today's financial scandals. The directors were accused of reckless mismanagement, accounts were deliberately falsified, securities were entered into the accounts at inflated values and debts were shown as assets instead of liabilities. Any shareholder reading the balance sheets would have thought their investments were safe. The Bank directors were also accused of expanding too fast by opening more branches than was commercially or financially prudent.

But surely the worst indictment made against the directors was that they used depositors' money to fund

> hopelessly rotten firms in the East India trade. Investing in doubtful or speculative securities ... including American railway stock, buying land in Australia and New Zealand, and generally behaving like an insane gambler mad to be rid of his fortune.[11]

The eight directors languished in jail while the enormity of their crimes reverberated round the city. The worse aspects of the whole business were that the shareholders had signed an unlimited liability guarantee, which meant they would be held liable for the bank's debts; these were estimated to be over six million pounds.

One thousand two hundred shareholders met towards the end of October to agree that the bank should be put into liquidation. All those present were aware that such a decision would ruin them, but there was no alternative. Once appointed, the liquidators wasted no time in demanding from the shareholders the sum of £500 for each £100 of stock they held.

Caught up in the disaster was Robert Young. Two of his sons were to play a major role in the business and personal life of the Templetons. Born in Kirkintilloch in 1822, the son of John Young and Janet Kirkwood, Robert had come to Glasgow as a young man to join his brother, John, as a ship broker and managing ship owner. Robert was elected a director of the North British Railway Company and of the Glasgow Tramway Company. He and John prospered, and by 1878 they were men of considerable wealth.

In May 1858 Robert had married Ann Henderson Lusk, the daughter of Daniel Henderson Lusk and Isabella Corbet. Robert and Ann lived in an elegant town house in the west end of Glasgow. They had six sons and two daughters. After the collapse of the City of Glasgow Bank, the lives of Robert and his family changed. As a creditor he was asked to contribute a huge amount to help cover the debts of the bank. Such a debt would have destroyed most men, but Robert was stoical and philosophical, and he set about recovering his losses and making sure his family did not unduly suffer. He succeeded, and it was due in no small measure to the resilience and enterprise of his sons. Whether influenced by his father's financial trauma or not, Robert Arthur junior, fifteen-years-old at the time of the collapse, became an accountant. He emigrated to America, and in Chicago, established Arthur Young & Co which became one of the most respected and influential accounting firms on both sides of the Atlantic.

John Stephen, like Al, was not one of the victims of the collapse of the Glasgow City Bank; during 1877/79 he was negotiating to purchase Iron Bank House, the home of the late David Tod, of Tod & McGregor. John had many alterations and additions made to the house before he and Elizabeth moved in. He renamed the house *Domira*.

At Lovedale, James Stewart was also building and extending the mission property: Stewart and Mina had spent much of the previous two years in Scotland. The Zulu Wars of 1879 could well have influenced their decision to return home, as well as ensuring that their two eldest daughters, Mina and Florence, spent part of their studies in Scotland.

The journey time from the Mission at Lovedale to Corona must have taken weeks, with difficult journeys over land, long sea journeys and then finally coach rides. Stewart and Mina made that journey often in the years they were at Lovedale. Of Mina's eight children, seven survived the harshness of Africa and the long journeys back to Scotland. Only Mina's second daughter, Mary-Ann, died in infancy.

Lovedale was rapidly expanding, and even in Stewart's absence there was little rest for either the Mission staff or the students. Stewart, as did many Victorians, believed that idleness was an evil and that only through labour could one find fulfilment.

All the Lovedale boys have to do thirteen hours of manual labour every

week, chiefly in agriculture, but also in tree-planting, road-making, gardening. ... Part of the mission farm had 2000 acres, of which 400 were arable.
It was called Domira, from the name of the Glasgow residence of Mr John
Stephen ... the donor of the land and for forty years a very generous supporter of the mission.[12]

John Stephen was not the only generous benefactor to the Lovedale
Mission, JS and James Templeton were equally supportive with very
large donations not only to Lovedale but to other foreign missions. It
was also inevitable that Stewart would seek help from the Revd Robert
Howie, even though he had little of his own money. JS and Al would
have been happy to endorse Stewart's belief that Howie was 'probably
the greatest and most successful raiser of money in Glasgow, if not in
Scotland.'[13]

Duty or Destiny

JAMES Murray Templeton was only three-years-old when his mother Mary Stephen died, and he could have had little or no memory of her. His father's subsequent marriage to Emily Campbell, and her untimely death, left him feeling lonely and disillusioned. It would also not have been surprising if he turned to his maternal grandmother, Elspeth Stephen, for comfort. She was after all the mother of eighteen children and she would have instinctively known how to comfort a grieving child.

But, like all the women he was close to, she died when he was eighteen and he was left to ponder his future without her wise counsel. He knew that it was expected, by his Templeton grandfather, his father and Uncle James, that he would follow them into the family business. As the only grandson his duty had been mapped out since his birth. It was unfortunate that he was the only son of the extended family. His Uncles James and Archie were not married, neither was his Great-Uncle Nathaniel. His Great-Uncle Archibald had a son, but he died in infancy.

There was a distant cousin, James Templeton, a West Indian merchant, who in 1852 married a second wife, Susan Lightbourne Trimingham. In the next twenty years they had ten children, six daughters and four sons. Two sons, James Heriot and John Preston, were of an age with James Murray, but there does not seem to have been any suggestion that they should enter the carpet business. They both became shipping clerks. The family lived at Drumgarve, Rhu near Helensburgh, the name coming from the farm on the Kintyre Peninsula.

The business of carpet making did not interest James Murray and he had little enthusiasm for the minutiae of commerce. He wanted to become a great artist. He had been surrounded by beauty all his young life. JS was a connoisseur of art, a member of the Council of Glasgow Art School, and a friend of artists. What could be more natural than that he should encourage his son in his artistic pursuit, especially as design played such an important part in the manufacture of carpets.

When fate decides a course of action rather than personal choice, the seeds of conflict are sown, and James Murray struggled for years to please both himself and his father.

James Murray was a wealthy, charming, handsome, sensitive young man, with deep brooding eyes, and a large bushy drooping moustache. He was a gifted singer, he loved poetry, art and the theatre. As the son of a successful manufacturer he should have been much sought after by dowager hostesses, with marriageable granddaughters, but he was an introspective young man. He admitted that he had a morbid nature and that he was constantly concerned over his poor physical health. His sister Alice told him that he should 'laugh at nothing with boys like his cousin Alex Stephen ...'[1]

There is a theme running throughout James Murray's account of his life which shows that he felt he was constantly being compared to his Stephen cousins. It must have added to his sense of isolation that he had grown up with just Alice as a companion, whereas the Stephen household had comprised three sons and three daughters. The families spent so much social time together, both in Glasgow and Dunoon, that comparisons were easy, added to which the Helensburgh Templetons also joined family gatherings.

The Presbyterian Religion and the work ethic were a part of the Templeton/Stephen philosophy: through adherence to their Church and to the production of goods they could find fulfilment. James Murray never inherited their certainties. He turned, like many before him, to spiritualism for the answer to his anxieties. In a conversation with his father, on his religious beliefs, James Murray later recalled that he had caused him some pain. He explained that his religious convictions lay between Unitarianism -- the belief that God is not a Trinity but one person -- and Theism -- the belief that God will be supernaturally revealed. According to Doctor Johnson, theism was the refuge of the weak, a point, which if he had known it at the time, JS could well have mentioned to his gullible son.

JS was defeated by his son's pronouncements and duly packed him off to see his friend and spiritual adviser, the Revd George Reith, Minister of the Free Church College. Reith, with that special logic of one who never doubted his Faith, simply told the troubled young man: 'Oh your state of mind is temporary, you'll come back all right.'[2]

When the teachings of the Free Church and orthodox Presbyterianism played no part in James Murray's beliefs, he turned for solace to the teaching of mesmeric and clairvoyant preachers. While in London he visited a Mrs Watson, and it was her alleged ability to speak to the dead that allowed James Murray to encounter the spirit, who according to Mrs Watson, was the spirit of his mother:

> A spirit said her name was Mary and why had I not done as I was told? She wished to communicate with me, and I must sit alone for it and write automatically. ... Then came another spirit who spoke of this last, said she was beautiful [and] was a spirit very noble in nature. ... Then said she worked in art [and] was anxious to bring me into sympathy with her ...[3]

The spirit then went on to tell James Murray that he must, immediately, or in the near future, abandon all notions of going into the carpet business and should follow his desire to be an artist. Even James Murray, naive as he was, believed then that Mrs Watson and her spirits were not being all that honest with him. She knew he was struggling between his desire to be an artist and his father's wish to see him enter the family business. Yet knowing this, James Murray still could not find it in himself to reject, totally, the words of the spirit:

> I find it impossible to think that Mr & Mrs Watson [are] impostors, difficult even to think them deluded: yet it is more difficult to believe in spiritualism as they make it out.[4]

James Murray's longing for his mother was never fulfilled and he constantly sought images of what a mother should be. In trying to find a subject for a picture he conjured up such an image:

> A mother sad-faced but with all the dignity of womanly pain, experience, thought, tenderness [and] love suggested in her face [and] bearing, rather in the back-ground, in front a youth or maiden yielding the mother's influence be beining [kindly and pleasant] care, tittering or singing with inspiration.[5]

In his diary James Murray does not mention exactly when he first met Laurence Oliphant, the South African born author, traveller, mystic, disciple and patron of Thomas Lake Harris, the American spiritualist prophet. The meeting between the impressionable young man and the well travelled writer and mystic was to have disastrous consequences. James Murray believed that Oliphant had the answer to all his problems.

It was James Murray who introduced Oliphant to Rosamond Dale Owen, granddaughter of Robert Owen, the socialist, philanthropist and pioneer of the New Lanark experience of community living. She had been born on 11 December 1846, at New Harmony, Indiana, the American equivalent to the Scottish community. But socialism and social principles did not last in the chaotic times of the Wild West and three years after the experiment began, it ended. Rosamond's father Robert Dale Owen was a congressman and liberal reformer, her mother Mary Robinson, was a descendant of the religious reformer John Robinson.

In 1880, Rosamond, then aged thirty-three, was still living at New Harmony with her brother Julian, a merchant, and his wife Anna Cooper, and their five children, three from their marriage and two from Anna's first marriage. Rosamond's father had died on 24 June 1877 at Lake George, New York; his most enduring legacy was to introduce a bill in the House of Representatives to create the Smithsonian Institution. Today the Smithsonian has among its exhibits the carpet made by Templeton for the Royal Reception Room at the 1851 International Exhibition in London. Later, the carpet was taken to Washington to grace the British Embassy; in 1930 it was returned to Glasgow for repairs, and when it returned to America it was placed in the safe keeping of the Smithsonian.

Again, it is uncertain when and where, James Murray met Rosamond -- the most likely scenario was that it was at one of the seances or lectures she gave in London during the late 1870s. Rosamond combined three of the elements that James Murray sought, spiritualism, socialism and a need to feel loved. In the early years of their relationship there was never any suggestion that they were more than friends.

On 1 December 1881, for a few brief hours, the Templeton/Stephen family came together to celebrate the Golden Wedding of James and

Mary Templeton. At the dinner, held at 7 Woodside Terrace, the guests included the golden couple's six children, including Revd Archie, who was back from Missionary duties in India, James's brothers, Archibald and Nathaniel, and Archibald's wife Jane and daughter Margaret, and Al, Mary and their six children. JS, Alice and James Murray were united in celebrating the happy occasion.

The celebration for Mary Templeton was marred by the absence of her sister Margaret and her husband Peter Reid. They had married on the same day as James and Mary, but their own Golden celebrations were spoiled by Peter's ill-health. Peter died on 26 December, just after he had celebrated his eightieth birthday.

For Al it had been a long day; it had begun at 9.30 with a meeting of the Necropolis Committee. He then went to Linthouse, but by 11.30 he was at a meeting of the Dean of Guilds to discuss what should be done about a dangerous building. At one o'clock he was at the Royal Infirmary for a meeting to decide the appointment of a surgeon and pathologist. It is hoped that he had lunch at the hospital, because at 2.30 he was presiding at the AGM of the Glasgow Medical Missionary Society. The Revd Archie had just been appointed Medical Officer to the Society.

Is it any wonder that the next day Al was complaining of the pressure of work. The week, however, ended on another high note when he learned that he had been appointed Justice of the Peace for Lanarkshire, and that he was required to attend the County Buildings on the 7 December to take the oath.

As the father of three daughters, growing into womanhood, Al Stephen must have been aware that sooner or later he would be approached by suitors pleading to be allowed to marry one of his pretty daughters. The choice of suitor exercised him somewhat. The intermarriage between the manufacturing families of Glasgow had been going on for some years. It was, though, important for him that his future sons-in-law should be able to support their wives in a manner to which they had become accustomed.

George Scott MacLellan was very welcomed as a prospective suitor.

As the eldest son of Walter MacLellan, chairman of a prosperous engineering and iron contractors, and Margaret Walker, he had all the right credentials. The family lived in some splendour at Blairvaddick House in Rhu. Walter was twice married, his first wife Margaret had died in 1858 of scarlet fever. He then married Thomasina Turner, in February 1861.

Walter, and his brother Peter, inherited a small shop and smithy manufacturing rivets, nuts and bolts from their Uncle Donald after his death in 1831. Initially, the brothers were helped by their Uncle Peter before he retired in 1839. The business began a period of rapid expansion and the use of iron and steel in building structures and railway extensions was largely responsible for this growth.

In 1853 the firm of P & W MacLellan moved to Adelphi Street, Hutchinsontown, and from then on the name of Clutha Ironworks became a recognized part of the company. Further expansion followed with the move to the Plantation district of Glasgow and by 1881, according to the census, the company were employing a thousand men, including Walter's three sons, George, and Walter Thomas the sons of Margaret Walker, and William Turner, Thomasina's son. George, apart from working for his father, also employed 100 men in his own right.

The union of the MacLellan and Stephen families was confirmed when George Scott proposed to Maud. On Saturday 4 March 1882, Al recorded his thoughts on the engagement:

> This afternoon Mr George S MacLellan, came to call on me ... and asked me, as he said a precious favour, that I would give my consent to his engagement with my daughter Maud. I speaking of this serious matter put it, as that of first of all, of true affection between them, and then, as I was desirous that if any of my daughters married it was my highest wish that it would be to a good Christian man. On Mr George assuring me on these points, and from all that we have known of him, I made him welcome to be a future son-in-law.[6]

Convinced that Maud herself was happy with George's proposal, Al and Mary were delighted to have the young couple to dine with them that evening. Al was then able to announce Maud and George's forthcoming marriage to his other dinner guests: John and Elizabeth, Janet, Ann and

Duncan Wilkie Paterson, JS and Mrs McMorran, the wife of the Reverend Robert, Presbytery Clerk at Dunoon.

June 1882 saw more family celebrations. On Tuesday 20 June, at Linthouse, they launched *Sylvia*, a 136 ton yacht built for Al and his family. It could well have been a silver wedding present, for five days later Al and Mary celebrated twenty-five years of marriage. Mary named and blessed the new yacht; shortly after this ceremony the guests were served cake and wine in the model room. John proposed the toast and in a short but amusing speech he said 'the yacht had had a good launch and did not, unlike some of the larger ships they had launched, soaked the assembled party.'[7]

John referred briefly to the pride he felt in seeing his brother elevated to the position of Lord Dean of the Guild of the City of Glasgow. In closing, he wished his brother and his family many happy hours sailing in *Sylvia*. Replying to the toast, Al said that he had been very flattered by what his brother had said but added, amidst laughter, that of course, one brother never ran down another brother. There is a degree of inaccuracy in Al's remark: anyone who knew of his battles with James and Andrew must have realized that his remark was ironic. Al admitted that in building *Sylvia* he had been a little self-indulgent, although he conceded that occasionally he did enjoy sailing. His principle aim he said was to give enjoyment to his family. He paid tribute to the men who had built the yacht, they had been extremely attentive to detail and their dedication was to be seen in every corner of the beautiful ship.

It is worth, perhaps, giving a detailed description of the yacht, for she was an elegant and luxurious addition to the Stephen's fleet.

A deck saloon is entered from an alcove, with a finely-coloured Oriental portiere. The wood finishings are of tinted sycamore. At the fore end is an elegant combined cabinet and secretaire in walnut. On the floor is an Oriental rug. The seats are covered with soft blue velvet, the windows are screened with white and golden brown Chinese silk. From this the main saloon is approached by a finely finished teak staircase. The sides of this

saloon are finished in sycamore, with four panels of figure subjects in mod-
elled canvas finely coloured. The framing is richly moulded and delicately
stained in different tones, and relieved with gilding.[8]

The description continued in much the same manner, emphasising that
the saloon contained a piano and a sideboard in walnut. There were seven
state rooms, each fitted-out with every convenience for comfort. The
saloon fittings were suggested and executed by William Scott Morton,
a Carluke born decorative artist and manufacturer, and husband of
Elizabeth Alexander.

It is impossible to verify that the Oriental rug and other floor carpets
for *Sylvia* were supplied by Templeton, but it would be a foolish person
who categorically said they were not. There was a strong bond of friendship between William and Elizabeth Scott Morton and JS, and thus the
lines between the two families crossed once again.

Towards the end of the reception, the guests were treated to a most
surprising intervention from a member of the workforce. As Al gave his
final vote of thanks to the assembled crowd, William Gray, a blacksmith,
stepped forward. Dressed in breeches with his shirt sleeves rolled up and
a leather apron, he must have looked an unwelcome intruder. Apologising he quickly explained the reason for his intrusion, he said he had
come on behalf of the workers, to give an elegant diamond necklace, in
an oak casket, to Miss Stephen. The inscription read:

> Presented to Miss Maud Stephen, by the employees of her father, Alexan-
> der Stephen, Esq., shipbuilder and engineer, Linthouse, Govan, and Lord
> Dean of Guild of Glasgow, as a token of respect and good wishes on the
> occasion of her marriage to George S M'Lellan Esq., 29 June 1882.[9]

Gray spoke eloquently, though wishing he were better able to perform
the duty that had been given him that day. In a long speech, which must
have been unique in the latter quarter of the nineteenth century, he said:

> We are assembled in accordance with the earnest desire and best wishes of
> the subscribers to the testimonial ... but of also expressing our sincere re-
> gard for the welfare of Miss Stephen, the amiable and accomplished daugh-
> ter of our respected employer, and our earnest hope that she may be long

spared and abundantly blessed in that honourable position which in the providence of God she is shortly to occupy ... And still further we cannot fail to observe, with the deepest pleasure and greatest satisfaction, that this testimonial is a strong indication of the attachment and respect in which the honoured head of this distinguished firm is held by his workmen.[10]

In these days of global organizations and faceless management, it would be extremely rare for a humble workman to make both a generous presentation to the daughter of an employer, and pay such a generous tribute to her father. Much has been lost in the demise of the large family-run businesses, not least in the respect the owners had for their workers and the workers for their masters.

Al and Mary took their family and friends, on *Sylvia's* maiden voyage, to Loch Goil and along Loch Long, passing some of the finest scenery in the west of Scotland. The party aboard wished their hosts sincerest congratulations on their Silver Wedding anniversary, and coupled their good wishes that sailing in *Sylvia* would give them many hours of happiness. But during the homeward bound journey James Templeton was taken ill with 'one of his breathless turns'.

Death on the Clyde

THERE is no reason to believe that JS was anything other than a very indulgent father. He passionately wished James Murray would enjoy becoming a carpet manufacturer, but he also knew that his son had other plans. In the late winter/early spring of 1882/3, James Murray travelled to Florence to experience the grandeur of Italian art.

Before leaving Glasgow he had seen Al who had asked him to buy him two pictures while in Florence; he wrote to his uncle giving details of the pictures he had selected, but Al wanted more information before parting with his money:

> I wish you had given me a more detailed account of what you thought best of. You call these subject pictures, but of course I could not decide off hand without knowing something more about them. I would not object to spend a £100 or 2 for something good. If there was time and you cared to give me a more detailed acc[ount] with a note of the cost then I would gladly tell you what I would be pleased [with] ...[1]

After the cold and wet of a Glasgow winter, Florence must have seemed like paradise, and dreaming of spring in Florence Al wrote 'I wish I could look you up in Florence and then it would not take long to decide.'[2]

The Florence interlude was regrettably short, as James Murray had to return to Glasgow to fulfil his father's desire to make a manufacturer out of him. In his heart he knew he would never live up to his father's expectations, he wanted to go to the Slade School and study art. The forces ranged against him were too dominant, and with an explanation that was both unselfish and full of love he wrote:

> Must I throw up this certainty for the sake of Alice and Father. Painting is for the visionary good of the multitude plus an infinite pleasure to myself -- to go back is for the immediate benefit of two, a certain practical good but it includes some present [James Murray crossed out the word misery and wrote] trouble for myself, with the quite possible result that time has only been wasted.[3]

Al must have wondered if the Gods had deserted him on Tuesday 3 July 1883. The scene was set at Linthouse for the launch of the *Daphne*, a 449 gross tonnage steam ship built for the Glasgow and Londonderry Steam Packet Company, for service on their Irish trade. There was a family connection between the builders and the purchasers: Walter MacLellan, as chairman the G & L Steam Packet Company, had placed the order. It is significant that the *Daphne* was the first Stephen-built ship for the G & L, a fact that surely had something to do with the marriage between the two families.

The G & L wanted the ship launched before the Glasgow Fair holiday. Reluctantly Al agreed and the ship was prepared for launching with over two hundred workmen on board. It should not have been a problem for the Yard had launched many bigger vessels. The weather was good and there was no reason to suppose there would be trouble. The ship slid effortlessly down the slipway, she floated momentarily, then, to the horror of the crowd gathered, she rolled over and started to sink.

An eye witness at the scene recalled the incident in graphic terms:

> She [the *Daphne*] moved off all right when the dogshores [wood used as a brake when a ship is launched from the slipway into the water] were cleared away, and it was only when she took the water that she showed a tendency to heel over ... As she fell over upon her side a good many of the men who were on the upper deck could be seen clinging to each other and grasping the rails, chains, or any other deck fittings that could afford a hold.[4]

There were among the survivors some who had tried hard to save the ship, and one in particular, Henry O'Farrell, a riveter gave a moving account of his efforts in the first few moments of the launch. O'Farrell was in charge of the launch flag that day and as the signal was given to knock away the supports he noticed

> that she [the ship] was going very smartly, but paid no particular attention to this until in taking the water, the vessel heeled over to the port side. I threw the launching flag away and, thinking that perhaps the current had caused the vessel to capsize, I ran to the wheel along with the pilot, William

Francis, a rigger, and another man whose name I do not know. The three of us worked hard at the wheel so as to counter-act what we thought was the effect of the current. We turned it round several times, but it did not do any good; the vessel with every moment going deeper down in the water, and, getting alarmed for my safety, I jumped off the stern into the water. I can swim, but not very well. I managed to keep my head above the water, and shortly afterwards I was pulled on board one of the tugs which was assisting at the launch.[5]

Of the two hundred men on board, one hundred and twenty-four men drowned. They left fifty-two widows, one hundred and two children under the age of thirteen, and seventeen of the dead left widowed mothers. A stark statement of fact, yet what tragedies were unleashed that day. Andrew Henderson, who was to have been married two days later, on Thursday 5 July, was among the dead, as was Crawford Dick, a forty-three-old, foreman joiner, married to Annie Anderson Baird. He left three little sons, David Baird born in February 1872, who in 1881 was living in Govan with his widowed grandmother, Anne Baird, and his uncle Andrew, a ship's carpenter. Dick's other two sons were Christopher Fletcher aged six and Andrew Baird, an infant.

Al was not at the launch as he was at a meeting of the Dean of Guild and Directors, at the Merchant's Hall. They were in the process of electing a successor to Al as Dean of Guild when the news of the terrible accident was brought to him. It took him half an hour to reach Linthouse.

On Sunday 8 July, Al wrote up his diary for that week, expressing the immensity of the misery he felt:

> Grief, sorrow, pain, tears and anguish have come on me by what took place at Linthouse on Tuesday last ... My sorrow is so great that I can only look to God and cry. "O the poor widows and children, the fathers, the brothers and sisters bereaved in this sad calamity. God be gracious to them. O God have mercy on me and give the [numbed] strength to enable me to bear the burden laid on me."[6]

He went on the recall that over the many years ships built by his grandfather, his father, William and himself, had all been launched safely. He admitted that he prayed before every launch, asking God to ensure that everything went smoothly and without injury, loss of life or damage to property. He believed that each successful launch was only achieved with God's help and the skill and dedication of the men involved in the task.

The business of recovering the bodies and trying to refloat the ship went on without a break for eighteen days. The ship had been secured by hawsers and cables to stop her breaking up in the unforgiving tides. When she was eventually righted, the remaining bodies in her engine room could be removed. The bodies were taken to the spar shed, used as a mortuary and where the bodies were identified by their grieving relatives. On Saturday 28 July the remaining funerals were held.

There were many harrowing tales told by the survivors and the widows, but perhaps the most poignant report made at the time of the disaster was that written by an unnamed reporter:

> The faces of the dead recovered last night had by no means an unpleasing aspect; all looked as if they were asleep, and without exception the most of them had their eyes closed. A few had a look as if taken by surprise.[7]

In the aftermath of the tragedy it was inevitable that an Official Enquiry would be held. Sir Edward James Reed [1830-1906], a naval architect and Liberal Member of Parliament for Cardiff, was appointed to head the enquiry. Under Reed's chairmanship the enquiry was extremely thorough; evidence was given by many of the Clyde's leading shipbuilders, as well as the French born Francis Elgar [1845-1909], Reed's chief assistant in 1871 and later to become the first professor of the newly established John Elder Chair of Naval Architect at Glasgow University when it was established in 1883. The Enquiry, after some weeks, finally produced a seventy-three page report that totally and completely exonerated the Firm of negligence. Disasters such as the *Daphne*, thankfully, were not repeated.

A public appeal was opened and collected £30,000, the equivalent of over a million pounds at today's values. The company gave an immediate donation of £5,000, and paid another £1,000 towards the cost of the funerals. An Executive Committee was formed and it was not long before disagreements were being voiced regarding whether the bereaved were entitled to seek legal redress while accepting money from the Relief Fund. In September it was reported that:

> The first indications of agitation ... arose when the consideration of the
> relation of the sufferers to the Employers' Liability Act was mooted. Up to
> that time the country seemed prepared to subscribe ... but when it was dis-
> covered that they were being incited to press their legal claims, while at the
> same time they accepted charity, the generous impulses were checked.[8]

The first claim, in the form of a Sheriff's Court Summons for damages,
was delivered to Al, at Park Terrace, on Monday 29 July, the very day
the Sir Edward Reed's Enquiry opened. The claim was made by Annie
Morrison, the widow of Dugald Morrison, journeyman plumber. Annie
Morrison's claim was for £1,000, the equivalent of more than ten years'
wages.

The Morrison claim was shortly followed by another twenty. In a
little over three weeks the number of claims had risen to 68. Al's legal
advisers told him that he should wait until the Enquiry had reported before taking steps to fight the claims. Al admitted somewhat ruefully that
some of the claims had been made 'in respectful language and others in
legal determined language.'[9]

Al was also deeply upset by the tone of the reports appearing in the
North British Daily Mail. He said the *Mail* was making itself obnoxious in
urging the bereaved to make legal claims against the company before the
results of the Enquiry were known.

The Relief Committee were adamant that no money should be paid
to the widows or their families while they were seeking legal redress.
John McLeod, a Church of Scotland Minister at Govan, and a member
of the Relief Committee, objected to what he regarded as a change
in conditions. McLeod was adamant that no such under-taking not to
pursue legal redress had been given when the Relief Fund had been
set-up. It was reported in the *Glasgow News* that irresponsible outsiders
were inciting the widows into taking legal action. Sounder advice had
been given that such an action would fail, as there was no evidence
that Stephen's had acted in any way negligently. Indeed, such was the
controversy stirred up by the Press that donations to the Relief Fund
began to dwindle, and the Committee, chaired by Provost Thompson,

had to issue a statement clarifying the position of the Fund.

By the 19 October all claims had been withdrawn with the exception of that brought by the mother of James Carberry, a young engineer's labourer. Al had been told that even if the Carberry claim was pressed it could not possibly be heard by the Court before the beginning of 1884. He truly believed that before it went to Court, the claim would be withdrawn. His prayers were answered. On 20 November he recorded:

> I have received tonight from Professor Robertson mention that the legal agents of Mrs Carberry (Messrs Brown & Allan) write to him the case will be abandoned on condition we do not claim expenses of defence. This condition Professor Robertson agreed to and this ends this case. It is a matter of great thankfulness on my part for deliverance from trouble in this matter. We have not heard of any other claimant coming forward.[10]

It was obvious that the employees of the Yard did not hold them responsible for the tragedy, for at the next launch they presented Al and his fellow directors with an illuminated address, expressing the sympathy of the staff and the workers for what had befallen the ill-fated ship. The *Daphne* was refurbished and renamed *Rose*, and she was finally handed over to her owners, the Glasgow and Londonderry Steam Packet Company.

The terrible events of the *Daphne* sinking haunted Al for months to come. The Relief Fund, like so many before it and after, continued to experience difficulties. Payments were made to widows and children but there were some others who thought they should also have been compensated. There is a strange belief that the desire for compensation for trauma is a twenty-first century phenomenon. It is not. In 1884, as now, rows and litigation summons were an important feature of employer/employee relations. In January 1884, Al was informed that an employee called Sutherland was suing them for £200, for injuries caused by being 'precipitated into the water', at the time of the launch of the *Daphne*. It is significant that Sutherland had applied to the Relief Fund for monetary assistance but had been refused. Like all the other claims before it, the Sutherland claim never reached Court.

In 1883, JS bought Knockderry Castle, in Cove, Dunbartonshire. According to some sources the castle stands on the site of an ancient lookout tower built by Danish or Norse invaders in the twelfth century. Sir Walter Scott, in his novel *Heart of Midlothian*, immortalised Knockderry as Knockdunder Castle, a fact that is commemorated in a stained-glass window in the dining room. The castle had eighteen bedrooms, four reception rooms, a private chapel with panelled walls and a choir loft. William Leiper, the Glasgow born architect, carried out extensive external and internal alterations to the castle, including building a towerhouse

> of imposing scale, with a rich, colourful interior. Externally, but balancing full height oriels with flanking, smaller windows ... the impression of impregnability was not compromised.[11]

Sitting high on the edge of the loch, the castle looks impregnable and it gives spectacular views of Loch Long and the hills of Argyll. The scenery remains the same, though each day brings changes with the advent of the seasons. The loch is a shimmering blue grey on a quiet summer evening, and when the mist and rains lash the peninsular, it becomes sinister and frightening. A drive back to Glasgow from Knockderry along the road of the Gare Loch adds to the magic of the place. But how rudely that magic is broken when the grey forbidding buildings of the Faslane submarine base come into view. The foreboding is enhanced by the high black metal fence and the row upon row of razor wire that guard the interior from the eco warriors and peace activists who wish to see the base close down.

As JS travelled between his home in Park Circus and Knockderry Castle he would have felt a deep sense of contentment. He once said: 'My sense of the beauty and harmony of colour is strong.'[12]

JS's neighbour at Cove was John Stephen who had purchased Craigrownie Castle. This impressive baronial house was designed by Alexander "Greek" Thomson and completed around 1854. From the gardens of Craigrownie, John and his guests could look into the grounds of Knockderry and see JS and his young visitors enjoying themselves. There is a good deal of evidence to suggest that, although by 1883 JS had only two children, James Murray and Alice, he never objected when his adult guests asked to bring their own children. Knockderry must have been every small boy's idea of an exciting playground.

JS may have been concerned about the future of his son. Al, however, had no such worries about his two elder sons. Alex, after finishing his education at the Royal Technical College and Glasgow University, had spent a few months in America on a working holiday. He joined the firm in 1883 and from the very beginning used his particular skills in the Engineering Department. On 22 November, Fred graduated from Glasgow University with an MA. He had been a diligent scholar, taking class prizes in Naval Architecture. Before joining his father and brother at the Yard, Fred spent a very enjoyable grand tour of Europe.

PART THREE
1884 - 1897

' When a man is up in years the question may well be asked, "what has he made of his life?" "Has it been a blessing to himself and his fellow men."'

One Hundred Years
The Templetonian, June 1939, in the
Templeton Archives at Stoddard International plc.

A Clash of Beliefs

ON 7 March 1884, JS and his son signed an agreement whereby if James Murray continued to take an active part in the business, he would receive for the years 1884 and 1885, £250 and £300. If, after that date, James Murray left the business, JS would pay him, providing his capital would allow it, the sum of £200 per annum if he remained single and £300 if he married. This arrangement would end in November 1893; on the surface this was an arbitrary date, by then JS would be sixty and James Murray would be thirty-three.

James Murray was only too aware of his father's generosity 'Father is generous in this, where he might quite well say if I go, I go on my own account'.[1]

Nevertheless, father and son were diametrically opposite in their views on life, business and art. JS was annoyed when his son tried to compare himself with Alexander Miller and Guthrie, both elderly men who had worked and educated themselves through every department of the company. JS could not understand why his son would wish to leave a life of wealth and position to seek an inferior position as an artist 'begging men to buy [your] pictures, knuckling down to the monied men [and] conceited critics.'[2]

James Murray was disappointed with his father's attitude to art, which shows again that father and son did not understand each other. JS loved art, and he used his wealth to surround himself with beautiful things, and he counted artists among his friends. The argument between them can best be summed up by James Murray himself:

> If only he [JS] had a word to say as to the mission of art [and] the beautiful, the teaching of purity [and] sacrifice of money in business [and] certainly he holds out the power for good that an upright man has in business. Finally, he said it might be a positive evil to throw away a position Providence has given you -- spoke of one's not caring to feel myself in a lower social sphere than your relations. As for instance the Stephens.[3]

There is little doubt that JS was jealous that Al had sons who had followed him into the shipbuilding business. James Murray had a very poor opinion of Glasgow and its people, believing them to be devoid of ideas, unthinking and vulgar. He was equally scathing about London: 'How the foppery [and] fashion convenience [and] pride of select London society irritate me -- what various ills are mixed up in humanity ...'[4]

He was dismissive of his Stephen cousins' interests in sailing and physical activities. He thought he belonged to a higher plain as a romantic poet and lover of beauty. He once wrote that he would love to paint a portrait of a London dandy and write beneath it *Slave of Slaves*.

There is some justification for his beliefs, he most definitely had an artistic way with words and a perception for looking at people and things that few of his Glaswegian contemporaries were able to capture, either in words or paint:

> I was speaking for the first time to a girl in the factory, Marian [it has been impossible to identify her] who had been absent, sick until death [and] as she listened for a moment the mingled feelings that played upon her face while she smiled, and her eyes then filling with that indescribable sad wandering look [and] her lips trembling with emotion and weakness. She knew her escape, she felt the joy and gratitude of convalescence, while her nerves did not restrain her feelings. And some words from the "young master" were of course taken kindly. But that upward gaze [and] expression in a pure face! One might spend a life trying to record it ...[5]

In being concerned about the welfare of his father's work force, James Murray was following a lead set by his Templeton grandmother. James Murray wrote a number of essays that were aimed at opening the minds of the workers and showing them how to achieve self-improvement. His socialist principles were alien to JS, but he was still proud of his son's desire to improve the lives of his workers. If James Murray had believed in his own abilities, it is more than probable that he would have made a significant contribution to the advancement of the factory and to the lives of the workers.

Walter Lang of the Templeton Design Department, in an article printed in the house magazine, paints a touching picture of James Murray:

He had vision, and foresaw the need for something like many of the social and welfare schemes that are now in active operation. Music and art were to him a necessary part of life, and he was desirous that all should share in these good things. His singing at some of the factory social meetings, and his genial personality are still lovingly remembered by the older men, and the memory has been passed on by them to the younger generation.[6]

The conflict between the artist and the manufacturer was never settled and James Murray became increasingly disillusioned with his life.

He had signed an agreement with his father that he would, in return for an allowance, devote all his time to learning the business of carpet manufacture. However, having given that undertaking he did not always abide by it. If his duties took him to London, he used the visit to seek the opinion of as many prominent artists that would agree to look at his portfolio. In his heart he knew his dreams and his ambition did not exactly match, and his own shyness was sometimes a curse when confronted with an established artist.

On 7 February 1884, he visited William Morris, the artist, poet, political activist, and designer of stained glass, textiles and wallpapers. But Morris had also studied carpet design and dyeing, which made his opinions even more valuable to James Murray.

He visited Morris at his factory at Merton Abbey Mills near Wimbledon. The visit was not without incident, James Murray forgot to take his portfolio with him and then left his umbrella on the train:

I found the poet [Morris] a queer enough man. ... His factory was interesting, but a small thing, worked on principles quite unapplicable, as to a certain extent I knew before, to our own place. ... He does not, however, allow enough for the good side of machinery [and] competition owing I think to his isolated political position.[7]

It is a constant source of amusement that although James Murray did not want to be a part of the carpet business, he never missed an opportunity of referring to it. Frequently, he expressed his views on the way his family embraced the most modern machinery and industrial practices. His description of Morris, would later be seen in a cartoon by Max Beerbohn:

> He [Morris] was dressed in ... [dark] blue serge [and] a light blue cotton shirt
> [and] talked a mixture of shop and advanced politics to his work-people. ...
> He was most energetic -- almost restlessly so -- but a splendid robust florid
> man, large head, with fine expression but not suggestive of the author of
> Earthly Paradise.[8]

In spite of his youth and his artistic inexperience, James Murray felt able
to criticize Morris with an assurance that is most revealing in one so
young. In this, as in so much else, he was his father's son:

> In all his [Morris] designs there is a certain medievalism [and] originality
> that is very beautiful [and] striking. ... He is not a good colourist -- good
> where the copying if faded effect is concerned -- but generally his top shades
> were weaker than his shadows.[9]

James Murray was disappointed with the visit. He had not shown his
portfolio and he had not discussed his desire to be an artist with the great
man. He left bitterly unhappy.

However, back in London he visited Ernest Parton, the Ameri-
can-born landscape painter. This time he took his drawings with him.
Parton's response dented his fragile ego even more; he thought James
Murray had an eye for colour and a certain idealism, and that 'I would
succeed -- and take a second-rate position.'[10]

This was hardly the ringing endorsement James Murray was expect-
ing, and certainly not one that his father would consider appropriate. JS
would not have been content until James Murray could prove that he
was a highly acclaimed painter and a member of the Royal Academy.

Shortly after his visit to Morris and Parton, James Murray called upon
the Royal Academician, Sir Lawrence Alma Tadema. Tadema, much to
James Murray's astonishment, after looking at his portfolio, expressed
his admiration for the work. He said that although the work showed feeling it lacked the science of painting and he encouraged James Murray to
seek further professional training.

James Murray thought that the leading Victorian painters were
George Frederick Watts, the portrait and allegorical painter, and Edward
Burne-Jones, a member of the Pre-Raphaelite Brotherhood. Burne-
Jones's mystical and symbolic paintings were everything James Murray

aspired to achieve. After visiting Burne-Jones, he wrote:

> I went with the impression, having been told so, that he was rather an ego-
> tist [and] came away, seldom having been more favourably impressed. I was
> so at one [and] quite independently throughout of his kindness [and] praise
> of my work.[11]

He goes on to recount that Burne-Jones was a small man, with a fine delicate sensitive face, who after looking at half a dozen of James Murray's
drawings, said 'there was no doubt about it, I would certainly succeed
-- all I wanted was practice. I employed beautiful colour ...'[12]

It was only when they came to discuss the thorny subject of money
that the young man's spirits were depressed. Burne-Jones warned him
that if he wanted to make a good living from art, then the sort of subjects James Murray wanted to paint would not be commercially viable.
He should not have been surprised, after all, even the great French Im-
pressionists Renoir, Monet and Manet were hardly wealthy men.

Two days after seeing Burne-Jones, James Murray left London for
Glasgow. His visit to Templeton's London showroom and warehouse
was over and he had to return to his duties in the factory: 'Thus I go
home. I know that I could certainly take a position as an artist that at
least I could certainly earn a fair living ...'[13]

He goes on to say that it was Alice's impassioned pleading that finally
convinced him that he had to put duty before ambition.

JS and Alice were naturally delighted that he had returned to the
family fold, but in his heart James Murray was not sure that he had made
the right decision. After a late night talk with Alice, he retired to his
room and wrote movingly of

> her true humble self-sacrificing Christianity -- but on the other hand, how
> wide we are in sympathies of mind [and] emotions. This blooming paints
> and all ideals -- [and] books ... she hates. I must be natural [and] have friends
> belonging to my own position in life ... I may be [and] have been selfish
> -- yet somethings are hard for me she does not see. This is going to be a
> struggle but only necessary if just.[14]

On Monday 31 March 1884, James Murray went back to work at the factory. It cannot be said that he went with a light heart. He continued to be tormented by the knowledge that he would never succeed as a business man. He believed he had a mission to become a great artist, and to pass on to a philistine world his perception of beauty, intellectualism and spiritualism.

At the start of the Glasgow Fair fortnight in July, James Murray and his family were at Knockderry. He was suffering from a severe cold, a neuralgic toothache, sleepless nights and a black depression. His mood did not improve when one of the guests, Macfarlane, told him, during a walk on the moor, that he looked really well and in good spirits. James Murray was too exhausted and in too much pain to argue with him.

In the summer of 1884, Fred Stephen celebrated his twenty-first birthday and Al gave him a cheque for £100. At the same time the question arose again of where sixteen-year-old Bernard should complete his education. Mary and Maud had both been to England to finish their schooling, but Al, with Mary's approval, opted to send Bernard to Loretto, in Mussel-burgh, owned and run by Hely-Hutchinson Almond, a distinguished academic.

The ethos of the school was challenging, even for boys born and brought up on the Clyde:

> ... flannel shirts open at the neck, shorts or knickerbockers. ... Coats off when the temperature reached 60°, open windows and a cold bath every morning ... the value of organised games ... [an] intense belief that education must be one great whole, including every part of one's being, and that character could be trained only if body, soul and spirit were all being educated together.[15]

Bernard became a pupil at Loretto in the Winter Term of 1884, but if he felt even a pang of homesickness he was at least able to share his misery with three other new boys. These were John Campbell, James Allan and Arthur Cuthbert, the sons of Charles Cornell, another shipbuilder at Govan.

In 1851 when Stephen began to operate from Kelvinhaugh they appointed Charles Connell their shipyard manager. Ten years later Connell left to start his own Yard, a decision that Alexander Stephen thought to be particularly risky, and he foresaw Connell's dream would end in financial ruin. The venture very nearly did fail when, in the early hours of the morning of 28 September 1864, the new offices at the Yard were destroyed by fire. Fires on the Clyde were a hazard shared by all the shipbuilders. By the time of Connell's death on 14 February 1884 he left an estate worth over a quarter of a million. Al's comment on their ex-employee's demise was to marvel that he had, against all predictions, made a success of his business and had died a rich man.

JS admitted there were few certainties in life. He repeatedly said that he had to struggle with his conscience as he tried to resolve the dilemma of good over evil. He found it impossible to believe in his son's devotion to Spiritualism and Theism, he truly believed that the way to salvation and peace of mind was through repentance and forgiveness. JS even chided his missionary brother, the Revd Archie when his own Faith was causing him to doubt:

> You have an awful need of patience and faith, old fellow, but I do not a bit, as some might, commiserate [with] your troubles and privations. The consciousness of noble issues, aims [and] motives is far more than compensation even among dis-couragements and trials.[16]

JS passionately believed that with God's help he could find the true meaning of Faith and of the right way of serving Him. Rather unjustly he accuses himself of being weak,

> devious and deflected often, [I have] in the main flowed in a right course. By the Grace of God I have been helped to do a fair amount of good, and ... have been able to escape very much evil.[17]

In trying to put his life in some sort of perspective he wrote:

[I] have been subject less or more to dyspepsia, but, on the other hand ... except during gastric fever in boyhood ... have never been one whole day confined to bed by ill heath, in 1884, through the anxieties and overwork consequence on taking the responsibilities of the business at the time of my father's retirement [in 1878], my nervous system suffered a collapse from which I only recovered after six month's rest and relaxation.[18]

1878 was also the year that Emily died, shortly after giving birth to a still-born son.

On Friday 24 October 1884, JS and Alice left Glasgow for Liverpool where they boarded a ship for Egypt, followed by a visit to India. They arrived in Port Said on 8 November. The relationship between JS and Alice was an interesting one. In 1884, she was twenty-three-years-old, and for the greater part of her life she had been the constant female presence in her father's life. JS's assessment of Alice was revealing:

... she has shown herself most dutiful ... [she has a] strong good sense ... great amiability and kindness for which she is so distinguished and for which she is so generally loved and respected.[19]

JS was reasonably confident that he could leave James Murray for a little over two months. Perhaps he used the holiday as a way of testing his son's resolve and commitment to the business. JS would not have been convinced if he had read James Murray's diary:

I plod along in business sometimes branding myself as a failure, through want of energy [and] sometimes often true enough, pitting that against my physical weakness, but I feel pretty certain that I shall never make a man of business, unless my memory improves tremendously. Even then I don't know that I am practical [and] anxious enough to make profits [and] eagerly push matters. I suppose I shall find out soon enough.[20]

James Murray having said that he was not suited to the life of a business-man then wonders when his father is going make him a partner.

On 27 August 1885, James Templeton died at his home in Glasgow. He

was eighty-three and he had lived to see the Firm that he started in 1838 grow to become a company with an international reputation second to none. He had reason to be proud of his sons, JS and James, for they had proved to be equal to the task of running the great carpet manufacturing empire.

James's son the Revd Archie had served with distinction as a Medical Missionary to the Santals of India, until ill health forced him to return to Scotland. In 1880 he had been appointed to the Glasgow Medical Mission. James's daughters, Anne and Agnes Jane had not married, but Mary had been a loyal and dutiful wife to Al.

In his Deed of Settlement, James made it clear that his first wish was that JS and James should have adequate funds to run the business without incurring debts. He left generous legacies to his daughters and his grandchildren -- which, of course, included James Murray. The legacy to family members also included one to Elizabeth Mary, then teaching in Essex.

In dealing with family members James was scrupulously fair, and that spirit of generosity was also shown to the factory workers with more than twenty years service. In a list extending to thirty-seven names, he detailed not just the name of the employee, but also the actual length of service, and whether they were, in his opinion, very steady, steady or unsteady. To most he gave £10, but to those regarded as very steady he doubled the legacy. To his foremen he was even more benevolent. He also remembered his servants both in Glasgow and Dunfillan, including John Archibald, his long-serving coachman.

Mourning the death of his father, JS realized that he had spent the better part of his adult life alone. Alice was the most constant source of pleasure in his life but James Murray increasingly wanted to go his own way. JS was fifty-three, but had only had the pleasure of marriage for little more than four and a half years. On 4 November 1885, at 15 Belgrave Crescent, Edinburgh, the home of her step-uncle Edward Caird, a retired manufacturer, Maria Zelinda Glennie, became JS's third wife.

Twenty-two years younger than JS, Maria, was the second daughter of Charles Archibald Glennie, Her Majesty's Consul in Sanlos, Brazil, and his wife Leonora Flora d'Aguiar Andrada. When Charles and Leonora died, their children, Charles, Caroline, Maria and Leonora, were brought back to Scotland and their aunt Caroline Glennie became their guardian.

Caroline Glennie had had an interesting life, her first husband was a Writer to the Signet, James Bonar, the brother of Horatius, Andrew Alexander and John James, all highly respected Ministers in the Free Church. Andrew and Horatius, were both elected Moderators of the General Assembly. Caroline and James married in 1859, he died in July 1867, and in October 1869 Caroline became the third wife of Edward Caird, a prosperous Dundee jute merchant.

JS was enthusiastic about the prospect of marriage again, and marrying into a family with a Latin American pedigree, and a recognised social status, appealed to him.

JS gave free rein to his delight:

> My wife's parents ... I never saw. The father ... had attained wealth and consideration through the possession of a sugar estate in the West Indies. ... The family of d'Andrara ... was most distinguished [in Brazil]. ... One uncle of my wife was the Baron d'Andrara whom I met, one aunt was the Baroness de Penedo, whose husband ... was Ambassador Plenipotentiary at the Court of St James.[21]

On 23 December 1885, James Murray gave a lecture to the Dunfillan Temperance and Mutual Improvement Society. Most of his audience were workers from the Templeton factories.

In what was a long, and at times, highly complicated theme, he told his audience that with education they could make significant changes to their lives, and could aspire to higher things. He quoted from a letter he had received from Rosamond Dale Owen whereby she reiterated much of the philosophy of her grandfather Robert Owen. In 1813, Owen published *A New View of Society*, a series of essays on social reform. He believed that working men living as a group, working in cooperation and unity, would be more productive. He further contended that families should only have sole charge of their children until the age of three, from then on the community should have the responsibility of educating and rearing the child until adulthood. Owen also believed that such children would be graceful, genial, healthy, and content. He did not, however, say they would be loved. A reccurring theme in James Murray's writings was his desire to be loved.

In her letter, Rosamond, who was now back at her home in America, wrote that:

> It is false to hold that money and labour are equivalents. All the money in the world could be swept out of it with only temporary inconvenience: if labour were stopped death would ensue, and the last survivor, surrounded by heaps of gold, would realise fully that gold is a lifeless, senseless metal, while labour is an expenditure of life-force. The man who transforms a tree into a door has put so much of himself into his work as represents the difference between the tree and the door; his vigour and his brain have created it, and must for ever remain part of that door. When an employer believes he has paid fully for that work with a coin, he makes a mistake.[22]

JS never made any secret that he regarded both Laurence Oliphant and Rosamond Dale Owen as unsuitable companions for his son. In his *Memoir* written much later, JS wrote of his abhorrence of Owen's beliefs:

> I need only say that an account of this man's [Robert Owen] remarkable history as philanthropist, reformer and speculator in socialism and spiritualism will be found in any encyclopaedia. This, however, will not be told, after he left the vicinity of Lanark, the owner of the property pulled down the houses built for the community he had founded, ploughed the ground and sowed it with salt as a protest against alleged immoralities.[23]

JS could not have been happy when he heard, or was told, of the contents of Rosamond's letter to James Murray:

> Employers must return unto their workers some vital living effect besides the money that is owed. What do ... the heedless rich generally, and

wealthy employers, in particular, owe to these people who feed them, who clothe them and their families, without whom they would all go naked and hungry ...[24]

What social reformers like Rosamond failed to understand was that without the creation of wealth by the manufacture of goods and services, the poor would not survive. It did not occur to James Murray or Rosamond that in advocating their form of Utopia, they were wrong like many before and after them. Utopia is a concept that exists only in the imagination of idealists.

Radicalism and the unionisation of labour, preached by Rosamond and James Murray were, however, the least of JS's objections to their friendship. It was when Rosamond began to convince James Murray that she was receiving messages from his dead mother, that the God-fearing JS reached the end of his tether. It was also a cruel deception and one that would forever cause a schism between father and son. In their own way they were looking for unconditional love from a woman, and neither of them found that lasting relationship. James Murray's search for a mother was always doomed to failure; in Rosamond Dale Owen he found neither love nor happiness.

Happiness Eludes Him

AS a legatee under the Deed of Settlement of his Templeton and Stephen grandfathers, James Murray was at last financially independent and could turn his back on the carpet business and continue his study of art.

He returned to Florence early in 1886, and the Italian city was like paradise after the cold and wet of a Glasgow winter. James Murray took with him a letter of introduction from Burne-Jones to Maria Stillman, the second wife of William James Stillman, *The Times* correspondent in Rome. Maria Spartali was, before her marriage, a pupil of Ford Madox Brown and Burne-Jones, and a stunningly beautiful woman, who according to JS was the inspiration for Benjamin Disraeli's heroine in *Lothair*.

JS was impressed enough by Maria Stillman's art to purchase her painting of *The Childhood of St Cecilia*, and he had it hung in the drawing room at Park Circus. For once, father and son were in total agreement. James Murray found in Florence the happiness he had been seeking, and in the Stillman family, he found artistic and intellectual companions. When he returned to Glasgow in the winter of 1886, it was to tell his father that he was engaged to be married to Lisa Stillman.

JS was delighted by the news. He thought marriage would give James Murray the stability his life had so far lacked. He was a little troubled though that, at twenty-six, James Murray was too young to marry. That was amusing since JS was only twenty-seven when he married Mary Stephen. However once JS had established that Lisa Stillman came from a respectable family and that she was a young lady of good character, he gave his permission for an engagement to be announced.

Nothing in James Murray's life could be that simple, and as usual there would be no happy ending. A month after the announcement, JS received a letter from William Stillman that caused him much distress. Stillman thought it was his duty to tell him that the girl's mother, Laura Macks, had died in Crete, of 'profound melancholy, which became insanity accompanied by religious delusions from which she sought refuge in a voluntary death ...'[1]

The information mortified JS. He knew that his son suffered from black moods of depression and this, coupled with his interest in spiritualism and cult religions, would not be helped if his wife was of a similar persuasion. JS wrote to Stillman thanking him for his 'great candour and ... high sense of honour'.[2]

Within weeks JS was to receive another disturbing communication to the effect that as a result of all the excitement over her forthcoming marriage, Lisa had taken a quantity of laudanum. The dose had not been sufficient to cause her death, but enough to convince JS that she was not stable enough to become the wife of James Murray. The engagement was called off. It was a sad little episode, especially as Lisa died shortly after the end of her engagement.

One can only speculate at James Murray's emotional state at that time. He was a deeply unhappy young man. To add to his misery, in March 1887 his step-sister Maria Caroline Ada (Charry) was born, twenty-seven years younger than him. An interesting point was that her birth was registered by Uncle James and not by her father, and this could well have led to the confusion over the spelling of her name. Her birth certificate gives her name as Mary not Maria.

Whatever his feelings, there is a lasting reminder of James Murray that was handed down from that time in 1886. He presented to the Crownpoint Bowling Club, a handsome silver cup to be competed for annually by the Crownpoint bowlers. James Murray disliked sport, yet he cared enough for the factory men to give them something to compete for each year. For the next thirty years the names of the winners were engraved on the cup until there was no room left, whereupon in 1934 Alex Turnbull presented a base for the cup studded with small silver shields for future names.

It is hard to separate obsession and passion, but in 1886 Fred Stephen's love of the sea became a life-time passion for yachts and racing. In that year he designed and built *Coila*, a three-tonner yacht, and during her first few seasons *Coila* won a spectacular number of races. The highlight of the summer racing was the Clyde Club Regatta; JS remembered those blissful days as a guest of Al and his family:

> ... we enjoyed a sight not to be soon forgotten -- I suppose there would be
> 150 sail yachts within sight, at once ... the beauty of the picture set in the
> frame of our Highland hills and perfectly lovely midsummer day ...[3]

Al had hired a small steamer for the day, the music was supplied by a
regimental band, and the company consisted of, according to JS, a good
many young ladies, who apparently, thoroughly enjoyed the music and
the sight of the yachts racing. The glorious summer day was followed by
dark skies, pouring rain and chilly winds.

Twelve days after the birth of Charry, Maria died of puerperal convul-
sions -- a complication of child birth. This was the third time that JS
had lost his wife and he must have wondered to why his wives died so
young when his sisters, aunts, cousins and in-law aunts lived well into
their ninth decade. There is a myth that Victorian women died young
-- well yes, some did -- but then some lived into old age. One explanation that is worth a mention is that of those who lived into their nine-
ties, Agnes Jane (90); Aunt Elizabeth Templeton (97); Aunt Agnes (94);
Cousin Elizabeth Mary (92); and cousin-in-law Blanche Croudace (96),
all remained unmarried.

It could have been Maria's death that made JS think seriously about
who would become his successor. He was convinced that James Murray would never be persuaded to give up art for commerce. His brother
James was extremely unlikely to have an heir, and Revd Archie, although
unmarried, was beginning to have an interest in one of his parishioners,
Elizabeth Helen Aitken. But even if they did marry and have a son, the
child would be too young to be JS's heir. If was therefore inevitable that
JS would consider a young man who had first entered his workforce in
1884. Daniel Henderson Lusk Young, the eldest son of Robert Young
and Ann Henderson Lusk, was just a year younger than James Murray,
and the same age as Alice.

Dan had come to the factory on a recommendation. That recom-

mendation could well have come from Al, who knew the Young family
well. He was an immensely likeable young man, and soon won, not just
the respect of JS, but the respect and admiration of his fellow workers.
He was not averse to taking his coat off, rolling up his sleeves and lending
a hand on the factory floor:

> When pressure of work required a night-shift ... he took his place along
> with another to make a pair on a spooling machine.[4]

He was a graduate of Glasgow University. On joining Templeton, he immediately attended classes at the Old Weaving College, and could within
months assist in the maintenance of the machines.

It was not surprising then that JS was interested in this industrious
young man, nor is it surprising that Alice was made aware of the presence of a charming, compassionate and eligible suitor. Alice and Dan
announced their engagement in the autumn of 1887 and JS blessed the
forthcoming union by making Dan a junior partner.

In October 1887 Al's eldest daughter, Mary, announced her engagement
to Walter Wingate Gray. In marrying into the Wingate and Gray families
Mary was forming an alliance with another of the prominent families
of Scotland. Walter was born in January 1856, the son of Walter Gray
and Helen Richardson Wingate, who had married in December 1851.
Helen, the daughter of John Wingate and Janet Rollo Graham, was born
in November 1816, in Kilmaddock, Perth. John Wingate, the son of William Wingate and Isabella Carrick, died in 1856 at the age of eighty-nine
at his home of Kingsburgh, Perth. He was a man of property. The most
prominent Wingate families can all trace their ancestry back to William
and Isabella.

Walter Gray was born in 1802, to James Gray, a jeweller, and Cecilia Kuhill. Her father, Mark, was a sugar baker from Greenock. Walter
Gray, was a West Indian merchant, but he died on 13 September 1863 of
chronic hepatitis; Gray's business partner was Alexander Cunningham,
the husband of Isabella, Helen's sister.

Wingate Gray said that Janet Rollo Graham could trace her ancestry back to John Graham of Claverhouse -- first Viscount Dundee [1649-1689]. It would take a life-time study of genealogy to prove the connection, and even then it would probably not be proved beyond reasonable doubt. What is not in doubt is that Claverhouse was the scourge of the Covenanters. He was responsible for the persecution and murder of the Covenanter martyrs; he could also have been the reason why the Templetons left Hapland for Kintyre.

Walter Wingate Gray, under the terms of his father's Will, inherited at the age of twenty-three. Shortly after that he purchased the house and estate of Nunraw, in Garvald, East Lothian. In purchasing Nunraw, he bought into the history of an extremely fine and remarkable building. The original fortalice, was built by Malcolm Canmore -- Ceann-Mor, King of Scots, who murdered Macbeth in 1057, but was himself killed fighting the English in 1093. In 1178, the fortalice was converted into a convent for the Cistercian Nuns, thanks to the generosity of Countess Adia, the widow of Prince Henry.

In 1864, Robert Hay, who owned the Estate before Gray, began the task of restoring Nunraw. He wished to renovate the building back to its sixteenth century baronial magnificence. During the restoration, they uncovered the opulent painted ceiling:

> Eleven nine-inch joists are laid out in short panels enclosed by coloured lines which interlace each other ... margined with a guilloche border of red upon yellow, within which is a miscellaneous profusion of coloured ornament including birds, beasts, characteristic late 16th century, bunches of grapes, apples, and pears, with foliage, musical instruments -- a drum, shawms, crossed viol and lute -- muskets, gauntlets, human heads ... elements such as ... animal skull, shield-like cartouche, bow and quiver of arrows ...[5]

In the days when the nuns were in residence, the room with the beautiful ceiling was used as a refectory; in Gray's time it was used as a billards room.

In trying to be precise about Walter Gray's life before he purchased Nunraw, it has only been possible to rely on his obituary notices. Sometime before his marriage he joined the 16th Royal Lancers, thus maintaining the Wingate connection with the military. Gray's cousin [Francis]

Reginald Wingate [1861-1853] was the son of Andrew Wingate and Bessie Turner. Andrew just happened to be a shawl manufacturer in Paisley around the time that James Templeton was also manufacturing shawls in the town. Reginald and Walter were both made fatherless at a very early age, but unlike Walter, who was an only child, Reginald had six brothers and four sisters.

Al was to recognise Reginald Wingate as one of his closest friends and whenever Wingate's duties allowed, he and his wife Catherine Leslie [Kitty], were welcome visitors at Fearann Coille and Park Terrace.

In his diary and letters, James Murray said that early in 1887 he returned to London and later in the year he went to France to continue his art studies. Those months in Paris were among the happiest of his life; he had the great good fortune to become a pupil of Benjamin Jean Constant, that most gifted of teachers. Of Constant and his teaching James Murray wrote:

> The secret of French success ... consists more in this traditionary element of education than in aught else -- consists in the clear impress that is made of the best preceding ages on the forthcoming best, and upon the unselfish bestowal of a lifetime's acquisition of knowledge on those who have had no claim to it than that of being young striving followers, and fellow-worshippers at the shine of the Beautiful.[6]

Constant played a very important role in persuading James Murray that he could, after all, become an established painter. In paying tribute to Constant, James Murray wrote:

> Having been a former student of his *atelier*, I may offer with a peculiar gratitude my testimony to his uniform kindness and generosity of spirit -- a gratitude shared by hundreds of other British and foreign students. ... Twice a week, besides receiving on most Sunday mornings, he [Constant] visited his classes, criticizing, encouraging, and inspiring the students ...[7]

James Murray was not blind to the criticism that Constant expressed at what he regarded as the literary feeling and pseudo-cultural idealism that most of his British students wished to put into their painting. Constant thought that the symbolism and idealism that Rossetti, Watts and Burne-Jones used in painting, hindered rather than stimulated their art.

In France, James Murray met Laurence Oliphant again, the meeting, taking place at the time it did, was to have terrible consequences. When Rosamond Dale Owen returned to America in the 1880s, James Murray continued to correspond with her. Their friendship was undoubtedly a source of intense pain for JS.

The death of Maria only added to JS's sense of bewilderment over James Murray's behaviour. He believed his son should understand the depths of his grieving. He wrote, telling James Murray that his continued involvement with spiritualism, in all its religious connotations, was a constant source of unease and vexation to his family. In a very prophetic sentence, JS wrote that he had lost three wives in the most appalling circumstances, and if his son continued to adopt the style of life he was leading, then JS could see what lay before was even more grief than he had previously endured.

In the early summer of 1887, Al had been delighted to welcome home his sister Janet. She had spent the past sixteen months visiting James and Mina at Lovedale. On her return she would have spent many happy hours telling the family of her visit and of the sights and sounds she had enjoyed and of those that had frightened her.

Two weeks after Janet's return, Al received a telegram from John to say that he had received a telegram from Eleanor, telling him that Andrew was very ill. John immediately travelled to London but Andrew died in the afternoon of 19 July, in his fifty-fourth year. Of his six children, the eldest, William, was seventeen, and the youngest, Adela, was two. It appears that only John attended his funeral. It was unlikely that Al was there.

Three days after Andrew's death, Al took a party for a sail on board his new yacht *Nerissa* -- a replacement for *Sylvia*. The distress that Andrew had caused his ageing parents was something that Al could never truly forgive. He could accept Andrew's contrition but forgiveness could only come from God.

The Victorian industrialists and manufacturers measured their wealth, not just in the profit or loss of their company accounts but in the way they spent their private fortunes. Almost without exception, then as now, property was considered the way to measure success. The building of vast holiday homes was probably begun by the Prince Consort when he built Balmoral for his Queen. The Glasgow tycoons followed suit. JS bought and completely refurbished Knockderry Castle, his brother James bought Holme Hill House at Dunblane, John Stephen owned Craigrownie Castle. Al had owned Fearann Coille since 1866, but twenty years later he was seeking a better property.

James (Paraffin) Young's death in 1883 meant that his estate of Kelly, at Wemyss Bay, was put up for sale. The view from Kelly, across the lower reaches of the Clyde, on a warm summer evening, is still one that tingles the blood and has the pulse racing. The sheer beauty of the river, the sweep of the Cowal Peninsular, with Goat Fell on Arran black against the evening sky, is something to saviour. Wemyss Bay had another advantage for Al, commuting to Linthouse was easier than commuting from Dunoon.

If the location suited Al, the existing house did not, and almost immediately he had the house demolished, and then engaged William Leiper to design and build him a magnificent baronial mansion. Leiper, of course, had redesigned Knockderry and the façade at the new Templeton factory. The new Kelly would be built with local red sandstone and have sixty rooms; the external walls would be ornately decorated. The house was later rather unkindly described as being of 'Franco-Scotto-Anglo-Dutch' style. So much of Victorian architecture was decried in the 1950s and demolished. Now we know that much of that vandalism was misplaced.

The rebuilding of Kelly gave Al months of pleasure interspersed with anxiety and despair that the house would ever be finished to his exacting standards.

Death of an Idealist

MARY, Alex and Elsie were at Nunraw as guests of Gray over the New Year holiday of 1888; Mary was keen to get to know the place that would be her matrimonial home. What cannot be denied is that she fell in love with both the house and the district:

> One thing that was noticeable was her love of the place. A certain reserve in her nature seemed to find a congenial home among the quiet of our beautiful hills. She was never happier than at Nunraw.[1]

On Friday 30 December 1887, a presentation of a wedding gift was made by servants and tenants of the estate to Mary and Walter. The presentation was made by Anderston, the gardener and the oldest servant on the estate, ably assisted by Amos, McDonald, Halliday, Sked and Scott. In handing over the gift of a silver revolving dish, with an inscription, Anderson said it gave him pleasure, 'to present the gift to a master who was held in so high esteem by his servants and tenants.'[2]

Al's mind, while focused on the forthcoming marriage, spent the morning of Saturday 4 February at Kelly with Leiper, going over the plans and setting the schedules for the rebuilding. He returned to Park Terrace in the evening to host a party for Walter and Mary and the rest of the family. After dinner, Al and his guests were engaged in laying out the wedding presents in the Billiards Room.

It is rare, over a hundred years after the event, to be able to have an accurate list of those wedding presents. Some of the presents were stunningly beautiful; Gray gave Mary a double heart brooch of diamonds and rubies, and a small pearl initial brooch; Uncle James Templeton gave her a handsome coral and diamond bracelet; Al and Mary gave them a grand piano and Mary an oak writing table. The presents from the Gray family were no less impressive and included gifts for Nunraw. One particularly interesting present was the gift of a picture from James Murray, probably one of his own paintings.

The foremen and officials of the shipyard gave the couple a solid silver épergne, while the servants at Kelly gave them a china and silver salad bowl. Mary's Sunday School class gave her an inkstand, and her sewing class a silver pencil case.

The wedding of Walter and Mary took place at the Free College Church on Wednesday 8 February at 2 o'clock, and according to an entry in Al's diary the day was fine. Mary wore a white satin dress draped with Brussels lace: her tulle veil was fixed with three diamond stars, a gift from Uncle John Stephen. She wore Gray's brooch at the neck of her dress. Her four bridesmaids were her sister Elsie, Alice Templeton, Emma Tod, and Jane, who was Alexander Cunningham and Isabella Wingate's daughter. Each girl wore a gold brooch set with pearls, gifts from the bridegroom. Before the young couple left for a honeymoon in North Africa, the guests were entertained at Park Terrace.

In the evening at Garvald, two bonfires were lit followed by a firework display. The night before, the staff and their wives had been entertained to a supper and a dance.

Mary and Gray spent nearly two months touring Africa. It is not known if they visited Lovedale, but it would have been surprising if they had not visited Stewart and Mina. On their way home they travelled through Spain, France and England. They arrived back at Garvald on Tuesday 3 April, where they were greeted by villagers and servants, who had decked the street with triumphal arches and banners with welcome home slogans. They also wished them a long and united marriage, God's blessing and the hope that prosperity would be ever theirs.

Their carriage was met at the Priests' Brae. The men of Garvald unhitched the horses from the carriage and pulled the carriage home to Nunraw, stopping once so that Annie and Minnie (Wilhelmina Elizabeth) Broomfield, the little daughters of James and Wilhelmina Broomfield, a builder and merchant in the village, could present Mary with a bouquet of flowers. Al and Mary, Alex and Fred came through from Glasgow to welcome home the young couple.

How many words have been written in romantic fiction of the strict

Victorian autocrat who seduced a servant and, when she became pregnant, turned her and her unborn child out onto the streets? She gave birth in the workhouse, and only years later did the natural father, overcome with grief, seek and find his lost child.

There was a very different true story taking place in Glasgow. In May 1858, Margaret Hutton, a young seamstress, gave birth to an illegitimate daughter. Two years later, Margaret had a second illegitimate daughter, Elizabeth Helen; thirteen months later she had an illegitimate son. In January 1864 Margaret had yet another illegitimate son, who was registered under the name of Andrew Hugh Aitken Hutton. This is where the story began to take on a totally different complexion.

Hugh Aitken was a successful calico printer and dyer, living at 17 Whitevale Street, in the High Church district of Glasgow -- later known as Camlachie. Margaret Hutton was by now Hugh's housekeeper. Three more sons and a daughter were born between 1866 and 1871. The sons were all registered as Hutton, but were given the name Aitken among their forenames. The name of the father was missing from each of the birth certificates. Three of the children died in infancy, Margaret in 1859, Alexander Thornton Hutton in 1862 and Alfred James Aitken Hutton in 1871.

Hugh Aitken died on 13 May 1875, and on his death certificate he is referred to as a single man. The death was registered by his brother Thomas, also a calico printer but living in Manchester. Six years later, Margaret was using the name of Aitken, and described as being a widow, but still living at 17 Whitevale. She had five children with her, all bearing the name of Aitken, and all corresponding in name and age to her illegitimate children. Margaret died of consumption on 22 July 1881. She had been suffering from this for a number of months. The informant of her death was her son, Andrew Hugh, and he was in no doubt that his mother was the widow of Hugh Aitken. He also gave Margaret's parents as Thomas Hutton, a railway contractor and Elizabeth Hutton neé Smith. A marriage certificate for Hugh and Margaret has not been found nor has a declaration of an irregular marriage, a possibility at that time. An example of an irregular marriage is where the couple declare before witnesses that they now wish to be known as husband and wife.

All the above explanation is important for on 26 February 1888 Elizabeth Helen Aitken married the Revd Dr Archie Templeton. On their marriage certificate, Elizabeth gave her mother's name as Hutton, a seamstress, but there is no mention of Hugh Aitken, in spite of what her brother said a few years earlier. Hugh Andrew -- he had now reversed his first names -- was a witness to his sister's marriage.

There is a family story that Revd Archie met Elizabeth in Church. As he was preaching his Sunday sermon, he was aware of a pious young woman, sitting in the front pew, taking notes and hanging on his every word.

When the Revd Archie proposed to Elizabeth, did she immediately tell him of her unconventional upbringing, or did she wait a little while? It is obvious from her marriage certificate that she did not try to hide the truth. The marriage was most productive: they had nine children between 1889 and 1902.

The death of a child is always traumatic, but when that death is preceded by weeks of uncertainty the waiting for news becomes intolerable. William, the third son of William Stephen and Jane Skair Henderson, disappeared from his home in 1888.

On Thursday 22 March, William Stephen junior left his Helenslea home to meet a relative at Arbroath; unfortunately they missed each other and William junior returned to Dundee. He was not seen by a family member, nor surprisingly by any of the servants in the house. He spent some time in the vestibule of Helenslea, for later that evening, his gold watch was found under a chair. It was assumed by his father that William junior had returned from Arbroath and then gone out again, but his disappearance did not cause concern until he had not returned by the time the family retired.

The next morning, William and Elizabeth were shocked when the postman delivered a letter, written by William junior and posted around ten-thirty the night before at the General Post Office. The note was quite short, it said simply that William junior was tired of life and he asked his parents to forget he ever existed.

It can only be imagined by those who have not personally experienced the disappearance of a child just what William suffered in those early days of his son's disappearance. William would have found it difficult to admit, even to himself, that his son had been unhappy and mentally disturbed at the time of his disappearance. A month later when no word had come from him, William offered a reward of £100 for information of his son's whereabouts. A reward poster put out by David Dewar, Chief Constable of Dundee, gave a very revealing portrait of William junior:

> 5 Feet 4 Inches high; Dark Hair and Dark Moustache; Dark Eyes ... and wore Clear Steel-rimmed spectacles ...[3]

When last seen, William junior had been soberly dressed in a brown tweed jacket, vest and trousers, grey flannel shirt and black silk necktie, and a dark brown overcoat and black felt hat. He may have left his watch at Helenslea, but he took with him a pearl-handled pocket knife and thirty-five pounds in cash.

The statement issued a month after William junior's disappearance mentioned that his family still believed he was alive. They thought he could have sought work as a carpenter. He had served his apprenticeship in that trade. Dewar was of the opinion that William junior had been suffering a significant mental trauma prior to his disappearance. He had consulted a number of doctors, who thought he would be happier working with his hands, rather than taking charge, as he had been, of his father's Arctic Tannery Company. It was said, however, that he had showed considerable skill in running the business. He had, after all, been well educated, he spoke French and a little German, and had travelled widely. He was a deacon of the West Ferry Free Church. Dewar's statement ended with a very worrying pronouncement, that prior to his disappearance William junior had been suffering from symptoms of religious mania.

The obvious conclusion was that, like his cousin James Murray, he had become involved with an extreme religious cult. It is impossible to know whether James Murray had introduced him to Laurence Oliphant and Rosamond Dale Owen. The cousins would have met at family weddings, baptisms, funerals and other social occasions. There was only three years difference in their ages, and James Murray would have known the grief his cousin had endured at the age of thirteen when his mother died. James Murray would have sympathised with the betrayal that William junior felt when his father married again just fifteen months after the death of Jane.

Five weeks after his disappearance, a Glasgow newspaper ran the following article, and it is worth quoting for the implications which are still relevant today when someone goes missing and a reward is offered:

> Very great uneasiness has been caused to the relatives and friends of Mr W Stephen, jun. ... The young gentleman disappeared from Broughty Ferry ... and although a reward of £100 [about £3,000-4,000 at today's value] was offered for such information as would lead to his discovery, no trace of him was found until yesterday when a letter was received from John Graham, [of the] bookstall Citadel Station, Carlisle, who was formerly at Dundee East station, stating that exactly a month ago he saw and spoke to Mr Stephen.[4]

Later that day, 26 April, William received another communication stating that his son had been seen in Liverpool and that he had boarded the steamer *Aurania*, bound for New York, on the 24 March, and that his ticket was to take him on to Philadelphia. William, of course, had known that a week before his son's disappearance he had, indeed, been in Carlisle and could well have spoken to John Graham. It is also known that a passenger with the name of William Stephen did board a ship at Liverpool on the 24 March. The cruel irony of coincidence was hard for the family to bear; the last confirmed sighting of William junior was on the night of 22 March, when he crossed from Dundee to Newport on the last steamer of the day. 'He was recognised by one of the boatmen standing at the pierhead, apparently undecided which way to turn ...'[5]

Finally, the riddle of William junior's disappearance was solved for on Tuesday 1 May, a body was found floating off Tayport:

> The body of Mr W Stephen jun ... was in the river Tay. ... In the forenoon, James Ogilvie and James Sorley, mussel dredgers, happened to be at the pierhead, Tayport, when a body was noticed floating past with the tide. Getting a boat they went off and secured the body, which was immediately removed to the Mortuary.[6]

The condition of the body made formal identification impossible. But from a card case, a railway season ticket and two handkerchiefs found in the dead man's pockets, it was established the body was that of William junior. A telegram was sent to Dewar, and the family at Helenslea were informed. William was so grief stricken that he felt unable to journey to Tayport, and two of William junior's friends went in his place. They were able by means of the contents of William junior's pockets, and his clothes to formally identify him. Later that day his body was taken back to Helenslea.

On Friday 4 May, William junior's remains were laid to rest. Al and Alex travelled through from Glasgow for the funeral service.

Three weeks later, the Procurator Fiscal, Robert Wemyss Renton, pronounced that William junior's death was caused by drowning, probably as a result of suicide.

In trying to sum up the tragedy, the best epitaph to the unfortunate young man was given by Al, 'he [William junior] was a quiet and gentle young man, and liked by all.'[7]

As well as mourning the death of his nephew, Al was very much concerned about Bernard. He had left Loretto in the summer of 1887, but had shown little interest in furthering his education or in joining the Yard. In April, however, Bernard told his father he would like to go to Cambridge University. But if Bernard had expected his father to wholeheartedly endorse the suggestion, he was in for a shock:

> He [Bernard] does not show any particular talent for any special line or subject. I am somewhat at a loss what to do in this matter. ... The Lord may have something for him to do which we do not yet see and he does not see himself.[8]

It seems a pity that the Church did not attract Bernard, nor, apparently, did the sea. Al must have wished that Bernard had followed his cousin Robert into the Merchant Navy, for in 1888 Robert was awarded his Extra Master's Certificate.

Unable to find an immediate solution, Bernard spent a month travel-

ling with two friends, George and John Napier, the sons of James Smith
Napier, an iron merchant, who supplied iron for Stephen's ships and was
a close personal friend of Al's. On his return, Bernard became a reluctant
shipbuilder at Linthouse.

In 1888 disappointment in the attitude of their sons was not confined to
the Stephen family: James Murray set in motion a series of events that
would only increase his own sense of hopelessness and despair. He was
in Paris when he again met Laurence Oliphant and showed him a letter he had received from Rosamond Dale Owen. Oliphant, a widower
of two years, declared that he must meet the writer. He had already
planned to visit America, so after completing his business in New York,
he travelled to New Harmony. There was an immediate attraction between the sixty-one-year-old man and the forty-two-year-old woman,
and Rosamond agreed to return to England.

How right JS was to be proved. His son's friendship with Oliphant
and Dale Owen brought him nothing but misery; he may have hoped
that when Oliphant and Dale Owen married at Malvern, Worcestershire
in August 1888, their influence on his son would decline.

James Murray was not overly concerned about the union of his
friends. Shortly after their marriage, and after Alice had visited him in
Paris, he wrote to his father. He knew Alice would have passed on the
news that he had met the woman he wished to marry:

> I trust she [Alice] has reassured you about the young lady who is on my
> mind just now in so serious a way. I spoke purposely very dispassionately
> when at home, and gave you perhaps the worst possible impression. I ought
> now to try and say how lucky I shall be if I can get her for my wife. We
> have not yet settled that actually, though it is as nearly so as such a thing
> may be.[9]

James Murray went on to tell his father that although they were both art
students and that originally he was not enthusiastic at the idea of marriage, he now believed, once the marriage vows are made, they should
be forever. He assured his father that they had planned for a long engagement:

I am almost certain ... that I could scarcely find a woman for a wife, who might possibly so much please you. ... You wanted a woman for my wife who was a mere girl in experience. I require someone who has suffered, and knows the world -- and the battle that she is going to help me fight. Mrs Tuttle [this is the first time he names her in the letter] ... She is lively and humorous too, bubbling over at a good joke -- and quite capable of making one. She has both sentiment and artistic feeling, yet is quite practical in knowledge and quick decided actions.[10]

JS was delighted with the news, especially when James Murray imparted the news that Mrs Tuttle's sister was to marry a doctor, Arthur Lincoln, a nephew of Abraham Lincoln.

James Murray told his father that Jennie Tuttle was a young widow, but it would have been out of character for JS not to have made enquiries about his prospective daughter-in-law. He was horrified when those enquiries revealed that far from being a widow, Jennie Tuttle was a divorcee. Notwithstanding this revelation, JS invited both Jennie and James Murray to Knockderry for the marriage, on 3 October, of Alice to Dan Young.

The marriage of his beloved daughter Alice to Dan was something that JS could celebrate with gusto. A large marquee was erected on the tennis court at Knockderry, and a hundred guests were treated to a lavish reception. Even the weather played its part. The early October day was beautiful, the sun adding to the grandeur of the occasion. One of Alice's witnesses was her cousin Blanche Croudace, demonstrating once again the closeness of the Stephen/Templeton family. Blanche was to remain unmarried but she was always a favourite with the families, and she was rarely excluded from the guest list. Dan's groomsman was his brother Alfred.

James Murray, like his father, could delight in the happiness of Alice and Dan and he believed that their marriage would soon be followed by his own to Jennie Tuttle. Life, however, was not that simple; on 23 December, just four months after he had married Dale Owen, Laurence Oliphant died of lung cancer. James Murray went immediately to comfort Rosamond and to help her in her hour of grief.

A Terrible Accident

ROSAMOND Oliphant believed that she would inherit all Laurence's rather extensive estate, but when his will was probated she found he had left her only his property in Haifa. Even that inheritance was not without complications and she would have to return to Palestine to deal with the problems. It was inevitable that James Murray, acting as her guardian angel, would accompany her regardless of what Jennie Tuttle would say. He left Paris on 9 February 1889. At that stage there seemed to have been no hint of a relationship between James Murray and Rosamond other than that of a devoted friend helping a grieving widow.

In Rosamond's obituary published nearly four decades later, the writer suggested that on the journey out to Palestine she

> made the acquaintance of a drunken Arab lawyer, whom she took into her house, and who was for years to be the curse of her existence ...[1]

Such a companion would surely have been a source of great distress to James Murray and one can only express abhorrence at the arrangement.

When James Murray accompanied Rosamond to Palestine he was still in contact with both the Templeton and Stephen families. John and Elizabeth Stephen, and Mina Stewart left for a holiday to the Holy Land on 5 March 1889 and John arranged to meet James Murray there. They met early in April, a meeting that would have been both a pleasure and a worry for James Murray. John was not averse to expressing his views on his nephew's association with the Oliphants.

After Oliphant's death serious allegations were made against him, accusing him of having corrupted the moral welfare of young men. James Murray was among those named in the allegations. Anything to do with corrupting the morals of the young immediately came to the notice of the National Vigilance Association and its formidable secretary William Alexander Coote.

Not unnaturally, JS became aware of the allegations concerning his son and he wrote to Arthur Oliphant, Laurence's cousin, laying before him the charges. Appalled by the accusations, Arthur Oliphant considered taking legal action to refute them. But, aware that such action would only further blacken the name of Laurence, he let the matter drop. The Labouchére Amendment, passed by the British Parliament in 1886, making homosexual acts a criminal offence, quickly became known as the Blackmailer's Charter. It was used by unscrupulous people to make unsubstantiated allegations against young men and women of rank and wealth, in the hope and expectation that their families would pay rather than face the disgrace of fighting a legal action.

Among those also accused by the National Vigilance Association were four children of JS's friend, Alexander Allan, the ship owner. Allan was also a major client of Stephen and even the hint of a scandal appalled the Stephen family as much as it did JS and Allan. The allegation concerned Allan's children James, Charles, Elizabeth and Jane, all contemporaries of James Murray.

Allan and his wife, Jane Smith, the daughter of Robert Smith, ship owner and chairman of the City Line, were active and staunch members of the United Free Presbyterian Church. They also supported the work of the Home and Foreign Missions. Allan had since 1854 -- the year he married Jane -- been a member of the Temperance League, a director for nine years, and vice-president for twenty-five years.

The idea that his children were involved with Laurence Oliphant caused both Alexander and Jane hours of anguish. Indeed, in 1890 the burdens of his hectic life became too great for him and he and Jane left for an extended world tour. They had planned to visit many of the Foreign Missions they had supported for years, but in Ceylon his health became so bad that they returned to Scotland.

In 1889, work was progressing on the extension of the Templeton carpet factory in William Street for the production of Axminster carpets. The main engineers for the project were W & A Harvey, and the architect was William Leiper. Leiper's design for a Moorish-Italian façade based on the Doge's Palace in Venice was then, as it is now, unique in an industrial

building. The multi-coloured mosaic pattern was to be pinned to the
main frame of the building. Unfortunately there was a disagreement
between the engineers and the architect as to exactly how the pinning
should be done. As a result of this disagreement the façade was not
fully secured, and during a ferocious gale on the evening of Friday 1
November 1889, the façade collapsed onto a weaving shed where a large
number of workers were at their machines.

The tragedy could not have happened at a worse time for JS and
James. Five days earlier on 27 October their mother Mary Stewart had
died. She was eighty-two and had been a stalwart in the lives of her children. James Murray was called home and arrived in time for her funeral.

At four-fifteen in the afternoon of that fateful Friday, JS, James and
their sisters, Anne, Agnes and Mary Stephen had left Glasgow to spend
a quiet weekend at Cove, reflecting on their own loss. They had just
sat down to dinner when a telegram was delivered telling them of the
events at William Street. Their personal grief was now submerged with
grieving for their workers.

Twenty-nine workers were killed. One of the casualties was a Mary
Ann Stewart, a sixteen-year-old power loom weaver; she died of asphyx-
ia, certified by Robert Wilson, a local physician from Monteith Row.
Mary Ann was the daughter of John Stewart, a gasworks labourer and
his wife Margaret McDonald, who lived at 35 Norman Street.

Another young woman to die was Dinah Renton Gillies, aged nineteen, whose father John Caird Gillies also worked at the factory. In a harrowing report in the *Glasgow Herald*, the day after the collapse, it told of
a father's desperate search for his daughter. Gillies told the searchers his
daughter had not come home for dinner or tea. A factory clerk standing
by the father said he knew the girl and that a body had been found near
where she worked:

> When it [the body] was liberated, however, Gillies stated that was not his
> daughter, and with a sigh he stood aside and sadly watched the proceed-
> ings.[2]

Later, Gillies's worse fears were confirmed when the body of his daughter was finally recovered.

Shortly before eleven in the evening -- six and a half hours after the collapse -- the rescue workers, under the direction of George Bell, lifted a beam:

> In a row lay four young women. They were on their faces. Appearances seemed to indicate that they had been making for the exit when the crash came, and many were knocked down and pinned to the ground. They bore few marks on their faces. They had been suffocated.[3]

Later in the evening, Al, Fred and Alex visited the site of the collapse: in the deep gloom of a November night, the devastation was like a scene from hell. It is highly unlikely that JS and James were able to travel from Cove to William Street until the next day, but on the Sunday morning a statement was pinned at the firm's other factories:

> Messrs James Templeton & Co beg to express their heartfelt sympathy with the families of those of their workforce as unhappily killed in their service. They also grieve that other workers have sustained injury. To all those who with so much self-sacrifice, devotion and humanity assisted in the rescue they give their warmest thanks.[4]

The statement went on to reassure the workers that the factories not damaged would be back in business at ten o'clock on Monday morning, and that the management believed there would be 'no serious impediment to the regular work being carried on throughout the factory.'[5]

It told the worried workers that an order for looms to replace those lost in the disaster had already been issued and in the meantime the directors would endeavour to find work for all those weavers who had survived the collapse.

On Saturday morning, JS was in attendance when the site was visited by an official delegation, including The Sheriff-Principal Berry, The Lord Provost Sir James King, a near neighbour of JS's parents and a long time friend, and Whyte, the assistant Master of Works for the Corporation, whose job was to make a report for the Dean of Guild Courts. Whyte was accompanied by James Hart, the Procurator-Fiscal. As a result of their inspection a 'strong barricade was put up round the gable overlooking the Green. Police were ordered to keep back people from it.'[6]

All that Saturday and Sunday, crowds flocked to the scene to view the devastation.

William Leiper, the architect, was interviewed and gave a statement in which he denied he had been guilty of professional negligence. As early as the Saturday morning, serious questions were being asked as to whom, or what, had caused the façade to collapse. Leiper admitted he was:

> Of course ... responsible for the outside of the building only. The erection of the mill was in the hands of a very able engineer. I may say, however, that the foundations were excellent. They were of solid concrete, and the walls, I should say, were equal to anything; indeed, I believe they were even thicker than allowed at first. ... Of course the roof was not on, and, so far as I can judge, the hurricane is the cause of the disaster. ... In the morning the mill was a picture of stability, in the afternoon the men had to stop work on account of the rain ... of course, the entire front of the building was exposed to the full force of the gale.[7]

JS, when asked to what he attributed the cause of the collapse, was reluctant to speculate, and admitted that:

> He had no theory ... except [that] there was a great force of wind upon the building, which stood very high, and the upper part not being perforated with windows, it thus presented a plain unbroken surface to the wind, and offered great resistance to it.[8]

Over that terrible weekend JS visited those workers who had been injured but, who after treatment, had been allowed to return home. In the meantime Dan Young, accompanied by Cunningham, the Works Manager, visited the relatives of the dead, offering not only sympathy but practical help in arranging funerals. The Firm, apart from offering kind words and gestures, also paid for the majority of the funerals.

An appeal fund was launched and although Templeton were cleared of all blame by the Enquiry, they, nevertheless, agreed to pay compensation to the injured. They continued to pay this compensation annually until the last of the young girls died some sixty/seventy years later. Although found not guilty of negligence, it is worth noting that the company paid this compensation without recourse to costly litigation.

There is a very poignant story that perhaps should stand as a memorial to that dreadful night when so many young people died or were injured by a freak of nature. This concerns Lizza Seymour who received, from the Company a Bible, with a very appropriate dedication:

> Two women shall be grinding at the mill; the one shall be taken, and the other left./Watch therefore: for ye know not what hour your Lord doth come.[9]

Eighty-four years later in June 1973, Lizza Seymour's granddaughter, Mary Gallagher, returned her grandmother's Bible to the Company for safe-keeping in their archives. This gesture the Company were pleased to accept, and one that would have given JS a moment of sad reflection but also immense pride.

The factory and the façade were rebuilt, but this time the main building was constructed by the civil engineering company of Sir William Arrol. Leiper's magnificent mosaic was firmly tied and in 1892 the new factory opened for the manufacture of Axminster carpets. From that day in 1892, the façade has stood firm against the worst of Glasgow's gales.

Al had a multitude of concerns that autumn, Mary's grief at the loss of her mother and his children's grandmother deeply troubled him. He could, and did, share JS's distress at the loss of so many young lives, but he had also another reason to feel worried. He was concerned about the quality of Leiper's work at Kelly. In early November he called on James Smith Napier. Al told him that Leiper had failed to get approval from the Council before he made substantial alterations to the original plans for Kelly. He also thought Leiper was doing somethings without his authority. Napier suggested that he should consult the City Architect.

In the autumn of 1889 Al finally sold Fearann Coille, it had been slow to sell. It was with a degree of sadness when he made his last visit to the beautiful house that had been his summer home for twenty-three years. It had been a place where he went to renew his spiritual and physical energies. On 7 October he wrote:

> I like to record a visit to my sacred spot far up in the moor behind Fear-
> ann Coille in the gully of the running little water. I found my grassy seat
> washed away by the waters since my previous visit a year ago. My whole
> purpose was prayer to God on my last Sabbath here for the season, and I
> had this.[10]

The purchase of Kelly convinced Al that it was time he began to reduce
his workload and with reluctance he retired from the Govan School
Board. For twenty-five years he had been an active and conscientious
member; for twelve years he had been Chairman of the Board. It was
a matter of pride to him that in all those years he had rarely missed a
Board Meeting. In appreciation of his long service, the Board members
and the staff of the Govan Schools presented Al with an Illuminated
Scroll, signed by all members including John Lochore, the very first
teacher he had appointed, and John Craigie, the tireless Clerk to the
Board. In addition to the Scroll, Al was also presented with an engraved
silver cigarette box.

In the early months of 1890 Al was busy furnishing and fitting out
Kelly. Inevitably, the carpets were made by Templeton and Al was extremely grateful for the attention that he had received from James. He
wrote to express his gratitude, telling James that he was in no doubt that
the carpets would be worthy of J & J Templeton and Kelly. He was not so
appreciative of other tradesmen, to Scott Morton who was responsible
for some of the wood work he wrote:

> However desirous I am to see your account adjusted to your satisfaction, I
> cannot allow myself to be charged £1.8.0. extra for checking the hall walls.
> I was annoyed at the time at seeing the walls injured by your men; and there
> were other places injured by your men, where, if your work had been made
> to suit, no chipping would have been required.[11]

Al refused to pay for damage that had been sustained to the dining room
fireplace. He would argue with a tradesman over a bill if he thought he

had been overcharged even by a pound. His attention to detail was a measure of the quality of Kelly. Absolutely nothing was left to chance. But it was Leiper that Al held responsible for the minor faults that did occur:

> There is water coming into some of the rooms of the house: my own bedroom is one of them and several rooms upstairs. I would be obliged by your having this looked to as soon as possible, as it is necessary that the house should be water tight.[12]

The windows had already caused Al a good many problems, the stained-glass windows had been the subject of much annoyance between him and Leiper. That the fitted windows leaked was the final straw, although even Al must have known, even if Leiper didn't, that rain and storm-force winds coming off the Clyde at Wemyss Bay made it near impossible to ensure any window was leak-proof.

Al told Leiper that he would need to fix the leaks, as James Clark, who had been the Inspector of Works at Kelly, was no longer employed by him. If Leiper wanted Clark to carry out the work, then he would have to pay him, for Al definitely would not.

Problems at Kelly were not allowed to overshadow the arrangements for the marriage of Alex to Jessie Margaret (Daisy) Young. Daisy was the daughter of James Young, a muslin manufacturer, and Agnes Robson -- there may have been a family connection between James Young and Dan Young, but it has been impossible to confirm or deny it.

Agnes's grandfather, John Robson, who had married Agnes Renton, was Doctor of Divinity and Moderator of the United Presbyterian Church. He was the fifth member of his family to hold that office. Even with just a casual study into the ancestry of the Robson family, it is safe to conclude that there was a missionary and Presbyterian zeal in the inter-related families of John Robson, Henry Renton and Robert Frew.

The union of Alex and Daisy was to be the first between the Stephen and Young family. The witnesses to Daisy and Alex's wedding were her sister Agnes and his brother Fred. Fred and Agnes would marry the next year.

Al and Mary entertained their first guests at Kelly on 30 May, and included in the guest list were Daisy and Agnes's parents. The Visitors' Book at Kelly makes a fascinating record of the guests who enjoyed the splendours of that ornate yet oddly forbidding house. The names show the closeness of the extended family; the Helensburgh Templetons were frequent guests, as were William Wright and his third wife Joanna Gordon Lorimer. The Revd George Reith had been Al's minister and friend for decades; Dr John Pirie -- the husband of Jane Harvey, had been the family doctor and close friend. Reginald Wingate and his wife Kitty visited when on leave from his military duties in Egypt.

Al was later to admit that he would be happy to spend the rest of his time at Kelly, never again leaving it to return to his home in Park Terrace.

Loss of a Son

ON 25 January 1891, according to JS's unpublished *Memoir*, James Murray and Rosamond Oliphant were married, though it has been impossible to verify this by the production of a marriage certificate. Checks have been made with the Consular Offices as well as the Statutory Authorities, but no confirmation has been found. It is more than possible, in view of Rosamond's unorthodox views on marriage and religion, that they went through some form of secular ceremony.

In marrying Rosamond, a cold, frigid woman fourteen years his senior, James Murray was marrying a mother-figure and was again challenging his father, whose second and third wives had been twenty-two years younger than him and only six years older than James Murray.

It is always difficult for an only son to live up to the aspirations and ambitions of a successful and powerful father. There is no evidence that JS was anything other than a loving, generous father, but he had ideals and standards which he expected his son to observe. James Murray did try to join his father in the carpet business, but he was temperamentally unsuited to life as a manufacturer. He searched for fulfilment and happiness in his chosen field, but found like so many other young people that happiness is an indefinable gift and search as he might he would never find it.

JS saw his son for the last time in London on 2 April 1891, when James Murray called at the warehouse in Newgate Street, and asked him to accompany him to St John's Wood to meet Rosamond. Much to JS's regret he did not accept the invitation, later admitting that he had very recently received a letter said to have been written by Rosamond Owen to her cousin Mrs Clymer, in which

> she made some reference to my wealth, my "weak physique" and probable short life. ... How could I go to meet a woman whom I thought not only a cheat and a seducer, but a murderess in thought?[1]

James Murray and Rosamond returned to Haifa where she was still in disagreement with the Turkish authorities over her right to Oliphant's property at Mount Carmel. The Turks were reluctant to believe she had any claim on Oliphant's Palestine property.

The lack of money was a reccurring theme in Rosamond's life; James Murray's inheritance from his grandparents, and his allowance from JS, were never enough to satisfy Rosamond's needs. He made a little extra money writing the odd article for the *Magazine of Art* and selling the occasional picture. They were not poverty stricken, but in comparison with his wealth and position in Glasgow, life in Haifa was always going to be hard.

It was with a good deal of paternal pride that Al witnessed the ordination of Fred as a Deacon of the Free Church, on Sunday 29 March 1891. He expressed his joy thus:

> My prayers are with him as office bearer in Christ's Church. It is not a frequent occurrence in one family that three are office bearers in the same Church. I am an Elder and my two sons Deacons.[2]

Alex had been ordained the year before.

In June of that year, Fred married Agnes Robson Young. The marriage took place in Glasgow, with the Revd Black officiating together with Revd John Robson Elder. Elder was married to Mary Isabella Wilson, the sister of Uncle John's wife Elizabeth.

Fred and Agnes were surrounded at the wedding by a very large congregation of family and friends. Al was delighted to recall that his grandsons Walter and Alexander MacLellan were page boys, and performed their duties of holding Agnes's train with deference and concentration. Al later wrote in his diary:

> It is a union of true love and affection. I am personally sorry at Fred's going from our home, but yield with meekness to his having the object of his choice. ... God Bless them both throughout life ...[3]

Fred and Agnes honeymooned in Egypt, sailing along the Nile. It was from Kelly, where Al and Mary were spending a few days celebrating their thirty-fourth wedding anniversary, that Al wrote to the newly weds:

> Many thanks to you and Agnes for your congratulations ... on the 23 I was examining the presents ... you slipped out before I had a chance of giving you and Agnes a slap on the back.[4]

The weather that June had been unseasonably hot, and on the Saturday Al had not bothered to go to Linthouse, but had preferred to stay at Kelly. In spite of the heat, Blanche Croudace and Wingate Gray had played tennis that afternoon much to Al's amusement. In the evening, Al and Mary had hosted a dinner for twenty-three guests, including Mina Stewart and her eldest daughter Mina. Alice and Dan Young were among the diners.

It is quite extraordinary how many times when one side of the family is celebrating a birth the other side is mourning the death of a loved one. On 11 September 1892, Fred and Agnes's first son was born; he was, as was the custom in the family, named Alexander Murray. He would inherit all the gifts of leadership and business acumen that his grandfather Al had shown in such abundance.

Nineteen days later, on 30 September, James Murray was lost overboard while travelling by ship back to Haifa. He and Rosamond had been in Beyrouth [Beirut] trying to resolve the ownership of Oliphant's land at Mount Carmel. JS was on his way to America, and it was to Al that the British Consul in Haifa telegraphed the sad news.

The Consul did not go into details as to the reason for the death. Al's reaction to his nephew's death was to voice his puzzlement at the young man's strange life:

> Nothing else is said. ... For years he has been estranged from his father and all through his clinging to the views of the late Lawrence [sic] Oliphant. ... A strange life ... James was a young man of a peculiar mind. Tenacious of his opinions and beliefs. Yet sweet in temper and beloved by all. Very fond of Art and a considerable artist himself and of a highly aesthetic nature.[5]

Speculations as to why James Murray fell overboard became the order of the day; most people assumed he had committed suicide. JS believed that his son had been suffering from malarial fever. He had gone up on deck seeking the cooling night breeze, became dizzy and then had fallen overboard. It is true that marriage to Rosamond had not made James Murray a happy man. They had traipsed from London to Paris, Haifa and Beirut, seeking an end to their troubles. He had tried to paint but was dissatisfied with what he produced.

There is, however, another reason why his death may well have been suicide. When Rosamond died it became clear that her marriage to James Murray had been a sham. The presence of the Arab lawyer only added to his sense of hopelessness, and Rosamond had never stopped grieving for Oliphant. James Murray was aware that her love for him was nothing compared to her obsession and love for Oliphant.

She had tried to continue Oliphant's work. At Haifa she established a socialist community but without resources and without Oliphant's presence the place was never a success. The only person who remained was James Murray, and it must be asked, if it was his money that allowed her to purchase, Armageddon, a large tract of land where she lived for many years. It must also be asked why James Murray did not follow the example set by the Prodigal Son and return to his father and his family. Even if he had not sufficient money to pay for a ticket, there were a host of people in Glasgow who would have willingly and eagerly wired him the fare home. It is also more than probable that one of them would have gone to Haifa to bring him home. His welcome, when JS returned from America, would have been joyous beyond belief.

In early September 1893, William and Elizabeth Stephen, and their younger children, Mary, Charles and Edward, set out on a short tour of the Highlands. They journeyed along the Caledonian Canal which in late summer was at its glorious best. They spent some days in Inverness and they broke their journey home by visiting Grantown-on-Spey, intending to spend time with Janet, at Gowanlea. Shortly after arriving at Gowanlea, William felt unwell but neither Elizabeth nor Janet were initially concerned. William assured them he would rest and would soon feel better. Unfortunately his condition worsened and medical help was urgently sought. He died less than two hours later; the cause of death, as certified by Dr John Grant, was disease of the heart, though he could not say how long William had suffered from the condition.

Elizabeth and Janet were naturally distraught. While comforting each other and the children, they also had to arrange for telegrams to be sent to Andrew and Frederick Somerville in Dundee, and to Alice at Red Court. The telegrams were by necessity short, simply announcing William's death. Andrew and Frederick Somerville made immediate plans to travel to Gowanlea. Their journey was a tortuous one, taking them first by special train to Perth, then on to Granton by the midnight mail train.

Within the commercial and shipping world of Dundee the news of William's death was greeted with incredulity, and rumours soon spread as to the exact nature of his death. Sudden death, even in a man in his sixty-eighth year should not have caused a moment's speculation, a heart attack, could and does, strike with terrifying suddenness.

William's obituary was most complimentary of his life and his achievements. It listed in some detail his connections with the seal and whaling industry and commented:

> When the Greenland seal fishing threatened to become unremunerative Mr William Stephen sent his ships to the fishing off Newfoundland coast, and with so gratifying results that others were induced to follow his example.[6]

In summing up William's legacy, it was said of William's Arctic Tannery Company:

> Like his other ventures, this has proved eminently successful. The stock of sealskins, oil and whalebone in the tannery is perhaps the most extensive in the country.[7]

Shortly after William's death the shipyard was sold by his Trustees to the Dundee Shipbuilders' Company. Andrew was more interested in farming than shipbuilding; since the death of William junior, Frederick Somerville had managed the Arctic Tannery business.

William had taken over the Dundee Yard at a young age, but he had never really been his own master because his father had been a constant shadow at the Yard. And very much more so than at Linthouse, where Al and John had more autonomy than Alexander had allowed his eldest son. In his personal life, William also had reason to envy his younger brother; Al had enjoyed thirty-six years of happy marriage, whereas William's first wife, Jane, had died after twenty-six years of marriage. Al had had six children and all had survived into adulthood. Of William and Jane's eight children, two had died as infants, three had died in early adulthood, two of consumption and, of course, William junior had committed suicide.

With the loss of so many of his children, William had reason to envy Al. He had only two grandchildren, the son and daughter of Alice and Alex Gordon Thomson, whereas Al had, by 1893, four grandsons and three granddaughters. Seven more grandchildren were born before Al died and one was born a few months after his death.

William had also good reason to feel jealous of both Al and John; the Dundee Yard had never been as prosperous as Linthouse. William saw the building of Kelly as a testament to Al's financial security, and John's statement of wealth was Craigrownie. Helenslea, William's Dundee home, was a modest villa besides the splendours of Kelly and Craigrownie, and if he envied his brothers, how much more did he envy his brothers-in-law, JS and James Templeton with their grand country homes.

Two weeks after William's death, his daughter Alice was to mourn the death of her father-in-law William Gordon Thomson. He had been a generous benefactor not just to his only son, but to the St Enoch's Established Church. He had played an active part in politics, holding firmly to his Liberal Unionist views. In 1879 when the first Tay Railway bridge collapsed during a storm, Thomson had been asked to advise on whether the new bridge should be built on the existing foundations or on new foundations. A prudent man, he had insisted that a wholly new structure should be built. A hundred and twenty-five years later the bridge still carries trains, a monument to the foresight and expertise of a very professional engineer.

Frederick Henry Young [FHY] began life on 30 April 1874, the youngest brother of Dan; his birth was registered as Henry Frederick, but on baptism the names were reversed.

Thirteen years younger than Dan, FHY followed in his brother's footsteps, he went to Glasgow Academy, where he was an outstanding scholar, becoming school dux when he left in 1891. He played rugby and became captain of the School's XV, again following the same path as his brother Alfred.

FHY may well have been planning, as his brothers had, of going to University, but on 16 November 1893, his father, Robert, died. Robert had been travelling by overnight mail train from Glasgow to London. On arrival at St Pancras he had been woken by an attendant and immediately rose and began to dress but never completed the task, he slumped to the ground and died instantly.

It was a weekly occurrence for Robert to take that train to London and to return the next evening, and so he was well known to all the railway staff. He was seventy-years-old, and while thought to be in excellent health, the worries caused by the collapse of the City of Glasgow Bank, and the loss of a substantial part of his fortune had taken a terrible toll on his reserves of strength.

FHY, aware that he could not expect his widowed mother to fund his continued education, sought the advice of Dan, and early in 1894 he joined the staff of James Templeton. He admitted later that he had toyed with the idea of studying theology, law or medicine, but instead had chosen to go into business. His decision was to prove absolutely correct. Three years after joining Templeton's he became a director. FHY immediately inherited James Murray's mantle; they were both devoted to improving the working and social conditions of the Templeton workforce. They also shared a love of art and literature, and FHY became a frequent contributor to the *Templetonian*, the house magazine.

Odds & Ends

KELLY was to experience many social and family gatherings. There is, though, one event that must surely have stood out among all the other occasions. On Thursday 8 November 1894, Mary Stephen held an 'At Home', which in itself was not unusual for middle-class Victorian ladies, but Mary's party was something very special. Al hired a train and paid the fares for one hundred guests who left Glasgow Central Station at 7.25 pm and arrived at Wemyss Bay an hour later.

At Kelly House, the hundred guests from Glasgow were joined by another seventy guests who had made their own way to Kelly. Al recalled the evening had been very successful. He was immensely impressed that the electric lighting worked splendidly. Mary and Elsie had supervised a small army of servants and had personally seen that the catering arrangements went smoothly. The evening was a highly rewarding experience for both hosts and guests.

The train left Wemyss Bay at 1.30am on the Friday morning to return the hundred guests to Glasgow. Al and Mary were still left with fourteen overnight visitors, including John and Elizabeth, George and Maud MacLellan, Alex and Daisy, Fred and Agnes, and Florence and Nora, the daughters of Mina and James Stewart. The two girls were due to return to Lovedale the following week. Emily and Ann, the daughters of Anne and Duncan Wilkie Paterson and Margaret Templeton, Archibald's daughter, also stayed overnight.

Bernard, unlike Fred and Alex, was not a natural shipbuilder, he had joined his father and brothers at Linthouse, but he was unhappy with his role. In April 1889 he had left Glasgow for Dunkirk to spend six months studying French but even in France he was unhappy and returned early to Glasgow. If France had not lived up to his expectations, he did, however, still have a desire to travel. In the summer of 1893 he went to

America, visiting among other places Chicago and New York. Whether this trip was purely pleasure or whether he was on a selling mission it is impossible to know. It is certain however that Al would have provided his son with generous Letters of Credit and many letters of introduction. Bernard returned to Scotland on 1 November.

Four months later, Bernard took his first communion in the Free Church of Scotland. What is surprising is that he was now aged twenty-six. His late entry into membership of the Church rather shows that he did not altogether share his father's devotion. Perhaps it was during his tour of America that he began to see that his father's adherence to the Free Church Faith was something that after all he wanted to share. All his life he had attended family morning worship which set a pattern for the day. It is also worth noting that Al did not force his son to take Communion until he was ready to do so.

Later that year Bernard left on a four months visit to India, his travelling companion being Dr Petrie of Dundee. They were away until 20 March 1895, when Bernard returned to Glasgow. Al noted in his diary that Bernard had been just a day behind him and Mary, as they travelled home from Egypt.

Egypt, in the last decade of the nineteenth century, was the height of adventure for all those who had both the time and the money to explore. The Victorian archaeologists were among the most ardent collectors of Egyptian artifacts, and the stories of their remarkable finds made a visit to see the Great Pyramid and the Valley of the Kings an awe-inspiring experience. Al, clambering among the ruins at Luxor, fell and sprained his wrist, but the minor injury did nothing to dampen his enthusiasm for the wonders of ancient Egypt.

Cairo also gave Al and Mary a chance to visit and dine with Reginald and Kitty Wingate. The friendship between the two families had increased since the marriage of Wingate's cousin Walter to Mary. In 1883, Wingate had been assigned to the Egyptian Army, later becoming director of Military Intelligence. Wingate was also able to show Al and Mary a side of life in Egypt that would have been denied to them as ordinary tourists.

❖❖❖

1894/5 were important years in the management of the Linthouse Yard when Al and John handed over control to Alex and Fred. In April 1894, they formally signed a Contract of Sale, and in doing so they made ample provision for the new owners to repay the purchase price over an extended period. Al and John had spent almost half a century at the helm of the Yard and the idea of retirement was very sweet. Al would be able to spend more time at Kelly and John would retire to Craigrownie.

William Croudace had every reason to fear the sea. He had spent his adulthood as seaman, ship's captain and ship owner. He had experienced the loss of many of his ships. The *Cornwallis* was lost to the ice in the Davis Straits. The most terrifying of ordeals, fire at sea, had sunk the *Dundee* in 1880. *Pollux*, the new steamer he had commissioned in 1887, was abandoned in the North Atlantic three years later. The loss of ships was one thing that could be endured but the loss of his youngest son, Laurence in 1886, when he had been swept overboard from the steamer *Rover* as it plied its trade between Cuba and New York, was a terrible blow to him and Elspeth.

As a seaman, Croudace must have pondered the nature of his own death many times, but nothing could have prepared him for the actual moment. On the 15 November 1894, as he travelled by train from Edinburgh to his home in West Ferry, he suddenly died, aged seventy-three. He was found when the train reached Stannergate Station. According to his death certificate the probable cause was heart failure. To his widow Elspeth, his daughters Blanche, Elsie and Helen, it was a moment of deep despair that he died alone in a railway carriage without their loving presence. The press were strangely muted about his death and there were few obituaries, which is rather sad, considering that he had been one of the great sea captains of the nineteenth century. Even Al, who was so good at recording in his diary his feelings when a family member died, gave Croudace's death a short bleak mention.

Elspeth and her daughters had little time to mourn the death of William, when again they were plunged into another period of mourning. John Stephen, Elspeth's eldest son, died on 23 April 1897. He was the

Captain of the *Orion*, on a voyage from the Tyne to San Francisco, when he died of a heart attack. John had only returned to life as a sea Captain after the death of his father, having spent some years as a ship chandler in his native Dundee.

As Samuel had done two decades earlier, John, had his wife Isabella Jane Mitchell, and two of his children on board. John and Isabella married in April 1881 and had five children, two daughters Elspeth Helen and Dorothy Isabel, and three sons, William Deuchars, Patrick Douglas and Gordon Logan. Gordon died in February 1891 of whooping cough when he was twenty-five-days old.

There was a very definite alienation between Al and William Stephen and William Croudace, stemming from the many disputes they had over the payment of dues for ships built by the Dundee Yard, and the management of those ships. The disputes had intensified after Alexander's death. Croudace and Elspeth were both unhappy with the terms of Alexander's Deed of Settlement, and blamed Al and William for the way the Estate was handled. Strangely, the brothers had very little control over the main Estate, Al and John were only Trustees of the Special Trust Fund. The Trustees for the whole Estate had been prominent Dundee citizens, appointed by Alexander.

There is a period in the lives of most families when the sad times seem to out-number the happy times. Early in 1895, William Wright, as executor *qua dative*, probated the estates of three of his children. William Towers, died before his second birthday, Mary Louisa died in January 1880 of hydrocephalus when she was thirteen and Elisa Mina died of heart failure while travelling on a tramcar on Great Western Road, Glasgow on 7 January 1894. She was twenty-three. The size of the children's estates indicated that their mother, Mary-Ann, had made over her share of her father's Trust Fund to them when or if they reached the age of maturity.

In the 1880s it was rare for middle class young women to consider any profession, and nursing was certainly well down the list of those careers thought suitable for well brought-up young ladies. This was in spite of

Florence Nightingale establishing the first training school for nurses at St Thomas's Hospital, London, in 1860. Emily Wright, however, enrolled at the Royal Hospital for Sick Children in Edinburgh.

Iris Deacon Campbell, the future wife of FHY, wrote graphically about the conditions of a student nurse at the turn of the century. Iris had been born in India in 1883 where her father William Augustus Campbell was a Government Inspector of Works. After his early death, his wife Elizabeth Deacon and her two daughters Iris and Minnie returned to England. Elizabeth and her daughters were impoverished and the girls had to earn their own living, Iris as a nurse and Minnie as a Governess/Domestic.

The appalling conditions of low pay, long hours and harsh discipline that Emily and Iris experienced are unimaginable today. Iris's salary for the first year was £8 per annum. The second and third years she was paid £10 and £12 respectively. Uniform and lodging were supplied. Conditions were very basic. Her working day started at 7am and ended at 9pm with just a two hour off duty period each day. She was, however, able to recall with pride her days spent at the hospital in Chesterfield:

> The work we got was wonderful. Many of the patients were miners, some of whom were brought in after bad-accidents. They were a courageous, happy-natured lot of men.[1]

She admitted that 'it is difficult to make nursing a very easy job without spoiling its real object, which is definitely the good of the patients.'[2] It is a sentiment that has echoed down the ages.

After three years at Chesterfield, Iris worked for six months at the fever hospital in Liverpool, and once again her description of the conditions that she encountered caused her deep distress and anxiety. She said that the hospital was desperately under-staffed, and that the modern treatment of patients with diphtheria was not practised by the senior clinician:

> Antitoxin ... was in use in some hospitals, but our chief did not hold with its curative properties, and we had to do hourly, two-hourly ... mopping-out of membraneous throats, with membranes ... flying all over the place, and in the end not as many recoveries as should have been the case.[3]

She went on to wonder why some doctors refused to use treatments that had proved so successful in other places.

Iris's next hospital was University College, London where she expected to spend the next four years as a student, but just five weeks after arriving as a probationer, she was doing the work of a Staff Nurse, and even acting as Ward Sister when called upon to do so. She confessed that she had difficulty in finding the money needed to pay for her studies, but, such were her qualities, her so-called four years training period was spent as a full member of the nursing staff. She did, though, still hanker after becoming an Army Nurse, and even went to see the Matron-in-Chief of Army Nursing at the War Office. Regrettably, she was told she was too young and would not be considered until she had completed her certificate course at University College Hospital.

The history of romantic fiction is littered with books about pretty nurses marrying handsome doctors. It did, and indeed, still does happen in real life, but not that often!

Emily Burlton Wright was one who did marry a doctor. She married Robert Durward Clarkson, on 18 April 1895, forming a union with a doctor who was foremost 'a man of great charm and ability ... By his love, sympathy and understanding he brought happiness and a new hope to the lives of so many.'[4]

Born on 9 May 1867, Robert was the son of Robert Clarkson, a provisions merchant in Govan, and his wife Emily Thomas. He graduated from Edinburgh University in 1886 at the age of nineteen; in 1890 he obtained his M B and C M. His early years were spent at the Edinburgh Royal Infirmary and the Sick Children's Hospital. Paediatric medicine was important to Clarkson, but his interest went further than just the physical health of children. As a young boy he saw much which influenced his adult life. For instance, while

> holidaying in the country he found the defective son of a farmer tied up in a byre for his own safety. His talks with the boy and the sympathy aroused made a deep impression on him an impression which remained with him all his life.[5]

Clarkson admired the work of a fellow doctor, John Thomson [1856-

1926], a physician and writer on children's diseases. In 1889, Thomson was appointed as extra physician at the Edinburgh Children's Hospital and it was there that Clarkson's friendship with him deepened. Through his friendship with Thomson, Clarkson also met Leonard Findlay, ten years his junior, the son of a Glasgow doctor, and a man passionate about the care and treatment of children. In particular, he made a study of rickets, the scourge of all poverty-stricken children. Clarkson, Thomson and Findlay were pioneers and did much to enhance paediatric medicine in Scotland. But their reputations went further than that, they were often to be seen teaching and lecturing to young medical graduates from around the world.

It is difficult to know how close Emily's relationship was with her father. The early death of her mother and her father's remarriage so soon after Mary-Ann's death could not have been easy for her. When her father died, it robbed her of the last remaining link to her mother. William died without warning on the morning of Monday 12 August 1895. He had travelled by train, from the family's summer home at Aberfoyle, and was walking from Queen's Street Station to his office at 168 West George Street, when he collapsed, outside the offices of Maclay, Murray & Spens. He was helped into Maclay's premises and medical help summoned but it was too late, William was pronounced dead. The cause of death was given as rheumatic heart disease, from which he had suffered for ten years. It was later reported that eighteen months earlier William had, when stepping from a car outside his Belhaven Terrace home, sustained a bad fall from which he had never truly recovered.

Many tributes were forthcoming, most concentrating on the esteem in which he was held by his business associates but very few spoke of his personal qualities. Al, as he had done with Croudace's death a year earlier, recorded Wright's death but made no other comment.

1896 saw the death of Archibald and Nathaniel Templeton. In their respective ways they were the opposite to their older brother James. Nathaniel remained a bachelor and only ever referred to himself as a carpet manufacturer's assistant. When he died, the size of his estate showed that he had never shared in the wealth of his brothers. Archibald, of course, had married the third Stewart sister. His only son died young, and so began the myth within the family that a child named Archibald would die early.

In 1878 when Archibald had retired, he, Jane and Margaret returned to Scotland and purchased a house at Rhu, naming it Hapland, after the hamlet in Ayrshire from where the Templetons had originated. In common with many of the Templeton women, Margaret did not marry, and there is a suggestion that she was a sad, lonely person.

There is, however, much evidence to suggest that Archibald and Jane were good employers. Sometime shortly after Archibald took up his post as London director of Templetons in the mid 1860s, he employed John Benjamin Dent as coachman and when Archibald retired to Hapland, John Dent and his family came north with him and continued to work for the family until he could claim fifty-three years service. Dent's youngest daughter, Florence Matilda, was born in June 1880 at Beneli, Ardnadam. Beneli was owned by Archibald and would continue to have an association with the Stephen/Templeton family, for many decades to come.

Africa, in the last years of the nineteenth century, was a continent in turmoil; that turmoil was bound to spill over to Lovedale. James and Mina Stewart began to wonder if all they had sought to achieve at Lovedale would be torn apart by war. Stewart, believed passionately that

> man cannot live by bread alone, and that he cannot live without bread. His [Stewart's] aim was to make Lovedale a real Alma Mater ... it was his ambition to provide for all the needs of the native in body, mind and soul. He did not wish him to be a learner for learning's sake, but to be a learner that he might be a doer, a maker, a lover of labour, and a man.[6]

The trouble with Stewart's philosophy was that it took no account of the greed of the *uitlanders*, foreigners, who flocked into Africa to exploit the natural resources of the country. In prospecting for gold, as they did from 1884, the *uitlanders* did not want an educated, self-reliant native population, but a subservient, exploited work force. The Boers, the Dutch farmers, were equally frustrated by the incomers, they were farmers and they wished to carry on as they had always done. They tolerated the missionaries but had no great desire to see the native population treated as equal to the white man.

Lovedale had always been supported by the Foreign Mission of the Free Church, and by many generous private benefactors, including John Stephen, JS and James Templeton. Money was always short, and when the Church began to withdraw support Stewart had no option but to appeal to his family. In February 1896 JS wrote to John Stephen:

> In intimating to Dr Stewart on the 8th Oct 1895 the transmission of £1,000 -- this is what I wrote: "my brother and I wish you to understand that it is given to you for the purpose of the liquidation of the debt upon the 'Lovedale Institution', but subject to any conditions you may see fit to impose upon the Foreign Mission of the Free Church [and] subject to any postponement by you to them which may be involved in the adjustment of the conditions." This ought to give Dr Stewart [and] you power enough to protect your own interests.[7]

Trouble erupted at Lovedale when the native assistants decided that the time had come to form their own Church. The missionary assistants had little power but did a good deal of the day-to-day work of the Church. They were not ordained ministers and could not celebrate marriage, baptise persons or give the Sacraments at Communion. They were paid less than the missionaries, they had no status among the local white settlers and yet they were alienated from their own people.

> Being somewhat educated, they wished to better their position, and the more ambitious wished to make a rapid ascent of the social ladder. They had also an awakening sense of power and racial responsibility.[8]

It is true that, with the exception of a very few individuals like Stewart, Cecil Rhodes and Lord Milner, most white settlers treated the native Africans as second class citizens, who neither needed nor wanted equality. Stewart was passionate in his desire that the Africans should achieve equal rights. On one occasion he was moved to remark, that the Africans were by hereditary born to fight, that now this

> tendency cannot be gratified on the battlefield, it often reveals itself in politics, in church life, and especially in litigation. "all the Kafirs are natural lawyers ... and very sharp ones too."[9]

The use of the word 'Kafirs' by Stewart was not meant as a term of abuse, but was, as shown by a dictionary of that time to mean 'a member of the chief native race in South-East Africa, a branch of the Bantus, *esp* one living between Natal and Cape Providence: their language: a native of Kafristan in Afghanistan.'[10]

In 1898, Stewart wrote a *Kafir Phrase Book and Vocabulary*, and then followed this up in 1902 with *Outlines of Kafir Grammar*.

It was not only at Lovedale that changes were being made. At the Stephen Yard at Linthouse and the Templeton factories on Glasgow Green, changes were also taking place. Al and John Stephen and JS Templeton were handing over the day-to-day control of their businesses to the next generation.

Alexander Stephen

JAMES TEMPLETON
1802 - 1883

Williamina (Mina) Stewart

Alexander (Al) Stephen

John Stephen (Uncle John)

The Golden Wedding of James and Mary Templeton
Back row (left to right): James Murray T, Maud S, Elsie S, James T, Mary S, Fred S,
Al S, Alice T Front row (left to right): Mary S, Ann T, Mary T, James T, Agnes Jane
T, JST Photo on chair: Reverend Archie; seated on floor: Bernard S.

The wedding of Alice Templeton to D H L Young.

Frederic J. Stephen

Sir Alexander Murray Stephen

Fearann Coille, Dunoon

Knockderry Castle, Cove

George Scott MacLellan

Maud MacLellan

Elizabeth Helen Templeton

Auchenfail, the Ayrshire home of Alex E and Daisy Stephen

Kelly after the fire

Mary (Marie) Caroline Ada
Templeton

Agnes Robson, Mary Templeton, Margaret Frew, daughters of Alex E and
Daisy Stephen.

*Frederick Henry Young
(FHY)*

Iris Deacon Young

Agnes R Young, Daisy Stephen, Margaret, baby Patricia

Above: Reverend Archie and Elizabeth Helen T, Dorothy, Joanna, Isabel and Constance.

Right: Kenneth Templeton with J S Templeton's casket

Sir Arthur Young, Duke and Duchess of York, Fred H Young

Cecily C MacLellan

Eric Aubrey Hawks and Nancy Whitcombe

PART FOUR
1898 - 1923

" While the War was being waged many well-meaning but irresponsible
people went about declaring that never again would the industries of
the country be carried on in the old ways, and that when Peace came it
would herald the beginning of a social millennium..."

The Spirit of Progress in our Factories
F H Young.
J T & Co Magazine, February 1920, in the
Templeton Archives at Stoddard International plc.

A Sad Farewell

AL had kept a private diary in addition to his Scribbling diaries for forty-five years, but towards the end of 1898 his entries became intermittent. A penultimate entry was made on 15 October 1898, and it accurately reflected his attitudes and beliefs:

> Every one has a right to do with what he has as he may decide himself. When one gives a subscription or donation to any cause and gives it on condition that a similar amount is given, or that a certain other amount of money will be given -- and sometimes in a stipulated time -- I think that is a principle of giving that I cannot approve of. Consequently when I see this I do not like it. When one gives let it be given to the cause on one's own judgement, and that freely, without what appears to be a threat.[1]

The last entry, written from Kelly, was dated 15 January 1899. Since the New Year, Al had been deeply concerned over the health of Fred who had been suffering, since the previous Monday, from an extremely high temperature, after having caught a chill at Linthouse.

There had been a large family gathering at Kelly to celebrate the festive season, including ten grandchildren: Walter, Alexander, Elspeth and George MacLellan; Alex's three daughters, Agnes, Mary and Margaret -- a fourth daughter, Alix, would be born in 1907. Fred's three sons were also present, Murray, and the twins, James Howie and John Graeme; a daughter Agnes Maude was born in December 1898.

Fred needed a period of convalescence after his illness, and he and Agnes set out for South Africa, a journey that would include a visit to Lovedale. Agnes had mixed emotions about making the trip, she wanted to accompany her sick husband, but it meant leaving her three-month-old daughter, Agnes Maude at home. Fred and Agnes made the long journey by sea, calling at Madeira on the way where Fred was later to learn that he had just missed getting a telegram from his father.

Among the many hundreds of letters in the Stephen archives, the letter that Fred wrote to his mother from South Africa, on Good Friday 31 March 1899, gave a fascinating and detailed account of his itinerary, his experiences and his emotions. As a child Fred had heard stories told by Stewart, and they wetted his desire to see the *Dark Continent* for himself.

The South Africa that Fred and Agnes visited was a very different place from that first experienced by Stewart and Mina back in 1867. Thanks to people like Cecil Rhodes, travel by train was possible, and while vast swathes of the continent were still inaccessible, the towns along the Indian Ocean coast were thriving centres of commerce and trading.

Fred and Agnes arrived in King William's Town on 30 March, having previously travelled from Durban to Pietermaritzburg, the administrative capital of Natal Province. Leaving from Durban, they travelled the remaining sixty-seven miles by train, taking just over four hours. As Fred told his mother, the railway line 'is very steep with many sharp curves. It is part of the line to Johannesburg.'[2]

They went on a rickshaw ride and met up with old friends. On their return to Durban, Fred described the scenery as being like a gigantic botanical garden where everything grew at an extraordinary rate.

They continued to dine with friends and acquaintances, including Bishop Bains, who Fred thought was too young to be a bishop. Back in Durban they had to make a booking for their return to Scotland; they were unable to get berths on the ship of their choice and had to settle for cabins on the *Mexican*. Fred assured his mother that although the ship was old it was perfectly sound. He told her they would leave Cape Town on the 19 April. But before that they made a very special visit to Lovedale. They left for East London on 1 April where they boarded the train for Alice. From Alice to Lovedale the journey was less comfortable, horse and wagon being the mode of transport.

Strangely, Fred's impressions of Lovedale have not survived, but it is very unlikely that he was not impressed with the buildings, the educational achievements and industry of the students, and the sheer beauty that Stewart and Mina had worked so hard to achieve.

The visit to South Africa had, as Fred explained to his mother, been a great success: 'We are getting on very well and enjoying ourselves -- I am getting stronger all the time.'[3]

He complained that it had been hot in Durban, but in East London it was much cooler, and he admitted to having a bit of a head cold. Fred also expressed his gratitude for the letters he had received from home and was particularly pleased to have good reports of his children.

The sailor in Fred could not resist telling his mother that he had a sail in a friend's yacht; he had wanted to race but the wind was too light. He thought the yacht very different from the Clyde boats, as the bay was very shallow. He also remarked that on the sea voyage from Durban to Port Elizabeth, the weather had been bad with high winds which caused the ship to pitch a good deal. It is surprising that high winds and a pitching sea were worth mentioning, he had experienced far worst winds on the Clyde.

A man's worth is too often measured by his monetary wealth, but in James Stewart's case this was definitely not so. Personal wealth was never his ambition. In 1893 he had been awarded an Honorary Doctorate of Divinity at Glasgow University but it was not until 1899 that he achieved the highest office possible in the Scottish Church. He was appointed Moderator of the General Assembly in May of that year, the fifth such missionary to hold the post since the Free Church Separation of 1843. He was the first African Missionary to hold the post. Interestingly, ten years earlier, Dr John Robson, an Indian Missionary and a relative of Agnes Stephen, had held the same position.

Stewart and Mina left Lovedale with a certain degree of reluctance, it had been their home for over thirty years. The manner of their parting made them aware of how much they would be missed. The staff of Lovedale presented Stewart with a loyal address and sufficient money to buy his Moderator's gown. The address not only paid tribute to Stewart's work but included a special mention of Mina:

> She has had a very great share in the work of Lovedale, and her gracious influence has been felt throughout every department. Her wise advice ... will be much missed by us all.[4]

Edinburgh, in May 1899, would have seemed a strange and bewildering place to Stewart and he would have needed time to recall the places of his student days. It was a daunting task to face the sombre ranks of the Scottish Clergy. He knew that the divisions of the 1840s were again being discussed, and that during his year as Moderator, the Parliament in London would order changes to their structure.

His years in Africa had taught him that conflict could be minimised if he conducted himself with his usual dignity, tact, attention to detail and efficiency. He knew that if he spoke little, but allowed others to voice their opinions, he could, in his final address, argue his case with clarity and precision:

> We are on the eve of great changes. The widening of men's thoughts on the great unity of the Church has grown not only with the process of the suns, but with the progress of the Church ... reconsider our position and to ask whether more good can not be accomplished by throwing in our lot with the majority than by holding out any longer.[5]

He went on to say that they were

> like men in a mist; or like sections of an army in the darkness, mistaking each other, and attacking each other because we have not the same regimental facings on our coats ...[6]

If his words were true of the schisms in the Church, then how much more true would they become, when his beloved Africa was again torn apart by strife later that year. The Second Boer War of 1899-1902 would be costly in the lives of men, women and children, both European and African. Stewart, at the General Assembly, had spoken of African soil that 'would be soaked in blood and its sky filled with tortured cries.'[7]

Stewart's words have a familiar ring to them today. African cries of sorrow and anguish remain. They are heard in distant lands but little is done to heal their suffering.

When Stewart returned to Lovedale in 1902, he would hear of the horrors the Second Boer War had inflicted on the local population. The infamous settlements established by Lord Kitchener were euphemistically known as concentration camps. Stewart would also hear of the telegram sent by Kaiser Wilhelm II to President Kruger, expressing his hope that the Transvaal would keep its independence and expose Britain's colonial isolation. The mission of Stewart's life had been to bring education, industry, prosperity and a Christian belief to the indigenous population of Africa. Perhaps it would have been better if he had first taught Christian principles to his British and European neighbours.

Al Stephen died peacefully at the age of sixty-seven on 19 May 1899: he had been unwell for a number of weeks. He had been in shipbuilding for fifty years, having joined his father at the Dundee Yard in 1849. He had witnessed an unprecedented growth in the production of marine craft and had seen sail give way to steam, and wooden ships replaced by iron clad ships. He had seen the rise of the Trade Union Movement. The number of strikes at Linthouse had mercifully been few and those that did occur were promptly settled. Al had a respect for his work force, and they had a deep affection for him.

There were to be many fitting tributes paid, but surely one of the finest was by an unknown contributor who wrote, after paying a visit to Kelly:

> [I] was shown a delicate tool which in the practised hand now cold in death, had given form and outline to between 300,000 and 400,000 tons of shipping. Few men have paid more religious respect to the injunction, "Occupy till I come," than the genial high-principled owner of Kelly ... Mr Stephen took a keen and intelligent interest in the well being of the army of workers over whom he directly and indirectly exercised control, and by many of whom his removal, while still active and kindly force in their midst, will be deeply regretted.[8]

It is obvious from a letter James Templeton wrote to his sister Mary that he knew that she was concerned Al had not left her with a sufficient income:

> Since I was at Kelly, I have got the books of father's trust from 2 Claremont Terrace, and looked into the terms of father's "will" regarding the sum held

by the trustees on your account ... [and] of how you and Elsie are situated
in regard to it ... but you had better ask Alex or Fred if my interpretation of
their father's "will" is correct. You must, I suppose, now give some attention to money matters, altho' Alex and Fred will minimise your trouble in
these affairs.[9]

Mary's worries over money were not justified. Al had left her an income
of two thousand a year, free of tax. But not for the first time in the history of the Stephen family, Al's Trust Disposition and Settlement, like
that of his father, had given an interesting insight into the psychology
of the family. Alexander had made it clear in his Settlement, whom he
wanted to inherit his money and whom he most definitely did not want
to benefit by his demise. Al's Trust Settlement was a very detailed document written by a man who knew his own mind. He makes it clear that
he will be generous to Mary, so long as she remains his widow. Should
she remarry, her settlement would all but stop. The fact that Mary was
sixty-three and had been married for over four decades, apparently did
not rule out her remarriage in his book. Mary could remain at Park Terrace and Kelly, free of rent and burdens, but again only as long as she
remained a widow.

Al's orders for the disposal of Kelly were particularly interesting, in
view of his love for the estate. By 1899, Kelly was not just the new manor
house but also comprised a farm and hotel. Al hoped that Mary and his
children would keep the estate intact, but should they decide only to
occupy the house, he gave them permission to rent out the farm and
the hotel. If, on the other hand, they decided to sell, then first refusal to
buy should be given to Alex; if he declined then the same offer should
be made to Fred. Al stipulated that the price of buying Kelly should not
be less than £45,000. Retail Price Inflation would see the house fetching
almost two million at today's prices. House inflation would probably
triple that amount.

The future success of the Yard was Al's main priority, and he made
generous provision so that the Agreement he and John had made in 1894
and 1895, with Alex and Fred, should be honoured. And, if necessary,
extra funds should be made available to them. The residual of his Estate
was to be divided equally between his six children. It is when Al comes to

write a Codicil in November 1895 that one must ask what had happened between him and Bernard.

It is true that Bernard had never enjoyed shipbuilding. He had been reluctant to take an active part in the affairs of the Yard. He was never made a partner, and it must have irked him when his brother-in-law George Scott MacLellan was appointed to the Board.

In the Codicil, Al mentioned that Bernard was now unable to handle his own financial affairs, seemingly to imply that Bernard had considerable debts and could not, therefore, be trusted with his full inheritance. He ordered his Trustees to take over Bernard's affairs and to pay him an annuity of £300 a year, rising to £500 if they thought it necessary. The harshness of the decision was in direct contrast to two further Codicils where Al had increased the legacies to Alex and Fred, first to £13,500 then to £25,000. This was in addition to their share of the residual of the Estate.

Mary did not live long after Al's untimely death: she died at Kelly on Monday 8 December 1902. Her Estate, when Probated, was reckoned to be worth the equivalent of nearly a third of a million pounds at today's valuation. It was obvious that her money worries were greatly exaggerated, but then she would not have been the first or the last widow in history to worry about her future.

In the fourteen years since Andrew Stephen's death in 1887, his widow Eleanor's life had under gone something of a renaissance. There had been a period of mourning when her youngest son Willoughby died in the summer of 1892, but the marriage in March 1892 of Eleanor's daughter Beatrice to Major George Edward Moke Norrie had been the start of better times. Norrie and his family lived at 62 Queen's Gate, near neighbours of the Stephen family, who had lived at 58 Queen's Gate Terrace. Moke Norrie was sixteen years older than Beatrice, and had been born in New York, his family coming to London between 1871 and 1881. In 1881 he was an undergraduate at Brasenose College, Oxford; he had a fascinating career, serving in the South African wars and becoming a big game hunter. He later presented many of his trophies to the Natural History Musuem in South Kensington. In 1893 by Royal Licence he added the name Norrie to his surname of Moke.

In 1901 Eleanor Stephen was living at 12 Chichester Terrace, Brighton with Beatrice and her three children aged seven, six and three. Major Norrie was away on the night of the census, but his young sister-in-law Adela was also staying with her mother and Beatrice. The household comprised six servants, including two nurses, a cook, parlourmaid and housemaid. Beatrice's sister, Eleanor, was living a short distance away as a boarder; all three sisters give their 'profession or occupation' as independent or living on own means. The whereabouts of Eleanor's two sons, William Alexander and Ernest remain unknown.

Beatrice's eldest son, Charles Willoughby Moke Norrie, probably deserves a biography all of his own. He was a soldier, winning a MC and DSO, and reached the rank of Lieutenant General. He was later appointed Governor General of New Zealand, and awarded a GCMG and GCVO. He was appointed Baron Norrie of Wellington, New Zealand and of Upton in August 1957. Charles's daughter Rosemary married Francis Humphrey Fitzroy Newdegate, the nephew and heir of Viscount Daventry.

Andrew, if he had lived to see the success his daughters and his granddaughters had made of their lives, would surely have had a sly smile that in spite of his own misadventures his children had prospered beyond his wildest dreams.

In his unpublished *Memoir*, JS wrote a moving and rather sad reflection on his life as he saw it. He was proud to have been appointed a Justice of the Peace for Dunbartonshire, and Deputy Lieutenant for the County of the City of Glasgow. He was proud of his friendships, yet he failed to name a particular friend. There is a definite feeling in what he wrote, that he was a sad, lonely man:

> There has therefore been nothing extraordinary or dramatic in my career. I have been in no way conspicuous among my fellows and any memory of me must soon fade and perish. I have really no wish that it be otherwise. I have never had the faintest desire to have my name attached to some charitable gift, or costly tomb.[10]

How different JS's desires were to those of a fellow Scot, who had emigrated to America and made a fortune. JS had been introduced to Andrew Carnegie during one of his frequent visits to the States. John Sloane, the painter, had made the introduction. In 1899 Carnegie had retired from his business empire to devote his time to distributing his vast wealth to universities, libraries and institutions, and most would carry the Carnegie name.

In 1902, JS entertained Carnegie at Knockderry and was able to witness Carnegie handing over to Sir Samuel Chisholm, Lord Provost of Glasgow, a cheque for £100,000. JS may not have been able to match Carnegie's generosity, but he was a frequent donor to Glasgow Hospitals, the Free Church, including Lovedale, and he was proud that he had served as an Elder of the Church.

He had never neglected the welfare of his workers. He and James had been the driving force in setting up the first work's canteen in 1884, the Recreation Trust in 1886, and the Templeton Benevolent Trust in 1894. JS was particularly proud that he had urged on his workforce the need to save. In 1883 the company opened its first savings bank:

> For some time past the donors through their firm ... have accepted small sums of money as deposits from their workpeople at a rate of interest favourable to depositors, and have thereby, as they believe, advanced the moral and intellectual wellbeing of their workpeople by encouraging thrift and stimulating effort.[11]

JS and James went even further by granting a personal liability to the Savings Fund should it ever suffer from a shortfall of funds. Their guarantee was never called upon.

Money, and the pursuit of money for its own sake, was never the over-riding pursuit of JS's life. Although content in his working life, his personal loneliness led him to seek other distractions. He considered himself an aesthete, and explained his artistic leanings:

> During all my life music has been a great source of pleasure. Any knowledge or practice of it however has been self-taught. My singing is good, [and] might have become really excellent by cultivation. I play the flute in accompaniment to the piano or organ. ... I have been acquiring, without in-

struction, the ability to play simple hymn tunes on the harmonium ... I am fond of the arts which have found their expression in painting, sculpture, architecture and decorative design ...[12]

He goes on to say that poetry delighted him, but only the poetry of the great masters. He had a deep love and knowledge of Shakespeare and Robert Burns, but no interest in contemporary poets. He probably would not have read Oscar Wilde or Lord Alfred Douglas, for he admits that he had no sense of humour and saw in others a flippancy that he could not accept. In this, of course, he was reflecting his son's views of London society: James Murray had had no time for the dandyism and pretensions of his contemporaries.

Within JS's *Memoir* there is only a fleeting mention of his youngest daughter Charry -- it is difficult to know exactly what was the relationship between father and daughter. She referred to him as the 'Old Gentleman' and called her step-sister Alice, 'Mamma'. James Murray recorded in his diary that it was difficult for his father to express his feelings, nor was he given to physical displays of affection. Charry once admitted that she had been a disappointment to her father.

It is probable that in the exquisitely beautiful Charry, JS was reminded of the wife he had loved, and lost so tragically. If Charry had been a son, perhaps the relationship would have been different. The relationship with Alice and Dan Young was stronger, and JS was able to enjoy a grandfather's role with their three children, Arthur Stewart Leslie, born in 1889, Eric Templeton in 1892 and Anne Templeton [Nancy] in 1895.

In 1903 JS was again engaged in moving homes, but as always with him the distance involved was negligible. He moved from 1 Park Circus to 2 Park Circus. The house had been originally the home of his good friend John Anderson, who was also his neighbour at Knockderry. A few years earlier Anderson had crossed Park Circus and bought a house at number eighteen.

Moving next door, which while part of the terrace was a slightly larger house, JS could indulge his love of interior design and colour. Elsie

Stephen then moved into JS's old house at number one.

Entering 1 Park Circus today, one's attention is immediately drawn to the stained-glass windows, either side of the main door. The panels are made up of a shield with a dark grey Saltire and a Maltese Cross: Stephen's house flag was a blue Maltese Cross. Below the Saltire and the cross there is a representation of the sea, a fish, and a sheaf of wheat. Turquoise vertical stripes are crossed by two yellow and pink stripes in a wave formation.

Climbing the broad staircase to the drawing room it is possible to see the beauty of the original house, some of the wood panelling still exists, as does the wrought iron of the staircase. To enter the drawing room with its white intricately carved doors, elaborate cornices and splendid fireplaces, is to be transported back to the days of gracious and genteel living. To glance out of the large casement windows across to the small park, when the Park area is cleared of the parked cars, is to understand what pleasure the Templeton and Stephen families experienced in living in the heart of a great city.

A Church Divided

SEMI-RETIREMENT allowed JS to concentrate on other activities. As a former Elder of the Free Church of Scotland, he felt able to add his voice to the fury that followed when the Free Church joined with the United Presbyterian Church on 30 October 1900. The matter was further complicated when the House of Lords put forward a motion that the newly formed Church should rejoin the Church of Scotland and issue a new Creed which would serve the whole Church of Scotland. Then as now, the church does not take kindly to dictates from an English unelected Chamber. The fury really erupted when an English Court of Law, led by Sir Edward Fry, ruled that the merger should go through despite the objections raised.

Fry's judgement and its effects dominated the National and Scottish press for days in the summer of 1904. As with all disputes both sides quoted from history, and the reasons for the 1843 Disruption were aired again and argued over. Robert William Dobbie, minister of Blochairn United Free Church in Glasgow, was among those who gave the readers of the *Glasgow Herald* a history lesson. Quoting from the 1707 Treaty of Union he recalled:

> That no causes in Scotland be cognoscible by the Court of Chancery, Queen's Bench, Common Pleas or any other Court in Westminster Hall, and that the said Courts or any other of the like nature after the Union, shall have no power to cognosce, review or alter the acts of sentences of the Judicatures within Scotland, or hinder the execution of the same.[1]

There was vociferous opposition to the proposals from many members of the United Presbyterian Church, but none spoke with more right, or more authority, than the Revd Dr George Robson. As the son of John Robson and Agnes Renton, and therefore, uncle to Daisy and Agnes Young, his views were important to the wider family. He wrote of the House of Lords decision the deepest and most general impression created by the decision is that a great injustice has been done to the United Free Church in respect of its history, its libraries and its property.[2]

Robson went on to declare that whatever the future held for the UP Church, it would eventually be decided by God and by God alone, not by Man.

JS had not been happy with the way his Church had been behaving for years. In his letter he expresses the disappointment he had felt, explaining what had caused him the most anguish:

> About twelve or fifteen years ago I sent a formal intimation to the church session of which I was a member to delete my name as a subscriber to the Confession of Faith, which was obligatory when I became an elder. I explained that I had come to see that my subscription was not and never had been truthful (my early scruples having been overcome by casuistical representations, such as subscription meant only general approval of doctrines.[3]

He went on to say that he had had many theological discussions over the years, including some with two Doctors of Divinity and one Doctor of Law. Although JS does not name these eminent people it would be a fair guess that two of them were his friends, Norman Macleod and Robert Buchanan. JS declared that his theological friends and he had come to the conclusion that above all else honesty was the thing that moulded them into their beliefs.

The arguments between the Scottish Presbyterianism and the teachings of the Church of Rome had divided men ever since the Reformation. As JS admitted, somewhat reluctantly, there did not seem to be an end in sight. He acknowledged that there were those who advocated that all the Churches should be united, but he argued

> I have often said that it was a happy accident that we had three Presbyterian Churches in Scotland for the reason that one was a check upon and stimulus to the other.[4]

JS was not in favour of an Established Church, with its closer links to the Church of Rome. He saw there would be definite dangers of a Church being led and controlled by an autocratic hierarchy of priests. He wanted a Church where the layman had a voice, and it was with this in mind that he drafted a *Simple Creed or Confession of Faith*.

In October 1906 he published *A Layman's Mind on Creed and Church*. In it he tried to bring together all the strains of the controversy. He believed they could resolve their differences if they issued a new short Creed to replace the Confession of Faith. In the introduction to his book, JS gave the reasons for the task he had undertaken, referring back to the letters he had written on the subject and mentioning also the privately printed series of letters he had written to a friend, the father of three clergymen of the Church of England. He also acknowledged the debt he owed the late J B Mirrless, the sugar magnate, for his book *Old Letters: A Layman's Thoughts on Current Religious Topics*.

The new Creed was made up of fourteen parts and should not have caused controversy between the Churches. It was, however, the fourteenth declaration that gave cause for grave concern in the Established Church and the Church of Rome. It said:

> We believe that the government of Christian Churches is very much a matter of accommodation to time, place, and circumstances. That of the Presbyterian Church is founded on the precedents of the Apostolic age. That the only rulers then appointed were two kinds -- the Elder (Presbyter) alternatively called Overseer (Bishop) and the Deacon. These officers were selected by the whole body of disciples, on account of superior character and of fitness to preside and to teach, but never to perform any sacerdotal function.[5]

Writing to a fellow carpet manufacturer, Thomas Martin Southwell, in 1897, JS had said:

> Do not let us forget this, that from all bodies of men who assert for themselves special powers and privileges we have the right to ask their credentials: and, further, that in whatever laws and rules such men make for others we have always strong reason to suspect self-interest.[6]

It was about this time that JS made the acquaintance of a young man who could, if things had gone as he wished, taken the place of his dead son. Hubert Louis Simpson, had been born on 13 May 1880, the third son, of the eminent obstetrician and gynaecologist, Sir Alexander Russell Simpson and his wife Margaret Stewart Barbour.

Charry Templeton, writing in 1938 to her niece Dorothy Young, gave a vivid description of Hubert at the time he met JS:

> He had an excellent and clear brain ... ironic and somewhat biting wit that chimed with [JS's] dry humour. He was level-headed, urbane, understanding and sceptical, and detested fuss and melodrama as much as [JS] himself.[7]

Charry went on to say that Hubert also possessed a touch of eccentricity that he inherited from his notorious mother. Her comment is intriguing, for there is nothing that is known of Dame Margaret Simpson's character that would deserve such an epitaph. She was a woman of strong and forthright views, she wrote prolifically, including a very intimate obituary of Henry Drummond when he died in 1897. She was also involved, with her husband and Drummond in caring for the social and religious welfare of generations of Edinburgh medical students.

It was in this atmosphere of evangelical Christianity that Hubert grew up, and it was therefore, not surprising, that when he was appointed assistant minister at Kelvinside Church in 1905/6 and later as minister at Kilcreggan in 1907, that JS should find in the young man, the son he had lost.

In running a successful business, both the Stephen and Templeton families could well have been accused of nepotism. Alexander Stephen never saw this as a problem, nor did his sons. James Templeton was equally happy to hand over control of the carpet business to his sons, and later his grandson-in-law. Problems only began to arise when nephews and distant cousins thought they had an automatic right to a position within the family businesses.

It was when a matter of discipline arose that things became difficult; in June 1904, Fred Stephen was wrestling with such a dilemma. Frederick James Reid, the grandson of Peter, and son of Patrick, had argued with a senior member of staff, telling him that as a family member he had a special position in the Yard. Fred disagreed, a row broke out and Reid was sacked. The matter should have ended there, but Margaret Templeton wrote, on behalf of her great-nephew, to ask Fred to change his mind. This Fred had no intention of doing, and he told Margaret his decision was final.

When Patrick Reid had died in 1875, his father and the Templeton brothers set up a Trust Fund for his widow Anna, and her five children, Margaret, Edith, Ernest, Francis and Frederick. Anna was just thirty when her husband died, and her children were all under six-years-old. The sacking of Frederick Reid was an additional complication for Fred. He had been negotiating to purchase Beneli, in Dunoon, from Margaret Templeton, who had inherited the house on the death of her father, Archibald. Fred never wanted to buy Kelly as his father had suggested, but for sometime he had been looking to purchase a country house.

It is interesting that Fred chose to return to Dunoon, for it was at Fearann Coille where he had spent many happy hours as a child. In the early summer of 1905 George MacLellan and his youngest son [George] Douglas were guests of Fred and Agnes at Beneli. MacLellan senior had been feeling unwell for sometime, and all believed a holiday at Beneli would help his recovery. It was also about this time that Maud was diagnosed with rheumatoid arthritis, a condition that would plague her for the rest of her life.

Douglas, had spent the previous winter holiday at Beneli, tutoring Murray, James Howie and John Graeme. Fred was determined that he should be paid for his services, something that Douglas was loath to accept. Douglas had, since 1899, been a pupil at Merchiston Castle School in Edinburgh, where his brothers Walter and Alexander were also pupils. The MacLellan boys were joined at Merchiston by three of Revd Archie Templeton's sons, Archibald, Clement and Godfrey. Indeed, the Merchiston Year Book reveals that at the turn of the nineteenth century many of its pupils were the sons of the leading manufacturing families of Scotland.

When Fred began to consider schools for his sons he did not go with the choice of either his MacLellan or Templeton relatives. Murray had been a pupil at Kelvinside Academy, but had transferred to Cargilfield, a preparatory school in Edinburgh. Cargilfield had been established since 1873, when it became Scotland's first preparatory school; in 1898 the school moved to its Barnton Avenue West site where it has remained ever since.

Fred's choice of Cargilfield was an inspired one, and the school would go on to educate not just his three sons but his grandsons and great-grandsons. The school had, from the very beginning, an ethos of high academic standards that were achieved with classes of less than twenty children. The schools in Govan, where the workers' children went, still had classes of over sixty children. Sport was an integral part of the curriculum and it was at Cargilfield that Murray learned to play rugby and hockey. He would eventually play hockey for his country.

Fred Stephen must have believed that he had entered a period in his life when things could not have been better. His sons were happy at school and his little daughter Agnes Maude was thriving. In September 1905, he and Agnes were on holiday at Aix-Les-Bains, on the French/Swiss border. The first five days of their holiday had been marred by bad weather, but finally Agnes could sit in the garden of the hotel and enjoy the sun and the views across Lac du Bourget.

It was from there that she wrote to her sister Janie, now living in Vernon, British Columbia, with her husband William Armstrong. Agnes admits, somewhat sadly, that she would love to visit Janie and her family, but doubted that time would allow. She was also unwilling to allow her little daughter to accompany her sister Grace on her forthcoming trip to British Columbia. In a sad comment that all mothers, with boys at boarding school would echo, Agnes wrote 'I don't see how we could spare Baby! It will be bad enough with all the boys gone, [and] we wd not like to be bereft altogether.'[8]

As she wrote that letter Agnes could not have known that thirteen days later she would be dead. She died at the Hotel Berniscon on 1 October. She was about to celebrate her forty-first birthday when she died after surgery for appendicitis. In the early years of the twentieth century, the death rate from any surgical procedure was appallingly high.

Fred did not have time to grieve, he had to arrange telegrams to tell those back in Scotland of Agnes's death. He knew that telling the boys would be the responsibility of the headmaster at Cargilfield and he could only pray it would be handled sensitively. Telling Alex and Daisy added to Fred's despair, but he knew they would be better placed to inform Agnes's parents and her siblings. Arranging to bring Agnes's body back to Scotland was another of the daunting tasks Fred had to handle.

Such were Fred's distractions with everything that was required of him, it was early November before he was able to respond to Dr Leon Blanc who was one of the doctors who had treated Agnes. Blanc was looking for payment of the Clinic cost and medical fees. Apologising for the delay, Fred sent the cheque, and in doing so, asked Blanc to 'convey my thanks to those gentlemen for their kind attention. Please accept the same yourself.'[9] Even in his grief, Fred still retained the dignity that sustained him all his life.

In late November, Fred received a letter from Janie, who explained that she had been told by her mother that Fred wanted to hear of any recollections that she or Agnes Gordon -- a long-serving family retainer -- had of his late wife. Recalling a moment shortly after Murray was born in 1892, Janie remembered her sister sitting at Linnwood, her Glasgow home, where '[she] looked so absolutely content [and] happy, [and] it made me think of a Madonna.'[10]

Janie then went on to praise Agnes's care of her younger siblings:

> She was an awfully sweet wee sister to us. The day that Daisy got engaged I remember Miss Campbell (Grannie Robson's companion) saying "Oh I'm so glad it's not <u>Miss</u> Young who is leaving us." ... I am sure there are lots of things if I could only think of them, but so many associations are just connected with her voice [and] her laugh [and] her looks ... she was so dear [and] sweet that last night we all dined at Park Terrace [and] when we said goodbye she said "Well don't be surprised if you see us out I mean to come if I can."[11]

Agnes's death was not the only death in 1905 that caused grieving in the Stephen's family: four days before Christmas James Stewart died at

Lovedale. It is impossible to tell of the enormous outpouring of grief experienced by all those who had come into contact with him and Lovedale. Africa had been his home for over four decades, and Africa was in his blood.

A few days before Stewart died he was visited by the Revd Knox Bowke, the little Kafir boy who had, so hesitantly, made his first visit to Lovedale all those moons ago. Bowke had travelled over three hundred miles to be with his old mentor on his death bed. In their last conversation, weakened by illness, Stewart told his ex-pupil and friend:

> I wish I could have done more for your people and for Africa, but the opportunity seems at an end. The task is now for others to take up, and such as you as have shown the way ought to know what to do ... Wise and discreet leaders will ever be watchful not to disappoint or distrust the friends who are trying to do their best for them.[12]

Stewart's legacy to Lovedale was his true monument, but later a great stone obelisk was erected in his memory. Tributes poured into Lovedale, but words could never convey the sense of loss all those connected with Lovedale felt. Stewart would have been the first to admit though that he would never have succeeded at Lovedale or Livingstonia without the unswerving love and support of Mina. Shortly after their marriage they had journeyed together to Africa, and together they had built a family and served their God beyond their wildest dreams.

Africa would never again see a man like James Stewart.

Back in Glasgow, Fred began to contemplate his future without Agnes, and it was understandable that her sisters would rally round him. Agnes's relationship with her sisters had always been close, but with Janie in Canada and Daisy married to Alex, it was inevitable that Mabel would rally more than others to help Fred through his grieving. It is impossible to know exactly when her role changed from that of housekeeper to companion. But in June 1907, Fred wrote to his bank informing them that they were to honour all cheques drawn on his account by Mabel. It is a measure that their relationship was changing, but it must have been difficult for Murray, and the twins, to realise that their Aunt was now in a similar position to that once held by their mother.

The education of his sons was again a matter of consideration for Fred in 1907. Murray had successfully transferred to Fettes College in Edinburgh, but James Howie and John Graeme, for some reason did not join him there. In December 1907, Fred paid a visit to Uppingham, in Rutland, to determine whether the English Public School would be the right choice for the twins. On returning home he wrote to the Revd Cuthbert Creighton on 5 December:

> I quite understand what the registration means, but may say that up to the present at any rate, I have not changed my mind, and I don't think I am likely to do so, for I think my boys will be quite safe in your hands.[13]

He later had to apologise to Creighton for paying only one registration fee, when he should have paid for both boys.

James Howie and John Graeme, joined *The Hall* with Creighton as House Master in 1908. Creighton was the son of Mandell Creighton, Bishop of London and a historical writer of some note. His son was an admirable man to be given charge of James Howie and John Graeme. Under Creighton's guidance and encouragement the boys thrived intellectually, physically and morally. They were also lucky in that the school appointed a new Headmaster, the Revd Harry Ward McKenzie, who took up his duties in January of that year. McKenzie had previously been master at Wellington College. It was said of McKenzie, by the Dean of Lincoln and former head of Wellington College, Edward Charles Wickham: 'He is an indefatigable worker ... He understands boys as few men do. His rule is bracing, manly, absolutely free from sentimentality.'[14]

JS was elected Honorary Doctor of Law of Glasgow University in 1908. To honour the occasion, the staff at the factory presented him with a beautiful silver-gilt casket and illustrated address. The sides of the casket were formed to show a depiction of Knockderry and the Leiper façade.

The address spoke glowingly of JS's high moral character, his sense of honour, and his benevolence. The only sad note in the address, was where the writer expressed his wish that JS will soon be restored to health after his long and trying illness: JS tended to play down his failing health. In 1891, Rosamond Dale Owen had written to a cousin about JS's poor physical condition; she had been of the opinion that he would die before the end of the century.

In 1974, a Templeton worker, Robert Robertson, on a visit to Knockderry, found a wooden box containing the casket and address high up on a rocky ledge near Cove. How it got there, and how long it was there, remain a mystery. After restoration the casket was returned to Revd Archie's son, Kenneth, for safe keeping.

Fred had always been an enthusiastic traveller, but even he must have had a moment of doubt when, in September 1908, he left Glasgow for a world tour. He visited Australia and New Zealand, coming home via Vancouver, Montreal and New York. It was mainly a business trip, but he also enjoyed the odd social occasion when he visited old friends, including Janie and William Armstrong. He also found time for some sailing, and the journey from New Zealand, across the Pacific Ocean, would have given him time for relaxation.

It was during his time at sea, that he began to design *Coila II*, the yacht that would replace her very successful namesake. He had not sailed for some years, but the urge to do so was still as strong as when he had first taken the helm of *Coila I*. The introduction in 1908 of the six-metre class yacht for racing on the Clyde was an additional spur for Fred to work on an improved design. The new *Coila* was launched in May 1909: she would dominate the Scottish yachting scene for years, winning over a hundred and ten of her races, and achieving second place in almost as many.

Romance was in the air in the spring of 1909. FHY had met the stunningly beautiful Iris Deacon Campbell while on a skiing holiday in Swit-

zerland a year earlier. Iris, now nursing in London, had been treated to
a much needed holiday by her cousins. These cousins were probably
Charlotte Margaret Wilson, the widow of Charles Herbert Ball Wilson,
and their daughters Alice and Florence. In 1881, Iris's mother Elizabeth
Deacon Campbell and her baby daughter Minnie had stayed with Charlotte while they were on a home visit from India.

By 1908 FHY was free to marry. He and his brother Alfred -- now
resident surgeon at Drumchapel Hospital, the country branch of the
Yorkhill Children's Hospital -- had since their father's death in 1893, been
dutiful bachelor sons. But with their mother Anne's death on 28 March
1907, their commitment to her was ended. In 1897 FHY had joined Dan
as a co-partner at Templetons, and in the twelve years since he had become financially secure, he could therefore ensure that Iris would never
again face the poverty she had endured as a nurse. Iris later recalled that,
just before her skiing holiday, she had decided that she would return to
India, the place of her birth. But in Switzerland she met FHY, and instead
of going to India to nurse, she went to Bridgeton as a bride.

FHY and Iris were married at Park Parish Church, Glasgow on 29
April 1909; FHY's brother Alfred and his sister Katherine were witnesses.
Nine years younger than FHY, Iris with her wealth of experience tending
the sick and infirm, would blend into his life in Glasgow with ease. She
had that rare quality of dignity and compassion that would enable her
to mix with the grand ladies of the Park Circus area and also with the
Templeton factory girls out at Crownpoint.

She told a friend that she was going to Bridgeton, and she did become a frequent and much loved visitor to the Templeton factories. The
factory girls' welfare became her great passion. She and FHY bought a
house at Kirklee Road, just off Great Western Terrace where FHY had
been born.

A little over a month after the marriage of FHY and Iris, Fred Stephen,
after returning from his lengthy foreign business tour, married for the
second time. In marrying Mabel Frew Young, the sister of his dead wife
Agnes, Fred was making a commitment that may not have pleased the

traditionalists in the Church. The Church and State had no hard and fast rules about the marriage between in-laws, but there was still a degree of suspicion about such unions.

Fred and Mabel were married at Glasgow Cathedral, according to the Forms of the Church of Scotland, on 1 June 1909. The ceremony was conducted by James Black, D D of the United Free Church. Black had married Fred and Agnes, eighteen years earlier, and at that ceremony, Mabel had been a witness. It would have been hard for her to stand at the impressive altar in the Cathedral and not remember that earlier occasion. In taking her sister's place, Mabel would find it hard to eradicate her sister completely from her memory. Every time she looked at Agnes's three teenage sons, Murray, James Howie and John Graeme, the memory of their mother would be there. For Agnes Maude, her eleven-year-old step-daughter, the memories may have been easier: she was only six when her mother died.

The role of a step-mother is frequently a difficult one, but it surely must have been even harder when the role was played by a sister of the blood mother. Conflicts, between step-mother and step-children must have arisen, and conflict management must have been a difficult task for Fred to handle, though it may have been made easier by the fact the three boys were at boarding school: Murray had been at Fettes College for a couple of years, and the twins had spent their first year at Uppingham.

School holidays were a possible source of conflict, but at Beneli, or Craigrownie or Knockderry where they were often joined by Arthur and Eric Young, these conflicts would have no doubt been minimized.

An Uneasy Peace

THERE were significant changes taking place in Great Britain in 1910. Lloyd George's problem with getting his People's Budget accepted was causing a constitutional crisis. The House of Lords were appalled at Lloyd George's decision to raise, substantially, the level of income tax on the rich. His decision to levy a duty on unearned income caused their Lordships heart failure. The fight between the un-elected peers and the elected House of Commons rumbled on for months.

In May, Edward VII's death heralded a new beginning. With the new King George V declaring support for Lloyd George's Liberal budget, and his threat to create sufficient Liberal-minded peers, to thwart the wishes of the Tory House of Lords, they finally backed down. The crisis did however prompt the introduction of the Parliament Act -- a procedure by which the House of Commons would always hold sway over the Peers.

There were two General Elections in 1910, in January and December. Dan Young stood in both elections as Conservative and Unionist candidate for Falkirk Burgh, but as a Tory and a committed Unionist, he was never going to succeed. Dan was beaten by the standing Member of Parliament, the Liberal John Archibald Murray MacDonald. Dan had previously stood against MacDonald in the 1906 General Election.

The two main parties -- Liberal and Conservative -- won 272 seats each, Irish Nationalist 84 and Labour 42. The results ensured that, with the King's intervention, Lloyd George's National Insurance Bill would finally get its Royal Assent.

As far as it has been possible to ascertain, Dan was the first family member to openly support the Conservative and Unionist Party. The history of both families implied that they were more Liberal in their thinking and attitudes. Shortly before the 1889 election, Al had been admonished, by Fairfield Street, for taking part in a Tory election meeting. Street declared that: 'Connection with Toryism in any shape or form, be it Unionist or any other "ist" is fatal to moral rectitude.'[1]

The political crisis in London affected both Fred and Alex but somehow they were immune from its worst excesses. They were enjoying a few years of relative prosperity; the order book for new ships was good: the Anchor Line and the Clan Line had placed orders, and there was a feeling of optimism in the air.

Alex, less flamboyant than Fred, and less inclined to be a shipbuilder, was more drawn towards life as a gentleman farmer. In October 1910, he and Daisy left their house in Grosvenor Terrace Lane for an elegant town house in Prince's Terrace. His three eldest daughters, Agnes, Mary, and Margaret attended a school in England; Alix, the fourth daughter was only three. Alex, writing to the Station Master to book rail tickets for the girls, shows he had their welfare at heart but did not intend to indulge them. He tells the Station Master that he wants three 3rd class seats for the girls as opposed to the 1st class when their mother travelled. But Alex insisted that the seats should be in a Ladies Only carriage.

Alex had other things on his mind as well as the welfare of his daughters; he resigned from the *Institute of Metals*, then changed his mind. One of his domestic servants, Marian Samson, had been injured in an accident in the house and Alex was frightened that she would sue for neglect. He was willing to pay whatever was requested to get the girl the very best medical care, but he loathed the idea of a large compensation.

In July 1911 Murray left Fettes College and in October he went up to King's College, Cambridge, to read Mechanical Engineering. At Fettes he had rightly earned the reputation of excelling at everything he set his hand to, '[he had] a natural talent backed by an appetite for hard work and a willingness to study and absorb the details of every subject which concerned him.'[2]

If Murray worked hard, he also played hard, playing hockey and rugby and excelling in both sports. He was a member of the School's Cadet Force, obtaining the rank of sergeant. His father had also naturally passed on to his eldest son his love of yacht racing.

Murray had been at Fettes College with his cousins Arthur and Eric
Young. After school, Arthur had gone abroad to study, but Eric had gone
up to Magdalen College, Oxford. Eric, like Murray was a sportsman,
earning his Blue for rugby, and playing an active part in the Cadet Force.
If he had still been alive, James Murray would have despaired that his
second-cousins were dedicated to outdoor activities, and did not share
his love of all things aesthetic.

In 1904, the reputation of the Stephen Yard for yacht building was
probably second only to that of William Fife's Yard at Fairlie, who then
held the premier position as yacht builders. In that same year, William
Macalister Hall, of Torrisdale Castle, Kintyre, ordered a yacht from the
Stephen Yard. Hall wanted the yacht three months after placing the
order. Fifty-one working days later, she was delivered in full working
order. The yacht was named *Medea*, after the Greek sorceress, daughter
of Aeetes, and wife of Jason, and it would always hold a very special place
in Stephen's folklore. In November 1911, Macalister Hall sold *Medea* to
Frederick G Todd of Troon, but after just two years he then sold her on
to John Stephen.

The story of her illustrious career can be found in Craig Arnold's
book, *Medea, The Classic Steam Yacht*, published by the Maritime Museum
of San Diego, California. Today, a hundred years after her launch, she
still cruises the seas around San Diego. In 1971, after restoring her with
the same care that the Stephen Yard had lavished on her, Paul Whittier
her last owner gave *Medea* to the Maritime Museum.

It often follows that when a wife dies, her grieving spouse's death follows shortly after. Conversely, if the husband dies first his widow enjoys
many more years of life. There are, of course, exceptions to this rule. Six
deaths connected to the Stephen family occurred between November
1909 and March 1913. Anne Fleming Stephen and her husband Duncan
Wilkie Paterson died, their last years having been spent in Edinburgh,

in somewhat impoverished circumstances. But in those last years, Anne, with the practical common sense inherited from her mother, managed to maintain her self respect and dignity. Anne and Duncan had four daughters, who were, according to a contemporary source, strong-minded and inclined to outbursts of jealousy. Emily, the eldest daughter, remained single and became a notable artist and a member of the Royal Scottish Water Colour Society.

On 28 August 1910, Margaret Stephen died; less than eighteen months later her husband Robert Mudie died. They had, after Alexander and Elspeth's deaths, made their home at Corona, and Robert's shipping interests had prospered. There is a suggestion, however, that Margaret never owned Corona, for after her death Robert moved to Riverview. It is possible the house still belonged to Alexander's heirs, and only after Margaret's death were they able to sell. Margaret and Robert did not have any children.

The exception to the spouse rule, above, was Hannah. Her marriage to William Adams had caused a rift with her family but there is some evidence to suggest that it was partially healed. Hannah returned to Scotland sometime before 1881; in the census taken that year, she was living in Edinburgh with her teenage son, Alexander Stephen Adams. She listed her status as married and an annuitant. The latter implied that she was receiving an allowance, which could mean she was receiving an income from her husband -- or it could mean, that in spite of her father's wishes, she was benefitting from his Estate. As a single parent -- there is no mention of her husband -- she supplemented her income by taking in a lodger.

Alex Watson, Hannah's lodger, was a medical student, and obviously had some influence on the young Adams, for he went on to study medicine at Aberdeen University. Afterwards he moved to Rillington, Yorkshire in 1897, where he spent the rest of his working life as Medical Practitioner to the Norton Rural District Council, Public Vaccinator and as Registrar of Births and Deaths. In May 1897 he married Anne Chisholm, the daughter of John Chisholm, a wood contractor, and Isabella Burnett. Alexander and Anne had met in Inverness before he moved to Rillington and they were married by Special Licence shortly after he arrived in Yorkshire. The had two children, John Alexander and Violet. Adams provided a home for his mother and she was with him and Anne when she died on 20 December 1911.

Janet was the only one of Alexander and Elspeth's daughters who lived into adulthood and who did not marry. She had had an interesting life, and unlike most middle-class Victorian spinsters she travelled widely. She died at her Broughty Ferry home on 13 March 1912, aged seventy-one. Her nephew Frederick Somerville Stephen was the informant of her death; she was always closer to William's family than she was to Al's family.

The death of the three sisters coming so close together was hard for the extended family to bear. In 1912, of Alexander and Elspeth's eighteen children, only three remained, John who was in his seventy-eighth year, Elspeth Croudace was approaching eighty-six, and Mina, the youngest was sixty-four. Although John was in poor health and taking less and less interest in the affairs of the Yard, he remained concerned to see that his army of nieces and nephews upheld the family honour and traditions.

The sixth death was of William Murray Gordon Thomson, the only son of Alex Gordon Thomson and William Stephen's daughter Alice Murray. Since the death of her father and father-in-law in 1893, Alice had borne more than her fair share of suffering. Her husband had died just three years after his father, in September 1899: Alex Gordon had been ill for almost five years with a general paralysis. William Murray Gordon Thomson's death in March 1913, at the age of thirty-four, was particularly tragic. In March 1901 he had married Evelyn Maud, the daughter of Robert Malcolm, a jute spinner and manufacturer, and Elizabeth Cuthbert. According to the death certificate, issued by Dr Robert David Campbell of Kirriemuir, William Murray died of heart failure caused by chronic alcoholism. A year later in June 1914, Evelyn married Robert Campbell.

If tragedy had dogged William Thomson, then at least his sister Jean had a more stable and lasting marriage. In 1903 she had married Ernest, the son of James Grant, a linen manufacturer, and his second wife Jane Easton Beattie. Unfortunately, James died before Ernest was six months old. Jane Beattie was left to bring up four boys under five years old, nevertheless, she made an extremely good job of raising her sons.

Ernest and Jean Grant had two sons and two daughters, and after

her mother, Alice Thomson's death in October 1916, they inherited
Red Court and the family owned and occupied it for another eighty-six
years.

Kelly House had remained the property of Fred and Alex since their
father's death in 1899. They had been loathed to live in the house and yet
they were reluctant to sell. For a few years they had leased the house to J
Clark-Neill, a director of J & P Coats, Paisley, but in May 1913 Clark-Neill
moved to Curling Hall, Largs. The Coats connection is interesting in that
two of the great-granddaughters of Sarah Greenlees née Templeton,
(Thomas's daughter) married into the Coats family. Elizabeth Millar
Greenlees married Alexander Harold Glen Coats; Jane Muir Greenlees
married Stuart Auchincloss Coats.

It was a difficult decision for Fred and Alex to part with Kelly, knowing, as they did, just how much Al had loved the house. But they had
to be realistic, the house was too big and had to go. They put it on the
market at the staggering price of £70,000. House inflation was even then
a topic of conversation. Perhaps worried by Lloyd George's People's
Budget, the house remained unsold throughout that summer and Fred
and Alex were forced to reduce the asking price. That produced a buyer,
James Steven Spencer, a Glasgow ship owner. Contracts were to be final-
ised on 5 December.

Early in the morning of that day, Thomas Prentice, Station Master
at Wemyss Bay, rose from his bed at five-forty-five, and glancing out of
his bedroom window, was horrified to see a strange orange glow coming from the windows of Kelly. Even as he watched, the glow turned to
flames leaping out of the roof.

Prentice notified local police, who then contacted the fire brigade,
but they had to travel from Johnstone, a tortuous journey of twenty-
five miles. It took Firemaster Williamson and his five man team an hour
to make the journey, by which time Kelly was beyond hope. If the Fire
Brigade had arrived sooner, the fate of Kelly would still have been the
same. Water was taken from the Kelly Burn, but the pressure they were
able to maintain was very low. It would have been impossible for anyone
to save the house.

Thomas Prentice later told the police, who reported it to Fred and Alex, that when he approached the burning house, the front door had been forced open. He was of the opinion that incendiary devices had been planted. He told them that on the lawn he had found a roll of brown paper on which was written 'Retaliation! A Reply to the Cat-and-Mouse Act.' A copy of *Women's Suffrage, the Common Cause of Humanity and Votes for Women*, dated 28 November, was found in the shrubbery near the station.

During 1913, the Women's Suffrage Campaign had been engaged in ever more destructive acts of violence. In March they had resorted to arson attacks following the abandonment of the General Electoral Reform Bill. Emily Pankhurst had been sentenced to three years' imprisonment for fire bombing Lloyd George's home. In April the Government had passed the 'Cat-and-Mouse Act', whereby hunger strikers could be released from prison only to be re-arrested when they had recovered sufficiently. In June, during the running of the Derby, Emily Davidson had tried to grab the reins of the King's colt, Anmer. She brought the horse and his jockey, Herbert Jones, crashing to the ground, but her reckless folly caused her to fall and she sustained a fractured skull. She died in hospital four days later.

The police were sure the Suffragettes were responsible for the destruction of Kelly, but they had no hard evidence on which to bring a prosecution. The guilty women were never caught nor were their identities ever established beyond reasonable doubt. Rumours, however, have persisted ever since. One rumour that refuses to die, is that the culprit was Jane Allan, the youngest daughter of Alexander Allan. She had a colourful past, being implicated, with her brothers, in the Dale Owen/Oliphant religious sect. There was also a suggestion that she had been aided-and-abetted by Fred's wife Mabel. They knew the house was empty: there were no servants in the house that night and the house was about to be sold.

A second rumour concerned Elizabeth MacLean, the daughter of a highly respectable merchant family. But like all rumours it may have had some substance but, with the passage of time, impossible to confirm or deny.

Not content with destroying Kelly, the suffragettes also set fire to the steam yacht, *Emerald*, built by the Stephen Yard for Sir Christopher Furness in 1903. Her career had been less than distinguished but she did have the honour of being the first turbine-driven yacht to cross the Atlantic. She was later sold to Lord Inverclyde, chairman of the Cunard Steamship Company, and in the winter of 1913 she had been laid up on the Gare Loch. The fire badly damaged her and she ended her days as a coal barge. What a tragic end for a beautiful and graceful yacht!

In the spring of 1913, JS had brought out a second edition of his 1906 book, *A Layman's Mind on Creed and Church*. The arguments between the various strains of Scottish Presbyterianism had continued, with the 'Wee Frees' refusing to have any contact with the United Free Churches. In JS's opinion, his book:

> ... contains a fair, intelligible, and conciliatory presentation of the Christian Religion and might therefore be well fitted to serve as an explanation and 'apology' in arguing the question with the educated men of China, Japan or India.[3]

Such was his belief in his own interpretation of the new Creed that he hoped, with the aid of the Revd Hubert Simpson, to see his book translated into many languages for the benefit of non-Christian people. In the meantime he could bask in the admiration of those closer to home who had read his little book. In May, he received a letter from Victor Bulwer-Lytton, and his comments pleased and yet annoyed JS. Bulwer-Lytton pointed out that JS had incorrectly identified his father as the Earl Lytton, when he should have said Earl of Lytton.

The marriage of JS's eldest grandson, Arthur Young, took place on 21 November 1913 in Melbourne, Australia. His bride, Dorothy Spencer, was just a year older than him. She was the daughter of Walter Baldwin Spencer, Professor of Biology at Melbourne University and Mary Elizabeth Bowman. After a glittering career at Oxford, Spencer had moved to Australia in 1887. He became one of the foremost experts on the origins of the Aboriginal people and was later appointed Chief Protector of the Aboriginal people.

Dan, Alice and Nancy travelled to Melbourne to be at Arthur and Dorothy's wedding. It is doubtful if JS made the long trip as he had just celebrated his eighty-first birthday, and although a seasoned traveller, the long sea voyage would have been too much for his declining strength. Eric, probably, would not have been able to spare the time away from his studies at Oxford. It is highly likely that Charry went in place of her father; JS may even have hoped that Charry would meet a suitor on the trip.

In the event, it was not Charry who had the romance but her niece, the eighteen-year-old Nancy. On the way back to Britain, she met a young New Zealander, Eric Aubrey Hawkes Whitcombe. Whitcombe was going to England to manage the London publishing office of his father's company, Whitcombe and Tombs. Nine years older than Nancy, Eric was the son of George Whitcombe and Marian Hall. When Nancy and Eric parted at the end of their sea voyage, they exchanged addresses. Alice and Dan would have rejoiced at seeing their daughter so happy, but they must have been worried that Nancy would be hurt if it turned out only to be a shipboard romance.

After their marriage, Arthur Young and Dorothy returned to Scotland where Arthur was appointed a partner of Templetons, joining his father, Dan and FHY. It is likely that the partnership was a wedding present from his grandfather and father. Dan had been made a partner on the eve of his wedding. Arthur and Dorothy had four children: Barbara Mary born 1916; Alastair Spencer Templeton born 1918; Anne Stewart born 1919 and Patrick Templeton born 1925.

The exact date that a controversial young woman first made her presence known to the Stephen/Templeton families has been lost in the mists of time. What is not disputed, however, is that sometime in 1911/12, Cecily Caroline Hicks-Beach borrowed £5 from her father's chauffeur and travelled to Glasgow. She was the twenty-four-year-old daughter of Archibald William Hicks-Beach, a military man, extra ADC to the Viceroy of Ireland at the time of Cecily's birth. Her mother was Violet Isobel Slingsby Bethell, the daughter of Slingsby Bethell, Clerk to Committees of the House of Lords, and Caroline Chaplin. Cecily could trace her ancestry back to the sixteenth century, her great-uncle being the 1st Earl of St Aldwyn. The Bethell line was equally well connected through the Baron Westbury. On both sides of the family, the Law, Politics and the Military were occupations followed by their sons.

Cecily, unlike her male ancestors, had a tendency towards a hedonistic life-style. According to some of the more pious Stephen/Templeton women, she had a wayward disposition.

Family rumour has it that Cecily came to Glasgow, at the invitation of John Graeme, but as he was still a pupil at Uppingham when she arrived in Glasgow, this seems unlikely. It is possible that the invitation came from Charry; they could have met at a coming-out ball in London. The two women had much in common: both had lost their mothers when they were infants. Both had been over-indulged by absent fathers, and were cared for by nannies/governesses. They were both single-minded and determined to throw off the shackles of their Victorian childhood.

It was highly likely that some of Charry Templeton's friends, if not chosen by her father, were thoroughly approved of by him. He mentioned two in particular, Violet Roberton, and Edith King, daughter of Sir James King. It was probable that after the marriage of Alice, JS looked for a mature companion for his young daughter, Edith King being sixteen years older than Charry seemed suitable. Violet Mary Craig Roberton, the other young lady, was born in March 1888, the daughter of William Craig Roberton, a Writer, and Janie Leney Reid. The Reid name suggests that there could have been a collateral connection to James Templeton's old partner Peter Reid.

Shortly after arriving in Glasgow, Cecily Hicks-Beach was taken ill with appendicitis and was rushed into a nursing home for surgery. One of her frequent visitors was not John Graeme but Walter Scott MacLellan, the eldest son of Maud. With Walter being the perfect visitor for an invalid, it was inevitable that a romance would blossom. They were married on 8 September 1914 at Holy Trinity Church, Sloan Square. The outbreak of war disrupted their early married life, but the first of their two children, Violet Maud, was born in August 1915. Their son Roderick George Scott was not born until August 1918.

Cecily should have been a breath of fresh air in the Presbyterian households of Stephen/Templeton but her love of horse racing, dancing and house parties did not make her many friends. The unkindly epithet most often used about Cecily was a transposition of the name Hicks-Beach into 'Hicks-Bitch'.

The Great War

IT would have been a brave person who predicted on New Year's Day the coming events that would shape 1914. The murder of Archduke Francis Ferdinand in Sarajevo in June 1914 was the prelude to a declaration of war. Even when war was declared on 4 August most people in Britain thought it would be over by Christmas.

Fred Stephen had every reason to believe that life for him and his family would continue in the same manner as before. James Howie and John Graeme had gone up to King's College and Pembroke College, respectively, in the autumn of 1913. Murray was in his last year at King's and was certain of obtaining a good degree.

In February, Fred had been appointed Justice of the Peace for the County of Lanark, an honour he shared with his father. If Fred did have a concern it was over the health of Uncle John and Aunt Elspeth Croudace. John was approaching his seventy-ninth birthday and had been in frail health for some months; Elspeth, would be ninety-one on 21 November.

Mina Stewart, a widow for eight years, was concerned about her investments; she believed that an inheritance from John would solve her financial problems. She voiced her concerns to Fred and James Templeton and she wanted Fred to bring her concerns to the notice of John, but Fred was unwilling to help her:

> His [John's] state of health was such at the time that I could not have risked reading your letter to him. Certainly the doctor forbade me to do so. Since then as you will have been sorry to hear he has been getting worse ...[1]

Fred told his Aunt that in spite of what she had heard to the contrary

> no influences had been brought to bear on Uncle John which caused him to alter his will to the detriment of your family. Of this afternoon, I know nothing, and if there was any I can tell you that it has had no effect. I may say that I saw [James] MacKenzie, his lawyer, recently who told me that the

amounts left to you and your family in the last will the Uncle made, viz in May or June last year, [the will was dated 24 June 1913] are exactly the same as in his previous will. Except George [James Gordon Stewart] gets more.[2]

Mina should have been reassured by Fred's words, and if she were still in doubt she could have asked her son-in-law David Blyth Anderson who was one of John's executors. Perhaps though, it was Anderson who had sown the seeds of doubt in Mina's mind. Mina's daughter, Florence, had married Anderson in June 1898 while she was staying at Craigrownie. In April of that year, Florence's sister, Mina, had married Ronald Charles Grant, a lieutenant in the Cape Mounted Rifles. Before her marriage, Mina had been staying at Park Circus with JS and Charry.

Family concerns dominated a good deal of Fred's time that spring. In April he was in contact with Walter Wingate Gray because Rex Wingate -- Reginald's son -- apparently wanted to order a new ship from the Stephen Yard to replace the *Southern Cross*. But as Fred told Gray the new ship might be too small for them to consider, and there was also a question of payment that perplexed Fred:

I don't know what exactly [you] mean by the instalment plan, but if it means cost instalments during construction, of course, that would suit us all right.[3]

There is a hint in Gray's letter that Rex Wingate wanted to pay for the vessel after completion by the instalment method. Fred could not agree to those terms.

Money, or the lack of it, was a reccurring theme in Fred's letters at that time. With three sons at Cambridge he was frequently sending them cheques, but it was not only his sons who were pleading poverty. With students that was to be expected, but Fred had less sympathy when Wingate Gray sought a loan. In May, he told James Templeton that he had been away yachting and that was the reason for the delay in replying to his last letter. Not for the first time was there a disagreement between various members of the family over the distribution of money. Fred agreed with James that the interest rate on the money should be set at four percent. He explained that George MacLellan had been deputised to see Gray and explain matters to him. From the tone of Fred's letters it is clear that he had little sympathy for Gray's financial woes.

A couple of days later Fred wrote to James:

> I return Walter Gray's memo. I do not think it necessary to make any expla-nation to him. Speaking frankly, and in confidence, I may say that I prefer not to discuss these matters with him and especially not to get into a cor-respondence with him.[4]

July 1914 saw an official visit to Scotland by George V and Queen Mary. They had visited Glasgow before as the Prince and Princess of Wales, but this was the first visit since their Coronation. The tour was scheduled to last three days, but for JS and his family the first day's proceedings were of particular importance.

The Royal couple opened the new Royal Infirmary. JS had assembled a time capsule which included a piece of the carpet made for George V's Coronation, a photograph of the carpet's pattern, and a business folder giving a short history of the company and its mills. JS and his brother had been major donors to the hospital building fund. JS, Charry, Alice and Dan were among the guests to witness the opening ceremony. Re-plying to the loyal address, the King made reference to the building being a memorial for the late Queen Victoria's Diamond Jubilee, and he was confident that 'the Royal Infirmary will long flourish as a testimony of Glasgow's care for its sick.'[5]

Later, Charry had the honour of presenting Queen Mary with a bouquet of flowers. In 1915, a bronze plaque was erected in the main entrance of the administration block as a tribute to JS and James. The inscription read:

> By a resolution of the managers, this section of the Infirmary Building is named The Templeton Block. In grateful recognition of magnificent gifts to the rebuilding by the brothers John Stewart Templeton and James Templeton jn.[6]

With the official declaration of war on 4 August 1914 Fred's anxieties were very personal. Murray had graduated from King's with a 1st Class Tripos in Mechanical Engineering. He had been suffering with a knee injury and after surgery, according to Fred, he had made a good recovery. On 31 July, Murray and two friends, Arthur Cecil Pigou, a King's College economist, and a fellow graduate William Armstrong, had left London for Interlaken. They had planned to climb in the Alps, but on the day war was announced, Murray and his colleagues were stuck in a hut on the Eiger.

On 12 August Fred heard that all transport out of Switzerland was halted. He approached Sir Francis Dyke Acland, Under-Secretary at the Foreign Office, trying to find out when Murray and his companions would be able to travel home. It would be three weeks before Murray was finally able to leave Switzerland.

Murray then immediately enlisted in the Royal Garrison Artillery. The twins James Howie and John Graeme, according to their Army Papers, enlisted in the Argyll and Sutherland Highlanders on 4 August. The three Stephen boys were commissioned almost immediately on enlistment. Reading down the list of names who enlisted the moment war was declared gives a terrifying picture of the readiness of the young men to fight for their country. Douglas, Walter and Alexander MacLellan; Arthur and Eric Young; Archibald, Godfrey and Clement Templeton, all answered the call to Arms. They were awarded many battle honours: Military Crosses and Distinguished Service Medals were handed out by a grateful nation but the war left terrible scars on their young lives.

If, when they signed up, they believed the rhetoric that the war would be over by Christmas, they were soon disillusioned. Before the war was won, words like Passchendaele, the Somme, Ypres and Gallipoli became synonymous with death. The survivors would understand Siegfried Sassoon and Wilfred Owen's moving and evocative war poems, which even now bring back all the horrors of war.

On 17 May 1915, Captain Eric Young and Lieutenant Archie Templeton left Falkirk for the Dardanelles and Gallipoli, and among the other officers was William Newlands Sloan. His cousin Alexander Bankier Sloan was Medical Officer during the bloody campaign that was Gallipoli.

Off Gibraltar on 23 May, Eric took the Church Parade and it is just possible that he said a silent prayer for his two great-aunts, Mary Templeton and Marjory Stephen who had died on the Rock.

Eric Young and Archie Templeton both died fighting in Gallipoli on the 28 June 1915. The grief of their respective parents was echoed in many homes across the country. Alice Young and Elizabeth Templeton coped differently with their loss. Elizabeth was inconsolable. She was hysterical in her grief, she believed that 'missing in action' meant that her first born son was lying in some Glasgow hospital waiting for her to come and rescue him. Her search never brought her a moment of comfort. Revd Archie withdrew into himself and could find no comfort, not even from his God. Alice grieved with quiet dignity for she had learnt from her father's suffering on the deaths of his three young wives and his only son, that inner strength and courage he had shown. She drew comfort from JS, Dan and her daughter Nancy.

In Scotland, Fred was struggling to come to terms with adapting the Yard from commercial shipbuilding to war ships. From June 1915 until December 1917 they launched just two ships for private owners, but they built and launched eighteen destroyers for the Admiralty. The Yard, working in conjunction with the engineering firm of J Weir Limited of Cathcart, built and equipped planes. The carpenters of the Yard were able to adapt their techniques so that within months the two companies were turning out four or five planes a week. According to the pilots of the Royal Flying Corps these planes were superior to the German planes they encountered.

It was not just the men who were fighting the war; the Stephen Yard was forced to take on women workers. Adeline, the wife of Claud Allan, wanted to set up a canteen and a shop at Linthouse. She asked Fred if he would support her efforts, but Fred was less than enthusiastic. As he told her, the men made full use of the restaurants and shops in the district:

I really do not think I could advise you to start an ordinary shop ... For one thing ... we have not enough men to work a night-shift, as so many of our men left to join the Forces, and we sent so many away to other Yards which were doing Admiralty work before we received orders from the Admiralty ourselves.[7]

Not to be discouraged, Adeline set-up a canteen and shop next door at Fairfields. Lady Inverclyde as Head of the Women's Voluntary Aid Society did however open a canteen at the Yard.

Two weeks later, Fred was again using his good offices for a member of the Allan family. Tom Lander, the son of Thomas Eaton Lander and Eliza Allan, had been wounded while serving with the Highland Light Infantry, but he wanted to get back into the action. In September 1915 he was paying for his own flying lessons in Windermere and he asked Fred if he could help him. Fred wrote to Major General Sir David Henderson, Officer Commanding the Royal Flying Corps. Fred's intervention obviously worked, for Tom joined the Royal Flying Corps. But in 1918, while on a mission over Mesopotamia, he was shot down by the Germans and received serious injuries to his leg. Captured by the Turks, they failed to treat his wounds properly and he would have lost a leg but for being rescued by the Germans. They treated his wounds and before long he was rescued by the signing of the Armistice.

The brutal treatment Tom received from the Turks -- a brutality mirrored in part by their treatment of T E Lawrence, Lawrence of Arabia -- did not put Tom off flying. On his return to civilian life he took up gliding but tragically died in a gliding accident in the early thirties.

It was with a growing sense of sadness that Fred, knowing there would be little opportunity to sail during the war years, he wrote to Commander Wright, Senior Naval Officer at Ardrossan, returning the permit granted for his yacht. He told Wright, the yacht was laid up for the winter. Fred and Mabel were, however, able to spend a fourteen day holiday at Droitwich.

In January 1916 the war had been raging for seventeen months and showed little sign of being over by the time the third Christmas was celebrated. On 1 January, conscription was introduced, and British troops made a humiliating withdrawal from Gallipoli.

Fred was again battling with a period of ill-health, and the concern over the safety of his sons was taking its toll on his health. He was annoyed that one of James Howie's Cambridge bills was outstanding and the company were demanding immediate payment. In paying the bill, Fred was moved to tell them that his son was serving in Mesopotamia. In a letter written to the Post Office, Fred showed that things have not changed very much with the passing of time:

> Might I say that I think there must be a want of co-operation between your departments, which I hope you will look into and get rectified, for it is most annoying to get these threatening notices when there is no occasion for them.[8]

John Stephen died on 27 March 1916 shortly before his eighty-first birthday. In looking back over his long life, it was impossible to find a single occasion when he was ever cruel, vindictive or intolerant. In working with Al he had seen the shipyard grow and prosper, but in doing so he had always had the welfare of the workers and their families uppermost in his thoughts. The early deaths of his own children and Eliza's numerous stillbirths had robbed him of an heir, yet he had always been a caring, kindly uncle to his army of nephews and nieces. He kept a fatherly eye on his brother James's two boys, James and Robert, and on Margaret Mary Dundas, and he ensured they led useful and rewarding lives. In 1881, according to the census, Margaret and her mother were living at Ebury Buildings, London, where Margaret was working as a milliner. When John Stephen wrote his will in 1913, Margaret was still there.

If the shipyard was his memorial, then how much greater was his memorial to the Free Church, a commitment largely undertaken without the glare of publicity. His friendship with the Revd Robert Howie never wavered, nor did his generosity whenever Howie needed money. Howie needed only to ask once, and John would sign the cheque. His commitment to his home Church was only equalled by his commitment to the Foreign Mission Service. For twenty-seven years he had been head

of the African Lakes Corporation

> [he had] done yeoman service in opening up the Zambezi, the main artery
> for trade and commerce to Central Africa, together with the basins of Lakes
> Nyasa and Tanganyika. With the missionary ... [he] places side by side the
> teacher of industrialism, and it is this leaven of strong common sense which
> has made his work in these remote and distant regions so valuable.[9]

John was the peacemaker. Whenever a dispute arose among his seventeen siblings he sought to calm tempers. If Al had found it hard to forgive
the indiscretions of his brothers and sisters, John could always forgive.
He sought compromise instead of conflict, and with his quiet unassum-
ing manner he was invariably the winner.

Five and a half months after John's death, Elspeth Croudace died. Of
Alexander's extremely large family, only Mina Stewart remained.

In the midst of mourning the loss of Uncle John, Fred was worried about
John Graeme who he had been hospitalised with rheumatic fever, but
his greater fear was over the fate of James Howie. He had heard nothing for a few months and he knew the situation in Gallipoli was desperate. Then in early May he finally heard from the War Office that James
Howie had been badly injured with gunshot wounds to his right arm and
back. James Howie had been taken to a base hospital at Basra and then
after treatment had been sent to India for convalescence. At the time of
his injury he had been transferred into the pay of the Indian Army.

Fred's joy was short lived. By October James Howie was back in
Mesopotamia and was killed on 11 January 1917. The War Diary entry
for that day makes depressing reading. The battalion had been ordered
to attack, under cover of a bombardment, to a position at Kut-el-Amara
that they had lost the previous day. The Turks responded with heavy

> enfilade and frontal rifle fire and destructive enfilade shrapnel from their
> left (from the other side of the river) ... Attack reported failed, infantry re-
> turning to our front line trench. Apparently Turkish front line lightly held
> when attacking companies reached it, but their small numbers were im-

mediately strongly counter-attacked by ... Turks who bombed them out of their positions.[10]

The battle raged throughout the afternoon and the casualties were appallingly high before orders were given for the British to withdraw. The War Diary recorded that among the fatal casualties were Lieut J H F Stephen and two other ranks; five officers were reported missing, presumed killed, eight other officers and one hundred and two other ranks had been injured. As darkness fell, a search party was sent out to find the wounded and bring back the dead, but no missing officer was found.

The next day the Diary reported 'Battalion in same position as on previous night. Companies reorganised as far as possible, work of clearing up trenches and burying enemy dead etc carried on. Quiet day and night.'[11]

Another casualty of the war was Andrew's grandson George Stuart Moke Norrie. He died on the 7 October 1916, during the Battle of the Somme in Northern France. The battle lasted from July to November and cost the lives of thousands and thousands young men. George, a Second Lieutenant, died shortly before his nineteenth birthday.

Even with all the deaths that were going on around them, there were still moments of joy and expectation for a better future. In January 1916, Nancy Young married Eric Whitcombe, the New Zealander she had met on her return from her brother's wedding. The marriage took place at Park Parish Church Glasgow. [The marriage certificate gives the date as 1917, but the family say 1916]. Whitcombe was a Lieutenant in the Royal Field Artillery and had been badly wounded in the leg which caused him to limp for the rest of his life.

It was ironic that Alice's son-in-law should carry the same name as her dead son. In Eric Whitcombe she found a soul mate, and in Nancy and Eric's home, Alice found contentment and tranquillity. Alice would soon delight in the birth of Nancy and Eric's children, John Douglas, Hugh Templeton, Elizabeth Aubrey and Mary Templeton.

June 1917 saw the marriage of Alexander Stephen MacLellan to Annie, the daughter of James Tennant Caird McKinlay. They were married at Westbourne United Free Church, and once again Hubert Simpson officiated at a family wedding.

The war destroyed more than just young lives, it also destroyed the dreams and aspirations of the survivors. John Graeme had always believed that if Murray and James Howie joined their father in the Yard he would be free to follow his dream and go into the Church. He loved the sea and sailing but had no feeling for the building of commercial ships or the financial and labour relations side of the business. He would have been a reluctant shipbuilder as his Uncle Bernard had been, and as his cousin James Murray Templeton had been a reluctant carpet maker.

James Howie's death had robbed him of his dearest friend: his death had been compounded by the report that Murray was 'missing in action'. John Graeme knew that 'missing in action' was often followed by a telegram saying 'presumed dead'. If Murray's death was confirmed then he would have no option but to follow his father into the Yard.

Fortunately, John Graeme's pessimism was unfounded. Murray, a Acting Major for a Siege Battery had been captured at Le Drumez near Laventie on 9 April 1918 and taken prisoner. He later wrote in graphic detail of the incident: he was short of men, short of ammunition, yet had been ordered to hold his position for as long as he could. The Germans were advancing, but the British reinforcements were still not within reach. Murray was also highly indignant that the Portuguese who should have been holding the line were nowhere to be seen. In an Official Statement, written after the events of that disastrous day, Murray explained the action he had reluctantly taken:

> I sent out a patrol to the front of LAVENTIE for information ... [an hour later] the patrol reported Germans on the outskirts of LAVENTIE in small numbers. A few British infantry passed on their way up, saying that more were coming. I destroyed my papers, ordered rifles out [and] I posted a Lewis gun. I collected a few men of the 6th DLI [Durham Light Infantry] who were coming back without officers [and] I posted them in the orchard to my North ...[12]

It was not long before Murray and his small Battery saw the enemy were less than three hundred yards away from their position. They fought bravely; the post set up by the DLI was the first to be captured, and unfortunately they could not get a message back to Murray and his troops. They inflicted some casualties on the Germans, but their own casualties were unacceptably high. Murray and one other officer were the only ones to survive. Towards mid-afternoon, Murray recalled in the same Official Statement:

> Going down a small trench at Southern end I ran right into Germans. We both fired [and] missed. I doubled back towards my own men in the centre, intending to take them with me to blow up the guns. But at the other end of the trench I walked into another party of Germans covering me at a few feet. Being completely surrounded I surrendered.[13]

Murray spent the next seven months as a Prisoner of War. On his return home, in spite of being awarded a Military Cross for his action on the Somme, he had to face the indignity of a Court of Enquiry. The Standing Committee comprised three senior officers, Major-General Llewelyn Price-Davies, V C; Brigadier-General Charles Griffiths and Brevet-Lieut-Col Challenor. At the end of June 1919, Murray was finally informed that 'his statement regarding the circumstances of his capture by the enemy having been investigated, the Council considers that no blame attaches to him.'[14]

This rather begs the question of why there had to be a Court of Enquiry in the first place. It is intolerable to think that Murray would have been better treated if he had sacrificed the lives of his men rather than opting for Prisoner of War status. It is a very outdated belief that death in battle is honourable, surrender is dishonourable.

Murray's attitude to the war contrasted sharply with that of his cousin Walter Stuart Wingate Gray. Just three years older than Murray, Gray in a letter to his kinsman Reginald Wingate, sounded as if he regarded the war as a schoolboy's prank. He told Wingate that his brother Sandy (Alexander George) had been injured again:

> [He was] in a German communication trench when a bomb landed at his feet, which he could not dodge, and it burst, hitting in the head and ankle? The head seems a favourite spot in our family, as this is the third time he has been hit in the head and I have been hit there also on three separate occasions. However I am still one up on him in hits.[15]

In the final paragraph of Gray's letter, there was a statement that could equally have been made by his father. Father and son were so alike in their attitude to servants, workers and infantrymen:

> I am glad to say that I have got three subalterns who are gentlemen which is more fortunate than some other [Battery Commanders] nowadays. It makes a great deal of difference when one lives continually and in a confined space with them.[16]

In the *Ballad of Reading Gaol*, Oscar Wilde wrote: 'And all Men kill the thing they Love'. It was a sentiment that JS could well have echoed. He died just six days before his eighty-sixth birthday on 8 October 1918 and just one month and three days before the end of the Great War. He had achieved all that a man could have achieved in his life but he had suffered many tragedies. He lamented once that he had been married three times but had only enjoyed six years and one month of marriage. His long periods of widowerhood had been marred, too, by the death of his second daughter Mary, of Emily's still-born child, and of the death of James Murray.

The war years had robbed him of his grandson Eric and of four nephews. It was only Alice and Charry that gave him a measure of happiness.

He had been a good man, a caring employer and a considerate philanthropist, yet, he was highly critical of his own endeavours. It is worth repeating J S's opinion of his own character:

> Weak always, devious and deflected often ... By the Grace of God I have been helped to do a fair amount of good, and I have been enabled to escape very much evil. It has sustained me in temptation. It explains how I have never murmured nor repined under most severe domestic losses. It enables me to say that during my long career as a master and employer of labour I have never once (so far as I know) said an insulting word to a servant or workman. Nor (again so far as I know) have I ever defrauded any man by untruthful representation or otherwise. I have kept faith with women and have never been guilty of abuse of any.[17]

JS was too hard on himself. When Rosamond Dale Owen returned to Britain at the beginning of the Great War, she approached him, pleading poverty. He could have turned a deaf ear but with his usual generosity he made her a yearly allowance for as long as she should live. His only condition was that she should return to him James Murray's painting of *Christ in the Garden*.

His benefactions to the Glasgow Hospitals were his true Memorial, and perhaps the final word on this complex and unusual man, should be left to James Murray. In a letter written in May 1887, while he was in Paris, he wrote:

> I hope, dear Father, that we shall have a pleasant quiet summer together. Being past redemption, perhaps you will accept your fate of having a son so full of "nonsensical fads", and make the most of what of good there is left in him. Believe me <u>there is some</u>, and I shall hope to share it with you ere long. That I am at any rate, always grateful for having so indulgent and forbearing a "governor" is sure -- and I remain otherwise ever your loving son.[18]

Anglo-American Yachting

From the very beginning of his association with Templetons, FHY's concern was for the welfare of the workers, in particular the young female workers. It was something he did for the fifty years that he was at the factory. In a 1920 article for the house magazine, FHY made special reference to the new overalls worn by the girls which gave them an air of superiority:

> Are we mistaken in imaging that since they [the overalls] were introduced a good deal more "swank" is noticeable among our girls? Certain it is that they look well in their new garments, and it is a great help to be able to go home at dinner time and in the evening in clothes which have been protected from oil and dust ...[1]

In an enlightened attitude which many current industrial and commercial concerns could copy, FHY went on:

> We spend a great part of our lives inside the walls of the Factories, and these working hours should be as bright and as happy as possible. Any suggestions which anyone can make for improving our environment will be welcome and carefully considered. And let us never forget that most important element in our environment -- an atmosphere of cheerful goodwill and helpfulness amongst us which will always add enormously to the happiness of all.[2]

However, FHY's interests were not shared by every member of his extended family. Alexander Stephen MacLellan had a very different opinion of the value of welfare. He outlined his objections:

> There are some strange conceptions of what 'welfare' means: at present it seems to me that the working man looks upon it as a means of getting something more out of his employer in the way of extra pocket-money. In my opinion, if I may be allowed to express it, true 'welfare' aims at a better standard of living by which a healthier outlook of life, physically, mentally and morally is meant ... I maintain that we are all working in the wrong way as far as this Welfare work is concerned.[3]

216

MacLellan's views were diametrically opposite to those of FHY. James Murray was advocating a more socialist approach by the employer to his employees as early as the 1880s.

Charry Templeton had refused to comply with her father's wish that she marry the Revd Hubert L Simpson. Three years after JS's death she did marry and her choice of husband would probably have pleased her father. She married William Newlands Sloan, the son of George Sloan and Elizabeth Ann Newlands, in the Roseneath Parish Church on 18 May 1921.

Sloan was an interesting choice for Charry, four years her junior he was the third of George and Elizabeth's eleven children. The Sloan's had been ship owners since the beginning of the nineteenth century. George's grandfather William, an Ayrshire born man, had been told by his father, who was the main contractor for building canals in Scotland, that he should go out and buy wee ships for his canal. William, a dutiful son, did just that and the Sloan's became ship owners of some note.

In July 1803 William had married Sarah Tennant, from Ochiltree, Ayrshire. Descendants of the Tennant line became major chemical manufacturers, industrialists and politicians. Margot Asquith, the daughter of Sir Charles Tennant, could trace her ancestry back to Sarah Tennant.

Charry and William had two sons, Michael James Templeton born in 1925, and George Christopher born in 1928. JS would have been disappointed that neither of Charry's sons would become carpet manufacturers. The management of the business was left to Alice's son Arthur and his son Alastair.

Five days after Charry's wedding, Dan Young died at Overtoun, his home in Dunbartonshire. He was fifty-nine, but had been in poor health for a number of years. His father had died of heart disease and Dan was prone to the same condition.

Dan had learned many things from his father-in-law, not least the need to be tolerant in his dealings with Templeton workers:

On [one] occasion, a foreman was having considerable trouble with a man who wasn't fond of hard work. He refused to do certain work, which he considered outside his province, and Mr Young settled the matter by asking him to stand and do nothing while he did the job himself with little assistance. The man ... felt very sheepish and there was no further trouble .[4]

Dan was ambitious, he believed that if the company made good profits they should plough a sizable portion of those profits back into the business. He neither sought great wealth for its own sake, nor did he seek great honours, yet he achieved both. He was appointed Deputy Lieutenant for Glasgow and Justice of the Peace and was awarded a CBE for his charitable services.

In 1919, he and Alice left Crutherland, their home in East Kilbride, for Overtoun.

Dan had one ambition that was not realized. He was selected as Prospective Unionist candidate for Dunbartonshire and he had a real chance of being elected in the November 1919 General Election. That was, until it was pointed out, to his Constituency officials, that as he had accepted Government contracts during the Great War he was accordingly debarred from standing. It was a great disappointment for him but he accepted the decision with his usual magnanimity.

Shortly after Dan's death, Alice left Overtoun for Freston Lodge in Sevenoaks; Nancy and Eric Whitcombe had purchased Woodside there, and Alice moved to be close to them. There was little to keep her in Scotland now that Charry had married, and for the first time since Charry's birth Alice no longer felt responsible for her step-sister. Scotland held too many unhappy memories for her; in the space of five years she had been robbed of the three mainstays of her life: the death of her father and of Eric and Dan. Only Arthur and Nancy remained to give her any comfort.

Dan's death was not the only sadness to affect the family that year. Mary Wingate Gray died at Nunraw on 16 August, of breast and secondary cancer. She had just celebrated her sixty-third birthday. She was the second of Al and Mary's children to die. Bernard, had died on 28 March 1919, at Craighouse, Edinburgh, of heart disease. He was forty-nine years old and unmarried. He had continued to live with Fred at Park Terrace since the death of his parents. He had been unable to compete with Fred and Alex, and there is the feeling that he died from a broken heart rather than from a diseased heart.

Alex registered Bernard's death, but had not been with him when he died. Mary's death was very different, she died at Nunraw and her husband was with her when she passed away.

There is no telling whether her marriage to Walter had been a success. He was, as far as the family were concerned, reckless with money, and his frequent requests to Fred and Alex for financial help strained their relationship.

Walter's own contribution to the family's budget was never sufficient. He rarely had paid employment, believing that as a country gentleman and the landowner of Nunraw, he enjoyed a certain status. He took part in local politics but his role was very much that of a Laird; he hosted many shooting parties and lavishly entertained his guests.

On the other hand, Mary was not content just to play the role of mistress of Nunraw, even motherhood left her with time to fulfil her own desires. In 1883, before the disaster at the launch of the *Daphne*, she had been planning on going to India as a Missionary. If marriage had prevented her from going to India it did not prevent her from continuing to work for the Foreign Mission Service. She had, after all 'belonged to a family which included ... some of the most ardent and generous supporters [of Church Missionary work]...'[5]

For many years Mary was President of the Haddington Branch of the Womens' Foreign Missionary Association, and it was through her good offices that they were able to support a missionary of their own. She was frequently asked to address meetings, rarely was a request refused:

> The addresses she gave at such gatherings were always the result of careful preparation, and no one could listen to her without being impressed with the strength of her convictions, and the wholeheartedness of her interest in the cause for which she pleaded.[6]

To an interested listener the conversations between Mary and her Aunt Mina Stewart would have been fascinating. They would have been able to exchanged ideas and beliefs, one from the standpoint of having seen Missionary work at first hand, and the other from the comfort of Nunraw. In 1920, Mary was elected President of the Womens' Foreign Missionary Association; she took the chair at the General Assembly when they discussed the role of women in Missionary work. As with all she did, Mary

> had a graciousness of bearing and a dignity of presence which fitted
> her eminently ... she discharged [her duties] in a way that won her gen-
> eral admiration.[7]

But in helping the Church and the Missionary Service, Mary did not neglect the young people of Garvald. For many years she was involved with the Mothers' Union and the Girls' Friendly Society.

Mary was able to seek relaxation by maintaining close links with her family. She and Walter were frequent visitors to Kelly. Fred, Alex, Maud and George MacLellan and their families, Bernard and Elsie were also able to enjoy Mary's hospitality. Mary's elder son, Walter Stuart, married in 1915, Rose Beatrix Adam. The couple's first child, Mary's first grandchild, was born the following year thus adding to Mary's sense of the family continuing for at least the foreseeable future.

Mary Wingate Gray's death was followed a few months later by the death of James Templeton. He died on 21 November 1921, at his Dunblane home, Holme-Hill, after an illness lasting eighteen months. He was in his eighty-fourth year. Unlike his brothers, JS and Revd Archie, James never sought the limelight. He had a somewhat retiring disposition. At Templetons he had been largely responsible for the financial management of the Company. He saw his role as that of a benevolent uncle, a role he played to perfection. One duty had always been important to him and that was ensuring the wellbeing of his two unmarried sisters, Anne and Agnes:

[James] did not take a prominent part in public affairs, but was keenly interested in a number of religious and benevolent institutions in Glasgow, and of these organisations he was a liberal and unostentatious benefactor.[8]

In his will, he left substantial bequests to all his nieces and nephews, both Templeton and Stephen, and he left a sizable bequest to the Revd Archie and his wife Elizabeth Helen Aitken. He was equally generous to the children of Patrick Reid. To James Heriot Templeton of Drumgarve, his second cousin, he does not cancel the loan he gave him but does leave him enough money to continue to repay as they had agreed earlier. He also remembered his cousin Elizabeth Mary, who had lived with him and his parents when she was a teenager.

He left another donation to the Templeton Benevolent Fund and continued in the same manner by including donations to the Home Mission and Foreign Mission Funds of the United Free Church. His donations to the Royal Hospital for Sick Children, and the Glasgow Mission to the Blind showed that even in old age his interests in children and the disadvantaged remained undiminished.

It has been said that Victorian employees, especially those who worked in the house or garden, were frequently neglected by their masters. Nothing could be further from the truth in James's life. In 1891 he was employing two servants, Margaret Martin and Catherine MacLellan, they were still with him in 1921. He remembered in his will Mary and Agnes, the daughters of his coachman John Archibald, and Archibald's son Robert, who took over as chauffeur when the horse gave way to the motor car. The Archibald family had worked for the Templeton family -- father and son -- for more than half a century.

There were many who would mourn the passing of James Templeton. He had been a good man and a man who cared about the welfare and happiness of those less fortunate than himself. He neither sought nor wished for monuments to be erected to his memory, yet the monuments do exist. His name is on the plaque in the entrance hall to the administration block at the Glasgow Royal Infirmary. He would not recognise the hospital now, such has been its expansion, but for those who stop and read the inscription on the plaque they may wonder what manner of man was James Templeton.

In the spring of 1922, the horrors of the Great War could be forgotten. Murray Stephen married on 27 April, the twenty-three-year-old Kathrene Paton Mitchell, elder daughter of Alexander Moncrieff Mitchell, a Writer, and Bessie Craig Boyd. Officiating at the service was Donald Fraser, of Livingstonia, Moderator-elect of the United Free Church of Scotland.

The couple's wedding present from the foremen, staff and officials at Linthouse was an oak bookcase. The gift from the employees at the Yard was surely an indication that nothing had changed in the relationship between the family and their workers since Maud's wedding back in 1882. Indeed, in commenting on Murray's letter of thanks, the Editor of the House magazine said it 'truly reflects the spirit existing between both sides of the house at Linthouse.'[9]

One member of staff could not resist the temptation of sending a telegram to the happy couple, reminding them of their seafaring connections: 'Heartiest congratulations on successful launch -- with trim correct and stability ample, co-efficient of happiness will be maintained at maximum throughout voyage.'[10]

The sender of the telegram was right, the marriage lasted over fifty years, producing two sons, James Frederick and Alexander Moncrieff Mitchell, and one daughter Elizabeth Murray. This ensured that at least old Alexander's lineage would continue for another generation.

The end of the Great War had brought a desire in the Stephen family to resume sailing, and in particular to return to competitive racing. In 1921, an agreement was reached between the British and the American yachtsmen for a new class of six-metre racing. Four yachts from each country would be selected to race and the event would be held annually, with the races being held in alternative years in each country. There would be six team races, three windward and return races and three triangular races. Points would be awarded according to the finishing order. At the completion of the six races, the best boat from each country would race against each other for the Seawanhaka Cup.

The Seawanhaka Corinthian Club had, since its inception in 1871, transformed the concept of yacht racing. They believed in the true spirit of the Corinthians that all those taking part in the sport should be amateurs, maintaining and crewing their own boats. It was not a concept that appealed to all. At the time it was said that no gentleman would scrape, paint and rig his boat when he could pay a servant to do it.

The first International Races, at Cowes in 1921, surprised the American crews. They were shocked that after four long exhausting years of war the British boats and their crews could take on the might of the Americans and beat them. They admitted somewhat reluctantly that the British boats were of a superior design to their own.

The success of the 1921 Cowes races was the spur that Fred needed to set about designing and building a replacement for *Coila II*. The Americans had agreed that if a challenge was made by the British to race in America, they could do so under their own measurement rules.

If *Coila II* had been a successful racing yacht, then her replacement would be even more graceful, elegant and fast. She was launched at Linthouse in May 1922 and by happy coincidence she was the five hundredth ship to be launched since Alexander had started to build at Kelvinhaugh. Sea trials began in the Clyde, but it was at Cowes that the hard work began, as she raced against other yachts for the right to challenge for a place in the British team.

It was not only the Americans who were surprised by the ability of *Coila III* and by the agility of her young helmsman. Fred had originally planned to handle the yacht himself, but shortly before the trials began, he fell badly, puncturing his lung. The decision to allow John Graeme to take the helm would have been the right decision even without his injuries: Fred's next birthday would be his sixtieth. Murray would crew for his brother.

The trials successfully completed. The yachts selected were: *Reg* owned by Norman Clark-Neill, with Captain R T Dixon as helmsman, *Jean* owned by Sir John Ward with Sir Ralph Gore as helmsman, *Caryl* owned and skippered by Frank Robertson, and *Coila III* owned by Fred but skippered by John Graeme. Gore was an interesting character. Ralph St George Claude Gore, 10th Baronet was born in Ireland in 1877 and as an Irish nobleman he did not take kindly to being out-sailed by the son of a Clydeside shipbuilder.

Caryl had been a late replacement when Nicholson withdrew his yacht, *Rose*:

> The exclusion of *Rose* from the British team is a matter for regret, especially in view of the fact that, apart from her, only one boat, *Reg,* has been designed with a view to racing in American waters.

The yachting fraternity may have regretted *Rose's* exclusion but for John Graeme it was a matter of great delight. He and Frank Robertson were old friends and had raced against each other on many occasions. It is also worth noting that with the exception of *Jean,* the other three yachts had been designed and built on the Clyde. *Caryl* and *Reg* were the work of William Fife of Fairlie, probably the only yacht designer that could match a Stephen yacht for quality.

Agnes Maude accompanied her brothers to New York so that she could be there to cheer when they reached the finishing line. She had just come down from Girton College, Cambridge, after taking a degree in economics. She had gone up to Girton in 1918, the first female member of the Stephen's family to achieve that distinction.

The yachts, their crews and their supporters, arrived in New York on 26 August. Racing began on 6 September.

The American yachts were *Grebe, Clytie, Lea* and *L'Esprit;* the first race did not go well for the British team, *Lea* finished first, with the other American boats taking the next three places. *Jean* was the first of the British boats to finish. A small matter of National pride arose that night when the three Scottish owned, built, and crewed boats were described as English. It was a mistake not repeated in subsequent reporting: they were either British or Great Britain.

Next day, although *Lea* again won, the British yachts made a much better showing and their points score was somewhat healthier. Things then began to improve for the British boats. The third and fourth windward races were won by *Jean* and *Reg* and John Graeme and *Coila III* were able to add to the delight of British crews by winning the fourth and sixth triangular races. The final points tally was one hundred and eleven to the Americans and one hundred and four to the British team, a very credible performance, and doubly so for John Graeme who personally had an aggregate score of thirty-five out of a possible forty-eight points. He was chosen to race *Lea* for the Seawanhaka Cup.

Of the five heats, John Graeme and *Coila III* won three of them and with it the Cup, a remarkable achievement for a young man and a new boat, and one that he would be happy to defend when the Americans came to Scotland a year later.

The third, and last of the Templeton brothers, to die was the Revd Dr Archie. He died at his country home at Crookfur, Newton Mearns, on 24 June 1923. He, Elizabeth, and their family had also maintained a Glasgow house at 7 Bute Gardens. The Revd Archie was six months short of his eightieth birthday, he had resigned from the Indian Missionary Service in the late 1870s on health grounds but then his health improved rapidly when he was back in his native Scotland. He had enjoyed years of service with the Glasgow Medical Missionary Society and the Oxford Street Dispensary, his dedicated service to the poor of Glasgow never faltering.

Elizabeth's early years had been shrouded in some mystery but her marriage to the Revd Archie brought her happiness and contentment. It had also helped her to ease the lives of her sister, Jane and brother, George William. Her brother Hugh though equally well treated was subject to the restriction that his creditors did not have access to his inheritance. What a tangled web is woven when a man writes his will?

The Revd Archie had lived just long enough to see the marriage of his eldest daughter, Dorothy Grace, to Edward Taylor Wright in December 1922. Edward was the eldest son of Edward Wright and Anne Elizabeth Taylor; around 1900/1 Edward Wright and his family left Ireland for Glasgow. In the 1901 census they were living at Huntley Terrace, Shettleton, and Wright gave his occupation as Registered Practitioner as Medical Missionary. He had joined the the Glasgow Medical Mission and was one of the signatories on the retirement appreciation given to the Revd Archie.

Shortly before her marriage to Edward Taylor Wright, Dorothy journeyed to Australia, Tasmania and New Zealand with her brother

Anthony. On their return to Scotland they wrote a fascinating account of their journey that was later printed in the Templeton house magazine. Dorothy never mentioned any privations that she endured, she was an extremely fit young woman and an experienced climber.

In Hobart, Anthony and Dorothy had heard that the highest mountain on the island was called Ben Lomond, and so they made immediate plans to climb it. A journey by car and train took them to Storey's Creek, a small village, 2,500 feet up the mountain where Anthony described their arrival at the village. It was the home and working place of the tin and wolfram [tungsten] miners. He noted with glee that the manager was a Scotsman and was amused by the sheer number of Scottish settlers they had met on their travels:

> Arriving late at night we found the small boarding house already full ...
> At first we were told that we could not be accommodated; a startling an-
> nouncement, since the boarding house was the only one. However, our
> driver spoke up for us and said in a loud voice that we were travellers all
> the way from Scotland ... especially to climb Ben Lomond! Our hostess was
> duly impressed, but we think that it was more through pity that we were
> eventually taken in.[12]

The next day they duly climbed Ben Lomond. The view from the sum-
mit was spectacular. They were rather disappointed though that they never saw any kangaroos, only kangaroo tracks in the snow. Although Anthony and Dorothy said they were disappointed not to see any kan-
groos, it is highly unlikely the animals would have ventured onto the snowy slopes of Ben Lomond. The two visitors were, however, capti-
vated with everything they did see:

> [These] wonderful islands laid hold upon our affections, but, if any one
> wishes to visit one of the most delectable counties on earth, let him go
> there to be awed by the eerie wonders of Rolana and the nightmare of Wai-
> raki, to be enchanted by the beauties of the Wanganin River, down which
> we sailed for three days, to see Scotland over again in a different setting and
> under less cloudy skies, as we did in Dunedin.[13]

The holidays over, Dorothy and Anthony were forced to return to the realities of Glasgow: poverty, unemployment, trade union agitation and riots. These were what most people endured day after day.

Since he left the army in January 1919, John Graeme had not returned to his studies at Pembroke College, spending most of his nine months in the Yard's drawing office and only during the winter of 1919/20 was he able to continue his studies at Glasgow University. In the summer months he served as an apprentice plater with Ailsa Shipbuilders in Troon. His great-grandfather had insisted that his sons, if they were to follow him into the shipbuilding business, should have some knowledge of what it was like to work on the shop floor.

While at Ailsa, John Graeme had the dubious experience of being called out on strike, surely a unique experience for the boss's son. John Graeme's working life was further complicated in 1921 when the miners went on a long and bitter strike. A war that was supposed to have been fought to achieve a land fit for heroes saw only unemployment increase and wages slashed. Torn between duty to his family and loyalty to his fellow workers, John Graeme left Glasgow and spent three months at Leith helping with the work of distributing the meagre ration of coal to households.

But if his working life was fraught with difficulties, when the first signs of summer appeared, he was able to look forward to resuming his sailing interests. He challenged the Americans again for the International and Seawanhaka Cups. The six-metre races were sailed in mid August, the British team comprising *Coila III*, *Reg* the helmsman being Sir Ralph Gore, *Suzette* and *Capelle*. The American boats were *Hawk*, *Clytie*, *Ingomar* and *Lea*.

There was a delightful story, frequently repeated by the Stephen family, that at the end of a day's racing, John Graeme, seated in a cubical of the lavatory at Cowes, heard footsteps outside. A voice he could not identify asked:

"What are you going to do tomorrow?"

"Beat that damn Scot," replied the booming voice of Sir Ralph Gore.

Gore may have wanted to beat John Graeme but a study of the results of the races showed that the 'damn Scot' headed the points table
with Gore in second place. Indeed, the British team occupied the first
three places and sixth, thereby winning the series by 129 points to 86.

The boats then transferred to the Clyde for the Seawanhaka Cup
races. *Coila III* and *Lea* challenged each other once more. *Coila III* won
the first race, *Lea* the second, *Coila III* the third race. The fourth was declared void. John Graeme secured the fifth race and with it the Seawanhaka Cup for the second time.

The 1923 season was especially rewarding for Fred, John Graeme
and *Coila III*. After retaining the Seawanhaka Cup they competed for the
Evelyn S Parker Cup. The other three Scottish boats were Frank Robertson's *Caryl*, George Paisley's *Aracia* and Howden Hume's *Folly*. The four
American boats were *Hawk*, *Clytie*, *Ingomar* and *Lea*:

> The matches were to be sailed on a plan in general used among model
> yacht clubs but novel as regards yacht racing. Each boat in the team was to
> sail a match against one of the opposing team on each of four days, making
> sixteen matches in all.'4

At the end of the first day's racing the Scottish team were all square, but
by day two they had increased their lead by four points. From then on
the result was never in doubt and the Parker Cup was awarded to the
Scottish Team. For Fred and John Graeme it was a fitting end to what
had been a very successful season. They also had the pleasure of knowing that they had twice beaten Evelyn Parker's *Flya* during the Royal
Corinthian Yacht Club races from Hunter's Quay to Tarbert and back.

PART FIVE
1924 - 1950

'This suffering which I perceive to be perhaps the great good in the world in that without it man's perfect excellence would never be arrived at [and] from man's soul may never purified out of which is born the poet's song.'

The Diary of James Murray Templeton
Columbia University, in the City of New York,
Rare Book and Manuscript Library.
Thomas Lake Harris Papers.

Not the Best of Times

THE 1920s were a time of economic, political and social unrest. The Great War had been fought not just against a foreign enemy but also against the inequalities between the old aristocracy, the manufacturing elite and the workers. In the 1922 and 1923 General Elections, the Conservative Party tried to form a Government but their problems intensified to such an extent that the Prime Minister, Stanley Baldwin, finally resigned. A third election so shortly after the last two did however produced a workable result. Ramsay MacDonald was asked to form a Government with the assistance of the Liberal Party. This was the first time in the history of British politics that the Labour Party was invited to form an Administration.

Expectations by industrial workers were high, never more so than on the Clyde. The men of Clydeside believed all their prayers had been answered; MacDonald's Government confirmed this when one of their first acts was to recognize the newly formed Union of Soviet Socialist Republics. Red Clydeside prepared for a truly Communist Government in Britain. How quickly their dreams were shattered. In October yet another General Election was held, the Conservatives winning a landslide victory and Baldwin returned to Downing Street.

Shipbuilding on the Clyde now entered a period of real decline; Stephens', in keeping with the traditions laid down by old Alexander accepted the downturn with fortitude. They had prospered during the Great War, now they used some of their reserves to improve facilities at Linthouse for the Yard and its wokers. In 1920, the Company had bought twelve acres of land near Linthouse to build a playing field and recreational ground. They built a pavilion and a house for the head green-keeper, and it seemed only appropriate that the park should be named *Coila*.

Even in the midst of economic and social decline, there were moments of joy and relaxation for the Stephen family. In 1924 a challenge came from the Norwegians to compete for the Seawanhaka Cup; the races were held off Rothesay in late August. Fred, on home waters, decided that he was going to be the helmsman of *Coila III*.

> A challenge for the Seawanhaka Cup having been sent to the Royal Northern Yacht Club by the Norwegian Royal Club and accepted, the first of the series of races took place yesterday [28 August] at Rothesay. ... The challenger is the six-metre racer *Unni*, owned by Mr W S Skougaard and designed by Mr Hohan Anker, the defending yacht is *Coila III*, designed, owned and sailed by Mr F J Stephen.[1]

Coila III duly won the first and second races, and in the subsequent four races she and her gallant skipper gained enough victories to see off the Viking raiders.

There was little activity at Linthouse in 1925, only one ship was launched that year. Alex and Fred were nominally in charge of the Yard but they were leaving more of the day-to-day running to Murray and John Graeme. Alexander Stephen MacLellan had also been appointed to the board of directors.

Alex had always been a reluctant shipbuilder and was spending more time at Crosbie Tower, his home in Troon. Crosbie Tower overlooked the beautiful Royal Troon Golf course but Alex preferred to play at Prestwick; he was appointed captain in 1928. There was a certain snobbery in being a member at Prestwick, it was then, as now, the premier club in Ayrshire.

With the day-to-day running of the Yard left to his sons, Fred had more time for leisure. In 1925 he was elected Commodore of the Royal Northern Yacht Club, having been Vice-Commodore for many years. He also held the post of Vice-Admiral of the Mudhook Yacht Club, he was also a member of other Clyde clubs, including Largs, and he served as a member of the Yacht Racing Association. His diary of racing commitments during the season meant that he rarely had a free weekend.

John Graeme was a member and a Steward of the Royal Northern.

Fred's close friend, Evelyn S Parker, was Rear-Admiral. As the premier yacht club, its membership was a *Who's Who* of the business elite of south west Scotland. The Allan family were well represented, as were the Coats, the thread manufactures; George Sloan and Arthur Young, and John and Frank Robertson. All had raced with Fred and John Graeme for many seasons. The club members decided that Fred should be given a replica of the Seawanhaka Cup, to be a permanent reminder of *Coila III*'s achievements. The cup when duly presented contained a simple inscription together with a list of the thirty subscribers.

This award was made in 1925, although that year *Coila III* had fought gallantly to retain the Cup she was beaten as much by the weather as by the challenger *Lanai*. The races were held off Rothesay, the first race taking place on Saturday 11 July. *Coila,* a heavy water boat, was successful. By Monday the weather was decidedly docile:

> Owing to calms, the Commodore in charge hoisted the postpone signal no fewer than five times, and it was a quarter to three before the boats were sent away. By this time, the breeze was pretty general over the Clyde ... *Coila* put about on the weather bow of the challenger five minutes after the gun, but on the second tack the American worked through her opponent's lee and led to the weather mark at Kerrycroy by a minute. In reaching the defender [*Coila*] pulled in Lanai's lead, and was only twelve seconds astern at the end of the round ...[2]

The third race was held on the Tuesday, the fourth the next day, by which time *Lanai* had scored three victories to *Coila*'s one, and the Cup returned to America. *Coila* may have lost the Seawanhaka Cup, but during the Clyde Fortnight she more than proved that with the right weather conditions she was a match for any six-metre yacht sailing that summer.

As long ago as 1875 the relationships between the Glasgow and Dundee branches of the Stephen family were never close. The differences that occurred between Al and William at the time of the latter's second marriage to Elizabeth Henderson only increased the tensions. The sale of the shipyard after William's death, in 1893, did nothing to heal the

rift. Andrew, William's eldest son, was not interested in shipbuilding although like a dutiful son he served his apprenticeship at the Dundee
Yard. He was always more interested in farming and he spent much of
his time at Woodwraw, the farm of his Henderson grandparents. When
he died on 10 October 1921 his occupation was given as Farmer (Master). He never married.

Andrew's younger brother -- by their father's first marriage -- Frederick Somerville, also served his time in the Yard. But on the death of
his father, he took over the ownership of the Arctic Tannery Company.
With the decline of the whaling industry the business was forced to di-
versify, but it still provided Frederick Somerville and his family with a
comfortable living.

In 1904, Frederick Somerville had married Grace Mabel Billing, the
daughter of Arthur Billing, a paper manufacturer and Emma Hughes.
Between 1905 and 1921 the couple had five children, three boys and two
girls. Of the three boys, Ronald William became an Chartered Accountant, Frederick Arthur, a Lieutenant Colonel in the Cameronians; Alexander Murray, the youngest also joined the Cameronians, and later became
Deputy Governor of the Tower of London.

Frederick Somerville, in the interests of business, was a frequent
traveller. In the fourteen years between 1910 and 1924 he crossed the
Atlantic to New York at least seven times -- three journeys being made
during the Great War. Only JS could have claimed to have exceeded
Frederick's number of Atlantic crossings: JS made the journey nineteen
times. Frederick Somerville, in his younger days, was a member of the
Tay Division of the Submarine Mariners becoming its Commanding
Officer. He died suddenly on 21 February 1926, at the age of fifty-seven.
Six years before his death he had moved his family into Scotscraig, and
although not a wealthy man he left enough for Grace to care for her
family. Marriage had obviously dented Frederick's financial resources, his
bachelor brother, Andrew, left three times more.

Massie Stephen, the widow of Samuel, died on 28 April 1926 in Aberdeen; she was seventy-two-years-old and had been a widow for fifty-four

years. Her life had mirrored that of her sister-in-law, Hannah Adams, in that both were widowed after only a few months of marriage, and both had to bring up a child without the financial and emotional support of a husband or the wider Stephen family. Uncle John, though, with his usual generosity, left a substantial bequest to Massie's daughter, Mabel.

Alexander Adams and Mabel Stephen had been reared in an atmosphere of love and they returned that love with abundance. After qualifying as a doctor, and after his marriage, Adams always provided a home for his mother. Mabel Stephen followed her cousin's lead. In June 1909 she had married George Davidson, a medical practitioner, eleven years her senior. Davidson was the widower of Joanna Ferguson, by whom he had one daughter, Mary Birnie Ferguson born in 1891. She was given the name of his mother. George's father was a Church of Scotland minister at Logie, Coldstone, where George had been born in August 1863.

George and Mabel had one daughter born in 1910 and baptised in the name of her grandmother, Euphemina Mary Marsley Baxter Davidson.

The passage of time had healed many scars, but surely the wounds inflicted during the General Strike of 1926, and the protracted Miners Strike, which lasted from 1 May until 27 November, would never heal. The Stephen family, torn between the demands of maintaining a viable and profitable business and meeting the demands of an increasingly militant workforce, were in a no-win situation. The younger female members of the family helped to run soup kitchens in Glasgow; in 1923 Agnes Maude had studied for a diploma in Social Work and she put that training to good use. John Graeme went to Edinburgh to drive trucks used for ferrying people around.

The contrast between the plight of the working class and the landed elite can perhaps be no better illustrated than by highlighting that in 1926 Kenneth Clark (later Lord Clark) commissioned Stephen to build *Mingary*, a luxury 222-gross tonnage motor yacht. She was fitted out with every conceivable luxury and launched in June.

❖❖❖

During the black days of the 1920s, Templeton factories, under the benevolent eye of FHY, were also spending money to improve facilities for their workforce, once the terrible depression came to an end. In July 1925, they proudly announced:

> There are six new houses in the course of construction at the City of Templetonville, bringing the total now to 34 houses, while the population there is steadily increasing some low wag has been referring to the district as 'Bairnside' ... By the way all infants thus far have been girls.[3]

It would be too fanciful to suggest that FHY had had a word with the Almighty -- Templetons were always recruiting young women -- and the birth of so many female babies brought a twinkle to his eye. FHY had a wry sense of humour; he observed once, that a man should serve his time at every trade save censure. Critics, he declared, were born not made.

FHY was more than willing to accept change as inevitable, and while he may have mourned the loss of beautiful old buildings, he knew that in a modern industrial world things had to change:

> If a Bridgeton man were to return to his native city after an absence of 7 years, he would fail to recognise many of our buildings. If, for example, he walked down Tullis Street ... he would miss the decrepit old building with its dreary workshops and still drearier billiard saloon, which used to stand to the south-west of the school. Chimney stalks, the pond and the mysterious underground caverns which lay behind the old building are also things of the past and the whole area is partly covered by new buildings, partly by old ones completely modernized, which are bright and busy in the manufacture of carpets.[4]

For the first time since the death of James Templeton there was another Templeton on the workforce. Kenneth, the fifth child of Revd Archie Templeton and Elizabeth Aitken, joined as an engineer. His brother Archie had spent three months with the firm before being sent to Gallipoli, never to return. Kenneth, unlike his brothers, had been educated at Fettes College, not Merchiston Castle, which he had left in December 1917. He graduated in Engineering.

There is a true story, told by a retired Templeton worker, which reinforces the social and cultural gulf that existed between the Templeton family and the factory workers. Returning to work one Monday morning, a younger member of the Templeton family asked a group of factory girls what they had done over the weekend. They told him that they had been dancing at Barrowland and then gone to the café; one inquisitive girl asked: 'And what did you do?' The reply, when it came, showed the gulf between the bosses and the workers more clearly than he would have realised. 'Oh I hired a plane and flew to Kintyre for a round of golf.'

This gulf would never be bridged, but Kenneth was less aware of the social divide which existed. It was said of Kenneth that

> he could never have been content to bask in the reflected glory of his bril-
> liant grandfather. He created ... a career as colourful as any in his time ...
> [He] directed his inventive engineering abilities to the problems of Wilton
> manufacture to become one of the acknowledged experts in the field. There
> were many developments in Wilton of which he was the innovator ... The
> ideas which flowed from that time would be too numerous to list but the
> creation of Templex was perhaps the most important.[5]

Kenneth was a kindly, thoughtful man, much given to shyness, he loathed the limelight and did all in his power to avoid being the centre of attention. He was a typical boffin, with his head in the clouds as he worked on his latest invention. Later, those who worked with him spoke of him with genuine respect and admiration.

There is a delightful story, told by Kenneth himself, which best illustrates what a gentle, charming man he must have been. He had wanted to go to a Trade Fair in Leipzig because there was 'a special machine made in Eastern Germany about which I had had difficulty in getting any information and going to the fair seemed the only way'.[6]

Travel to Eastern Germany was not without complications, but having been given authority by the Templeton directors, Kenneth set about making hurried travel arrangements. The day of his travel was further hindered as he was expected to attend a wedding. He also found to his consternation that his passport was out of date 'but the passport people kindly opened their office specially on a Saturday morning to renew it for me.'[7] Kenneth, however, was not so pleased when he found the infor-

mation that the passport people had given him about money and visas
was wrong.

Eventually, after a somewhat tortuous journey Kenneth arrived in
Berlin, and had a spy-like interview with the guards at 'Checkpoint Char-
lie'. He was sent across the barrier to speak to the Soviet-style guards
about arranging a flight to Leipzig. His limited German hampered matters, but finally he could return to his hotel room happy in the knowledge that next day he could fly there:

> I had an early dinner and went to bed to find an amazing absurd touch of
> American high powered hotel service. On my bedside table was a good-
> night sweetie. (No! No! No! it was not what you are thinking at all, but just
> a chocolate wrapped in silver paper.) I giggled myself to sleep.[8]

The next morning he left the hotel and found to his delight that the taxi
he had ordered the night before contained another passenger, a French-
man also going to the Trade Fair.

He was a more experienced traveller to Eastern Germany than Kenneth, which was useful for Kenneth, finding to his embarrassment that
West German money was not accepted in the East and *vis-a-vis*.

The Fair was both a disappointment and a pleasure for Kenneth; he
was not amused by the Polish and Czech propaganda, but on arrival
at the Textile Section he was pleased to find there the machine he had
travelled so far to see. 'The people on the stand were helpful and co-
operative and I soon got the information I required.'[9]

Kenneth's return journey to England was not without a mishap,
he woke in his small Pension, thought the clock on his bedside said 6
o'clock, hurriedly dressed, left his room keys on the front desk, rushed to
the nearby train station, but then missed his train. Realizing that the next
train would not leave for another two hours, he looked for somewhere
to have an early breakfast. It was only when the police began to take an
interest in him that he looked at the station clock and realized he was not
late for his train, but five hours too early. He crept back to his Pension:
'I decided to waken up my nice little pension proprietor and get back to
bed. However, I managed with my knife to open the door and creep back
to bed without wakening anyone.'[10]

The success of the international races for six-metre yachts encouraged the development of the eight-metre class. Fred, always in the vanguard of new thinking, immediately set about designing a yacht that would race under his flag. *Coila IV* was launched in May 1927 and made her debut during the Clyde Fortnight. Unfortunately for Fred, the pleasure of sailing and racing *Coila IV* was short-lived. He was now rapidly approaching his sixty-fifth birthday, and his health, which had never been robust, was failing. His doctors ordered him to retire from racing, and so with reluctance he handed *Coila* over to John Graeme.

He may have been ordered to stop racing, but he had no intention of relinquishing his position of Commodore of the Royal Northern and Vice-Admiral of Mudhook. It was fortuitous that at the very moment when he must have been at his lowest ebb, he learned that *Medea,* the steam yacht that he had designed and built for William Macalister Hall back in 1904, was again up for sale. Since his appointment as Commodore, Fred had been using *Clio* as his Commodore's yacht, but she lacked the finesse of *Medea* even at the age of twenty-five. Fred was also conscious that when Uncle John's trustees had sold her in 1917, James Howie had written from Gallipoli to express his sorrow that the yacht was being sold. Perhaps in deference to his late son's wishes, Fred felt duty bound to bring the yacht back into the ownership of the family.

Medea's career in the intervening years had been rather chequered. She had had at least nine owners, including two years on war service with the French Navy, she had spent three years at Gibraltar, and a couple of years berthed at Cowes. After a quarter of a century of faithful service, Fred was delighted to have her back in his care and almost immediately began to make plans for her refurbishment.

Yachts & Politics

THE Stock Market crash in New York in 1929 sent shivers across the whole of the western world. The result of the collapse was that rich men became paupers, the army of unemployed stared into the abyss. Companies across the globe went into liquidation, believing there was no future for manufacturing and no way they could meet their financial obligations. The merger of great shipping lines and great corporations only added to the sense of failure; if the previous decade had been a decade of despair, the 1930s looked like being a time of total hopelessness.

There were, however, still those who had the money to indulge themselves; James Lyle Mackay, Lord Inchcape, placed an order with Stephen for a luxury yacht. *Rover*, launched in July 1930, was the largest and most extravagant yacht ever built at Linthouse. She lacked nothing in the way of comfort. Inchcape was not the only one interested in placing an order for a yacht; in 1929 Arthur Young placed an order with William Fife of Fairlie for a new eight-metre racing yacht. It was said of Fife yachts that they were 'perfect pieces of "cabinet work," wonderful little gems that would have gladdened the eyes of Chippendale or Hepplewhite.'[1]

Saskia, as she was to be named, lived up to Fife's reputation in every respect. In June 1931 she competed for the Seawanhaka Cup, that year held on the Clyde. *Saskia* took on the American challenger *Priscilla III*. Arthur Young and *Saskia* won the first race, and as a yachting correspondent joyfully reported after the second race had been run:

> Tactics played an important part in the race, but the Clyde yacht, skilfully handled throughout, showed that she was superior to the American in nearly every point of sailing ... *Saskia* also proved the faster boat in the spells of reaching which completed the first round, and thus demonstrated that she has the measure of the American challenger on the wind in a strong breeze, and also that she is better at reaching in a fresh as well as a moderate wind.[2]

Arthur Young and *Saskia* won four successive races and the Seawanhaka Cup returned to Scotland:

The victory of *Saskia* continues the splendid record standing to the credit of the Royal Northern Yacht Club in these contests for the Seawanhaka Cup ... Yachts representing the club have taken part in six contests for the trophy and have won five times so that Scotland's score is now equal to that of the United States.[3]

Young's victory was achieved in what were appalling weather conditions. John Graeme could hardly have enjoyed his role aboard *Medea*, stationed as he was four miles down the Clyde, just off Mount Stuart, a particularly unpleasant spot with a summer gale blowing. The summer storm covered much of northern Europe. On the Sunday evening of 14 June, the French excursion steamer *St Philibert* foundered in the Loire estuary and four hundred of her passengers perished.

Fred, in his role of Commodore, at the end of the racing, should have entertained both the victor and the vanquished to dinner in the club-house. Unfortunately, Johnstone de Forest, *Priscilla*'s owner had to decline the invitation owing to the recent death of his father. Johnstone de Forest did, however, make a comment that in America they had never encountered the kind of weather that they had experienced on the Clyde. He went on to say they designed and built light weather boats -- the very opposite to what John Graeme had claimed when he lost the Cup in 1925.

On 11 October 1931, Walter Wingate Gray died at Nunraw. The expense of maintaining Nunraw had always been more than his income could support, and he died leaving many debts. In the autumn of 1925 he had married Margaret Thornton, the daughter of the Revd Robert Thornton, a Minister of the Free Church. In a local obituary, the writer made much of Gray's devotion to the Church and to his having served as an elected member of the East Lothian County Council: he had been appointed Deputy-Lieutenant of the County. He had served on the Board of the Edinburgh and East of Scotland College of Agriculture, but most of these various appointments were unpaid.

Alex, Fred, John Graeme and George MacLellan travelled through to

Nunraw for the funeral service in spite of the many differences they had had with Gray over the years. It is hard to define exactly Gray's legacy; he was an extremely good laird and the people of Garvald were devoted to him. He had, after all, been their landlord for fifty years. He worked tirelessly for the local community, yet there lingers the doubt that he was not a truly likeable man. Arrogance and snobbery were part of his complex nature. He was laid to rest beside Mary, in the grounds of Nunraw.

There was both happiness and sadness on the morning of 17 February 1932 for Alex, Fred, Murray and Arthur Young, as they attended the funeral service for Robert Smith Allan. The eldest son of Alexander Allan and Jane Smith, Robert had been a life-long friend to the Stephen/Templeton/Young children. A ship owner and merchant, Robert had also been a noted educationalist. Yachting had been his passion, and with his brother Claude, he had played a major role in the Royal Northern Yacht Club and was Commodore of the Clyde Corinthian Club.

In the afternoon, Fred and his family had the pleasure of attending the marriage of John Graeme to Maida Tennant Sloan at Rhu Parish Church. Maida was the sixth daughter and seventh child of George Sloan and Elizabeth Newlands; her eldest brother William was the husband of Charry Templeton, forming yet another marriage link between the families.

Maida was eight years younger than John Graeme but had many things in common, not least the long friendship between their parents. They had both shared the sadness of losing their mother as children. Elizabeth Sloan had died when Maida was nine-years-old, the same age as John Graeme when his mother died.

John Graeme and Maida had two children, a daughter Mary and a son David. Not content with marrying a girl called Maida, a year later the Yard launched a six-metre international racing yacht also named *Maida*. It was not a gesture on John Graeme's part, the original *Maida* had been designed and raced by his father in the early 1890s.

There was also a Templeton wedding in the summer of 1932. On 24 June, Kenneth married Isabella More Papton Younger, the twenty-one-year-old daughter of Archibald Scott Younger, a consulting engineer, and Agnes MacNeil. Kenneth must have been the most maddening of husbands, his own assessment of his personality is delightful in its honesty:

> There are two kinds of people -- those who make mistakes and those who do not. I belong to the first kind: in fact I have a high rating in this class. However, there are compensations. If you are used to falling into holes, you are accustomed to getting out and it makes life interesting.[4]

There were occasions when Kenneth needed the help of others to get him out of a hole not of his own making. Sailing in a dinghy three hundred yards off Southend, Kintyre, a sudden gust of wind caused the boat to keel over: Kenneth was flung into the unforgiving waters of the North Channel. John Cameron, a local fisherman, and his motor boat came to the rescue; it would have been too cruel if the sea had claimed the life of yet another family member.

There had been many highlights in Fred's life, but he had, during the time he had been a director and chairman of the company, experienced constant downturns in the shipping industry. He had worked tirelessly to improve the industry he loved and was a member of a number of institutions. After the *Titanic* disaster in 1912 he had served on the Davits Committee, under the chairmanship of John Harvard Biles. Biles was for thirty years Professor of Naval Architecture at Glasgow University, and an old friend of Fred. It was the Davits Committee that ensured a ship would never again put to sea without sufficient lifeboats for all passengers and crew. They also insisted that crews should be trained for every conceivable emergency. Never again would a ship be described as unsinkable.

Fred had suffered from ill-health all his life. Even before his first birthday, his mother and his nurse had taken him to Moffat to see if the waters would cure his ailments. In 1930 he was again seriously ill, but dogged determination saw him recover. On Friday 16 December 1932 he lost his last battle. He had been at work the previous Monday but subsequently had taken to his bed at his Rhu home of Invergare with a severe chill.

His funeral service was held on 20 December at Glasgow Cathedral -- where a little over two decades earlier he had married Mabel, his second wife. As befitting a leading member of Glasgow's industrial society, five hundred mourners attended the service which was led by the Revd Philip Lilley, Fred's Minister from Rhu. In his eulogy, Lilley spoke of Fred's charm and kindness, commenting that there were many in Rhu and throughout Scotland who would miss him. Lilley mentioned that for years Fred had been an Elder of their Church, a man they turned to in moments of deep distress. Lilley paid a particular tribute to Fred's many benefactions: rarely was a request made that he did not generously support but always that support was done in an unpretentious manner.

Of all the various tributes paid, Fred would surely have relished the one that said he was recognised as one of the really great helmsmen in the smaller international class of yacht racing.

Murray succeeded his father as chairman at a time when shipbuilding on the Clyde faced an uncertain future. The biggest challenge he faced was how to overcome the significant debt owed by the Anchor Line. In 1932, £160,000 was still owed for the *Caledonia* they had launched in 1923. Attempting to get the debt settled brought Murray into contact with Treasury Officials in London. Together with Norman Hurd of the Union Bank they forced the Anchor Line into liquidation, believing that was the only way the creditors would get any money. The liquidation duly took place but by 1935 the Anchor Line was back in business, the assets being transferred to the new company.

Inchcape was appalled and annoyed that Murray had sought the help of the Government for he passionately believed that the State had no place in the affairs of industry, or in the personal lives of men of business.

To add to Murray's worries, the controlling shares in the Yard were held by the Earl of Inchcape, and when he died on 23 May 1932 in Monaco, aboard his yacht *Rover*, a solution had to be found. In the harsh economic climate of the previous decade the Stephen family had been forced to form a limited company and issue shares to non-family members. Inchape had purchased the bulk of the shares. As things turned out the family could not buy the shares back for some years, when they were forced to pay more for them than they had originally received from Inchcape.

Murray also played a significant role in the affairs of the Institution of Engineers and Shipbuilders in Scotland, the British Shipbuilding Research Association and the Shipbuilding Employers Federation. He continued the liberal tradition laid down by his great-grandfather, his grandfather and father, by ensuring that the workers at Lighthouse would have little reason to complain about their conditions of employment. A Linthouse apprenticeship was among the most prized possessions for boys who lived in Govan; with a Linthouse apprenticeship they could travel the world and find employment.

Royal visits were not something that Templeton Carpets had become ac-customed to: the Firm was ninety-three-years-old before the first Royal visit was made in January 1932 when Prince George -- later the Duke of Kent -- paid an official visit. In October 1932, FHY had the honour of welcoming to the factories the Duke and Duchess of York -- the future King George VI and Queen Elizabeth. The tour of the factory took the Royal couple through the showrooms where duplicates of carpets made for Royal occasions were on display. FHY was particularly proud to show the Duke the magnificent carpet made for the Paris Exhibition of 1867, *Christ Blessing the Little Children*, for which the firm had won the Gold Medal.

A year later, FHY and Iris were invited to Royal Lodge, Windsor, which had been newly prepared as a home for the Duke and Duchess of York and their two daughters, Princess Elizabeth and Princess Margaret Rose. Recalling the visit, FHY wrote:

> The Duke and Duchess showed us part of the house and took us round the garden. The two little Princesses took us into the miniature house which had been gifted to Princess Elizabeth by the people of Wales. ... Three last-

ing impressions have been left in my mind from that visit -- the simple sin-
cerity with which we were received; the personal charm of their Majesties
and of the two young Princesses; the happiness of the home life of the
Royal Family.[5]

The article, recalling FHY's visit to Windsor, was written in 1937, shortly
after the Abdication of Edward VIII, and the Accession of the Duke of
York.

It is often a mistake to spend vast sums of money with the sole aim of
achieving victory in a competitive event. The trouble with competition is
that it rarely goes according to plan. In 1934 the British-American series
of yacht races certainly did not achieve the results the British team had
anticipated. Arthur Young had commissioned a six-metre replacement
yacht, *Saskia II*. Thomas Sopwith had the noted designer and builder,
Charles Ernest Nicholson, build him *Endeavour*, a twelve-metre yacht
that was considered the best of her class. Regrettably, she failed to live
up to her name.

The races were held at Oyster Bay in late September. The British
team included *Saskia II*, and among her four man crew was Young's
teenage sister Barbara. She and her younger sister Anne had rightly
earned a reputation of being among the best yachtswomen of the age.
The other boats were *Kyla*, *Melta* and *Voras*; the American quartet were
Anis, *Challenge*, *Bob Kat* and *Lucia*.

Weather conditions at Oyster Bay were unfavourable to the British
yachts which were becalmed during the first race and had to be recalled.
In the subsequent races, the Americans scored a decisive victory. Racing
for the Seawanhaka Cup, the Clyde-built *Kyla*, owned and raced by
William Russell, was no match for *Bob Kat*.

Memorials to Scottish business men do not figure very highly in the
minds of the City Fathers, indeed apart from the flamboyant edifice

of the Templeton factory at William's Street there is not a permanent memorial to JS. On Sunday 28 April 1935, Alice Young dedicated a memorial window at Lindown Church, Kilcreggan, to the memory of her father, JS. This was designed by MacWhirter-Webster of the Stephen-Adam's stained-glass studio in Glasgow. In the upper part of the window there is a scroll, with the text taken from Psalm 92: 'It is a good thing to give thanks unto the Lord, and to sing praises unto they name, O Most High.' In the centre of the window there is a representation of:

> David the Psalmist clothed as king and standing in front of a great throne, on top of which his name is carved. In his arms he holds a musical instrument and in front, down the steps of the throne, are four children singing and playing instruments. Above are three angels, the left one swinging a censer, suggesting the Church; the right one holding a praise scroll bearing the Hallelujah; the central one having his head bowed and his hands clasped in prayer.

> The lower panel is an illustration with again a text taken from Psalm 92: 'O Lord, how great are thy works ... The righteous shall flourish like the palm tree, he shall grow like the cedar of Lebanon.' On the left hand side there is the youthful figure of the Psalmist, with arms outstretched to embrace the beauties of the earth ... [He is dressed as a pilgrim, and round his shoulders is slung a water bottle]. In the lower foreground are conventional flowers and shrubs, amongst which appears a hare, and on the right are tall graceful trees. Beyond the swelling hills there is the sea, blue and green and foaming against the base of tall purple cliffs. Above the cliffs there is a rainbow which breaks into long, sweeping flames upwards and joining with the scroll of the upper panel.

> On the scroll below, there is a small kneeling figure of an angel holding the letter "O". The border is a grisaille effect, with a vine stem running round. At the base of the window is a simple and brief dedication: 'To the Glory of God and in Memory of John Stewart Templeton, DD LLD Born 11 September 1832, died 8 October 1918.[6]

There is great symbolism in every part of the window, the four children being highly significant: JS had four children. The three angels could well have represented JS's three wives. The tiny kneeling angel holding the letter "O", could represent the son he lost. James Murray was always searching for the truth, and never finding it. The two little side panels beneath the scroll show JS's commitment to his Church 'the left one showing the building of the temple, and the right one a view of the church.'[7]

JS's opposition to the merger of the Free Church with the Church of Scotland went very deep and he would certainly not have been happy that the Lindowan United Church was united with the Church of Scotland in 1929. In 1954 it became part of the Craigrownie Parish, and the Church became the Craigrownie Church Hall. The question must be asked. "How many people today using the church hall look up at the window and know who it honours?" Sadly, the answer is not many. History has not been kind to the memory of JS.

In November 1935, Arthur Young succeeded where his father had failed three times. He was elected Conservative Member of Parliament for the Glasgow Partick constituency, beating his Labour opponent by two thousand three hundred votes. The National Government, under the leadership of Stanley Baldwin, ruled during the Abdication crisis. George V's death, the abdication of Edward VIII, his marriage to Wallis Simpson, added much to the drama of politics for the newly elected MP. The forthcoming Royal crisis, though, was not on Arthur Young's mind when he made his maiden speech in February 1936, during the debate on the Scottish Rating System. Immediately before the rating debate, MPs had been discussing education and schooling, and the resolution which was carried must have warmed the hearts of all school age children:

> That in the opinion of this House, it is undesirable that school children should have their evenings occupied with homework; to the exclusion of rest and recreation; and that, whenever practicable, preparation on the school premises should be substituted for homework.[8]

As a former pupil of Fettes College, Arthur would have been amused that preparation would have been done anywhere else but in school. However in the rating debate, which Lieut. Col. Sir Charles Glen Mac-

Andrew, Member for Bute and North Ayrshire, moved the Motion:

> That the time has now come when anomalies in the existing system of lo-
> cal taxation in Scotland should receive close consideration of His Majesty's
> Government ...[9]

The anomalies that Mac-Andrew highlighted were that while in England, the occupier of a building paid the rates, in Scotland they were
shared by both the building's owner and occupier. A position that had
not changed since 1663, which incidently was the year patronage was
restored to Scotland. In seconding the motion, Arthur made reference to
1663 and to the numerous Inquiries, including a Royal Commission that
had been held since that time. But he spoke both as a passionate Scot and
a director of a very large manufacturing company:

> [If] a works which for reasons of bad trade had to close down and said that
> it had not only lost the benefit of derating, but the owner still had to pay full
> owners' rates. I believe that that is strictly the law, but in effect -- and I have
> had experience of these matters -- when a works becomes unoccupied the
> local assessor is empowered to reduce the valuation to some extent. ... I do
> not think that the owner of unoccupied premises should pay any rates. He
> does not do so in England, and I do not see why he should in Scotland.[10]

He then went on to complain that the only way the owner of a house or
factory had of avoiding rates was to remove the roof. This he declared
'is a very bad thing, because good times may come along again, and
it costs a lot of money to recondition a building.'[11] Arthur was right.
Many beautiful Victorian buildings were destroyed by this crass piece of
legislation.

Arthur was congratulated on his maiden speech and it was hoped
that they would hear more from him in the future. It was a hope that
Arthur was quite able to achieve; he obviously made an impression on
David John Colville, then Under-Secretary of State for Scotland, grandson of David Colville, the steel magnate, and a Kintyre man. There is
not enough evidence to say, with complete accuracy, that Colville and
Templeton were closely related, but there is sufficient evidence to suggest that there was a collateral connection. In November 1936, after

Colville had been appointed financial secretary to the Treasury, Arthur was appointed Parliamentary Private Secretary to H J Scrymgeour-Wedderburn, Colville's successor.

Colville was not the only Scot who kept a friendly eye on Arthur; his friendship with Walter Elliot, MP for Kelvingrove, would be important to both of them. There was yet another of those collateral family links that were so much part of the Stephen/Templeton family. Elliot's second wife, was Katharine, Sir Charles Tennant's daughter, and therefore a collateral descendant of Charry Templeton's husband William Newlands Sloan and John Graeme Stephen's wife, Maida Sloan.

Drift Towards War

IN December 1935, the Government set up a Committee under the chairmanship of Rt. Hon. Lord Morison to look into the *Law of Scotland Relating* to the *Constitution of Marriage*. To the man in the street it would probably have come as a shock that -- apart from those which took place at Gretna Green -- irregular marriages were still being performed. Irregular marriages differed from co-habiting. An irregular marriage, as defined by the Committee, was one that was not recognised by the Church, was not registered, and had not been witnessed by another person. It was possible to call yourself married if both partners declared to independent witnesses that they should, from then on, be known as man and wife. It would be another three decades before irregular marriages were outlawed in Scotland.

Such a marriage could explain why it has been impossible to find a statutory record for the marriage of James Murray Templeton and Rosamond Dale Owen. She died in Worthing in June 1937, and in a long obituary in *The Times*, which was headed Mrs Templeton, and sub-headed Laurence Oliphant's Second Wife, James Murray was not mentioned, only that she married after Oliphant's death. The omission is a poor reward for the generosity she received from the Templeton family, and a definite snub to James Murray. His memory would have faded completely had not Rosamond's adopted son, C A Rozenvalle, donated her papers to the University of Columbia, New York. Within those papers was James Murray's diary, and from that rare document his true and gentle nature shines through. The diary ended on 31 July 1884 when he wrote: 'Some women are near what God made them, most men are what they have made themselves.'[1]

He had such high expectations of women, but in Rosamond he found a woman who could not give him the love he craved. She had wanted moral purity in mankind but she found the ideal did not match the reality. J M Barrie died about the same time as Rosamond but the writer of that delightful fairy tale *Peter Pan* would be remembered long after those who tried to live up to Rosamond's fantasy world were gone.

No-one in the Stephen/Templeton family mourned the death of Rosamond, but two months later the families did have a good reason to grieve
when Maud MacLellan died, aged seventy-seven. For the past thirty years
she had suffered from rheumatoid arthritis, a crippling disease for which
in 1937 there was almost no treatment. Her life had seen more than its
fair share of tragedies, her youngest son had been killed in 1917, her only
daughter Elspeth Mary had married Arthur Lennox Skinner, a major in
the Indian Army, but she died in December 1930 of a cerebral haemor-
rhage. Maud, though, had been surrounded by grandchildren. Walter
and Cecily had a son and daughter, Roderick and Violet, Alexander and
Annie had two daughters and two sons, Louise, Elspeth, George and
Donald.

Maud's fifty-five years of marriage to George had given her happiness. She had shared with him his deep interest and commitment to the
Glasgow Mission to the Blind, and although her illness prevented her
active participation she had supported him during his fifteen years as
their President.

There were happier family occasions in 1937: on 25 March, Anthony
Godard Templeton, the thirty-six-year-old son of Revd Archie, married
Mary Gibson Anderson. She was the daughter of William Anderson, a
consulting chemist, and Jessie Gibson McKerrow. They had four children, Elizabeth, Ian and twin daughters, Lois and Ruth. The Anderson connection links into the family of James and Susan Templeton of
Drumgarve. Their daughter Annie married William Anderson, Provost
of Helensburgh. She was the only one of James and Susan's nine children who married.

It was inevitable that with a family as vast as the Stephen family, funerals would become almost a monthly occurrence. Indeed it must have been hard for the senior members to attend all the services, but if their presence was missed they could not escape the task of being an executor to the deceased. A study of the books of Confirmations of Wills and Deeds shows just how much they trusted each other, only one exception being noted. On 10 February 1938, at a nursing home in Leeds, Doctor Alexander Stephen Adams died. The son of Hannah and grandson of Alexander and Elspeth, he had had very little contact with his Scottish roots. Uncle John had with his usual generosity remembered him in his Will, but John was always the exception.

If the family did not grieve for Adams, the people of Rillington most certainly did. He had been their doctor for four decades and his passing was a time for generous tributes. The Revd Thomas Mountford Burnett, Rector of Settrington spoke for many:

> I had a very great respect and affection for him ... In his profession he had great skill and kindliness, as was recognised by all, and he was devoted to the service of his profession. I owe him a lasting debt of gratitude for his care of myself and my family ... He had a great desire to be brought home among you for burial to the place where he had spent the best years of his life and where he had so many personal friends.[2]

Adams left a widow, Anne, a pillar of the local community, a member of the Kirkbymoorside Rural District Council and a stalwart of the Ryedale Women's Institute. Their only son, John Alexander, trained as a doctor in Edinburgh, but shortly after his father's death he returned to Rillington as junior partner in the local medical practice. John's sister, Violet, trained as a nurse and at the time of her father's death was on the staff of the Yorkshire Orthopaedic Hospital at Kirkbymoorside.

Reading down the list of mourners at Adams's funeral, one name leaps out, that of Ruth Clarkson, Robert and Emily's daughter. Like Violet she trained as a nurse, and it is just possible that her path and that of Violet's crossed sometime during their training. How delighted they must have felt when they realised they were the great-granddaughters of Alexander and Elspeth Stephen. Ruth had trained at Great Ormond

Street Children's Hospital in London before returning to her native Scotland. She joined the staff at Yorkhill Children's Hospital, later becoming
a much admired Matron.

To mark FHY's sixty-fifth birthday, a complimentary dinner and presentation was held at Grosvenor Restaurant on 24 March 1939. One hundred and ten current and former members of staff were present to honour him. One notable absentee was Iris, who had been in poor health for
some years.

John Anderson, acting chairman for that night, presented to FHY
on behalf of his fellow partners, a fine oil painting by Sir David Young
Cameron, entitled *The Baths of Caracalla*. In his speech, Anderson paid a
warm tribute to FHY. He said that under FHY's guiding hand the company had expanded considerably in the past twenty-five years. If the directors needed help to solve a problem, whether a simple day-to-day matter
or a more complex long-term issue, FHY gave his advice generously.

Anderson also added that although FHY had reached the age of sixty-
five he sincerely hoped that he would continue to serve the company for
a good deal longer. Anderson did not know then in the dark days of
March 1939 that before the summer was over the country and the Firm
would once again be plunged into a destructive war with Germany.

George Adam, on behalf of the staff, presented FHY with two silver
salvers -- one for him and one for Iris -- and a walnut clock. In his short
speech Adam made particular reference to FHY's interest and devotion
to the welfare of the employees, and that there was hardly a sporting or
social activity that FHY had not supported.

FHY replied thanking the assembled company for their gifts and for
their warm wishes. Arthur Young also spoke, acknowledging FHY's contribution and emphasising that the other directors were also mindful of
their obligation to the wider community.

Some years earlier our firm bought a small piece of ground at the corner of
London Road and Tobago Street. It was covered by very old buildings, but
the firm considered it wise to secure the ground so as to preserve the amen-

ity of the district around Templeton Street. ... The buildings have recently been cleared away, and the ground was offered to Glasgow Town Council on condition that it would be preserved for all time as an open space and decorative feature for the neighbourhood.[3]

The autumn of 1939 was for many the start of the phoney war. The declaration of war, on 3 September, caused a feeling of fear and apprehension in the population as they contemplated an invasion by the Nazi army. Nancy Whitcombe's youngest daughter, Mary recalled, poignantly, that Chamberlain's declaration of war was the first time she had ever seen her mother cry. She had good reason to fear war, the death of her brother Eric and of her Templeton/Stephen/MacLellan cousins in the Great War was a wound which never healed. Her husband Eric still carried the scars from the wounds that he had received; her cousin Clement, was yet another casualty of war who had good reason to fear war and its aftermath.

It was not just the family members who feared war, the Templeton workers were also concerned about their futures. On 6 November, some of the workers received a printed slip inviting them to a meeting in the Clubroom. Many felt their fears were justified when it was revealed that the invitation was only for veteran workers One recipient found comfort in the term veteran, preferring it to old stager, elderly worker, or even senior employee which implied a status he did not think appropriate. But the general mood, as they assembled on that bleak Monday evening, was that they would not be hearing anything that would cheer them up. They were taken upstairs and given sandwiches, cakes and tea, and as they struggled with their cup, saucer and plates, FHY moved among them, chatting, never forgetting a name or the position they held in the Firm.

Replenished with food and tea, they were asked to return to the Grand Hall, and to take their seats. The atmosphere in the hall became noticeably more sober as the partners filed on to the platform, although as one of the veterans unfortunately identified only as Walvic, later recalled: 'There was no ceremony attached to the meeting, and certainly not the boisterousness of a bowler's social.'[4]

Walvic was able to describe the real reason for the invitation that night, and he paid particular attention to the way in which FHY rose to address them. According to Walvic, FHY immediately had his audience's attention:

> His [FHY's] language is simple and his message direct. He dwells on the value of the individual to whatever sphere of life he may find himself, and how important a part each one of us plays. ... He then stresses the value of co-operation, and points out how in business that it is the essence of success.[5]

Even with FHY's reassuring words, there was still a feeling that they were only a prelude to the announcement of bad news. FHY then made reference to the centenary celebrations of the Firm earlier that summer, before finally coming to the real purpose for which they had all been summoned that night. FHY said he was pleased, nay delighted, to announce that the Firm was granting each employee with over twenty-five years service, a gift of fifty pounds. An amount roughly equivalent to ten weeks pay for the average worker.

To celebrate the centenary there were other social occasions; on 13 May there was a Centenary Cruise for men who had retired. One of the happy bunch was William John Russell, a seventy-three year old veteran with forty years service. Unfortunately, meeting old friends and colleagues was too much for William and he died on 18 May of heart failure. It was remarked by some who saw him on the cruise that he had looked fresh and youthful. His funeral was on the Saturday following the cruise. Mary Duffy, his widow, was a Templeton girl.

It is impossible to know how many marriages between Templeton workers happened during the first hundred years of the Firm's existence, but it was not a rare occurrence.

In an article written to celebrate the centenary, FHY gave a witty and informative short history of the Firm:

> From the first year, which closed with nearly 100 in the little factory, till the centenary year, which sees about 4500 working in our various departments, tens of thousands of men and women have made their livelihood in the

Templeton factories. For nearly all of us surely the work has been interesting and happy. It has been remarkably steady employment: there are few casual workers: to most it has provided a job for all their working days. Entry to the firm is nearly always at a young age, it being only in exceptional circumstances that an older person is engaged. The eight partners started in Templetons at ages varying from 16 to 22. With only a few exceptions all our leading people began as boys and girls. When one of our men, who had entered the factory when a little older than most of us, was put on the pension list, he remarked, with a twinkle in his eye, "But I've been here only 37 years. If I had known it was just a temporary job, I might not have taken it."[6]

One Saturday morning in 2002, two students from the RSAM&D, Rachel McCue and Jodie Wilkinson, carried out a random survey in Sauchiehall Street, Glasgow, and asked shoppers if they had heard of Templeton, the carpet factory. Four out of five, who answered, said that they had great-grandparents, grandparents, parents, aunts, uncles or cousins, who had worked for them. There are still a few men and women who say, with the same twinkle in their eyes, that they themselves had worked for the Firm. They all speak with pride of their years working for the Templeton family.

A lifetime loyalty to one company is now an alien concept. Career changes are now the norm, not the exception. FHY was committed to the idea of the manufacture of goods, not just creating wealth by the manipulation of money.

He could have added, that in turning the raw materials into useful articles, the Templeton factories also turned them into things of beauty. The design book of carpets is, perhaps, one of the greatest treasures in the Templeton archives. They designed and made carpets for the great Transatlantic liner, the *Queen Mary*, for Kings and Queens, for lairds in their castles, for town houses and for the homes of the middle classes, for the Dorchester and Charing Cross Hotels in London and for the House of Lords. In 1941 the Chamber of the House of Commons was destroyed by German bombers, and when it was rebuilt and refurbished, the green carpet, with its wide red stripes just two sword lengths apart, was naturally a Templeton carpet.

During 1938/9 FHY was engaged in writing a history of the Firm, from its modest beginning in 1839 through a hundred years of industrial, social and economic change. It is a comprehensive record of the changes that took place during those turbulent years. It gives a graphic picture of the life of the hand loom weavers and the tremendous changes brought about by the invention of power looms. Publication was delayed by the declaration of war.

For the second time in the twentieth century, the Templeton factories were faced with helping the war effort. As in the Great War, the weaving machines at Tullis Street and Bernard Street were quickly adapted for the manufacture of blankets. Thousands of blankets were dispatched to the Ministry of Supply.

As well as blankets, Templeton workers turned out thousands of canvas sandbags, using the canvas normally used for the backing of carpets. The dyeing shop was equally busy on the war effort turning out many thousands of pounds of khaki cotton, and as a writer in the *Templetonian* explained:

> This has been perhaps our most difficult problem of adjustment for the technique of dyeing cotton is quite different from that of dyeing woollen yarns the shades fit to grace a bedroom or drawing room.[7]

The dyeing problems were obviously successfully solved for the factories produced yards of cotton material. To anyone who spent a night in a Reception Centre, after being bombed out of their home, those harsh, rough blankets re-awaken both good and bad memories.

Dark Days Again

HISTORY has a depressing habit of repeating itself. In 1939, Euphemia Davidson, Samuel's granddaughter, married in Gibraltar, an ex-naval officer, Austin Noel Rees Keene, the son of Revd Rees Keene and Louisa Margaret, of Gosford, Cumberland. Keene's career began as an Osborne naval cadet in 1914 and continued with tours of duty on HMS *Royal Oak* and HMS *Wakefield*. When the Fleet Air Force was formed, he trained as a pilot, serving at home and abroad. In 1933 he joined the Tactical School, and retired a year later for life as a civilian.

Euphemia, when she married Austin, must have silently prayed that her husband would not again take on a dangerous occupation. On the declaration of war, Keene immediately re-enlisted for active service, with the rank of Lieutenant-Commander. He joined the crew of the aircraft carrier HMS *Glorious*. In April 1940, *Glorious* was in action in Norwegian waters, its Swordfish and Skua aircraft attacking Trondheim.

Glorious remained in Norwegian waters, joined by *Furious*, and from their base at Bardufoss they continued to attack German positions on the mainland. Nine months after the declaration of war, *Glorious* had the misfortune to come up against the German battle cruisers *Scharnhorst* and *Gneisenau*, three hundred miles west of Narvick. The outcome was never in doubt, *Glorious*'s crew fought gallantly but she was finally sunk with the loss of all but forty-three of her crew.

For three weeks, all Euphemia knew was that her husband was 'missing in action'. Keene's death was finally confirmed on 27 June. In her grief Euphemia could recall that sixty-six years earlier her grandmother Massie had lost her husband to the sea.

As they had done at the beginning of the Great War, the Stephen Yard immediately went into full production and repair of war ships. They built cruisers, minelayers, escorts, and one aircraft carrier; in all, over thirty ships were launched and over five hundred vessels repaired or modified. The losses of Stephen built ships were to be horrendous, two escorts, *Holcombe* and *Tynedale*, were sunk by the same submarine *U-593*. *Croome*, however, would get a small revenge when she sank *U-372* off Palestine in August 1942. In 1943 the Yard launched the sloop *Amethyst*, destined to have a distinguished war record before embarking on an even more illustrious peace-time adventure.

The bombing of Clydeside, for a short while, hindered the work of the shipyards, but the grim determination of the workers and the resilience of the management ensured that production was never stopped for long.

Although the war effort was important, the Templeton factories also managed, even with all the restrictions on raw materials, to turn out carpets and rugs for the wardrooms of navy ships. But as FHY prophesied, in late May 1941 the situation was going from bad to worse:

> [We] do not know what the decision of the Government may be; our carpet manufacture may be stopped, or we may be appointed a "nucleus firm" to go on making a little for ourselves, and also making some goods for other carpet firms.[1]

He admitted that while the textile side of the business was in dire straits, the engineering business was only awaiting further Government contracts, but these could not begin until the new machines arrived. When they did, he hoped to re-employ some of the girls who had lost their jobs.

There is a story, told by Donald MacLellan's father, that in the early days of the war, Templetons, along with many firms, local authorities and households, built air-raid shelters on their premises. The Personnel Department sent round a memorandum asking the staff, including the factory girls, if they suffered from claustrophobia. They were somewhat alarmed when ninety-seven percent of the girls replied they were terrified of claustrophobia. Not convinced, the Personnel Department called in a number of girls and asked them to explain why they replied in the way they had. The girls, admitted that they did not really know what claustrophobia meant, so they had asked a colleague, and she had told them it meant CONFINEMENT. And that the girls declared they were 'awful feart of'.

January 1942 was only twenty-three days old when George Scott MacLellan died at his home Dunard, Downhill. A widower since Maud's death in 1937, he had been a director of Stephen and Sons since his marriage. He had also been a director and vice-chairman of P & W MacLellan and for twenty-two years he was Chairman of the Laird Lines. Even with an extremely busy working life he still found time for his charity work. For fifteen years he was chairman of the Glasgow Mission to the Blind. Reading through the Visitor's Book of Kelly, it is obvious that George was a much respected son-in-law to Al and Mary. He shared many of their beliefs and ideals. The premature deaths of his youngest son and his only daughter left a gap in his life, but he was proud of the success his sons, Walter and Alexander had made of their lives. He also saw a secure future with the birth of his grandchildren.

If an attempt is made to sum up George's life, it would be that it was long, successful and rewarding in the love of his wife and his children and his grandchildren. He and Maud had enjoyed fifty-five years of marriage, before her death robbed him on his dearest companion. On asking Al for the hand of Maud, George had assured his future father-in-law that he loved her with true affection and that he was a good Christian man. Al never had reason to doubt George's assurances.

A link with the past was severed when, in August 1942, Alex Stephen died at his Auchenfail home. He was eighty-one and had been in poor health for some time. Life at Auchenfail had given him much pleasure, and although he remained a director of the company, he took little day-to-day part in the activities of the Yard. He was more than content to leave that in the capable hands of Murray and John Graeme. He had spent all his working life in the Yard, and his legacy was in furthering the development of the engineering department. When he died, the engineering department at Linthouse had a reputation of being one of the finest in the country.

For a few days during the war, Allied servicemen could periodically enjoy a break from its horrors. The Dominion and Allied Services Hospitality Scheme, organised by Lady Frances Ryder and Miss MacDonald of the Isles, were responsible for giving servicemen a taste of British hospitality. Two of the earliest members of the scheme were Robert and Emily Clarkson. They were in their early seventies and probably looking forward to a quiet retirement when war broke out. But such was their generosity of spirit that they opened their home at Little Cambus, Doune, Perthshire to Allied Servicemen.

Robert and Emily were only two of more than five thousand such people who joined Lady Ryder's scheme. The visitor's book at Little Cambus shows just how much the Servicemen enjoyed the Clarkson's hospitality. The comments of the men in the visitor's book and in letters of thanks, followed a similar pattern; without exception they spoke of the enjoyable relaxing evenings and the sheer pleasure of hot baths; and in spite of food rationing, they remembered the delicious suppers. Mary, the Clarkson's youngest daughter -- she was in her early thirties when war broke out -- played an important role of friend and confidant. It was to Mary that many of the letters of thanks were addressed. When the visitors came from Poland she wanted to learn Polish and when the servicemen were from Australia, one of them wrote out a list of Aussie terms for her to master.

Domestic staff numbers at Little Cambus were very limited. Where once the family would have employed four or more domestic servants, now they had only one. Helen, a tiny little woman, probably younger than Mary, was the only servant and did most of the work of caring for the servicemen. Mary also recruited a small army of volunteers, to knit, darn and generally keep in good order, socks for the Royal Army Service Corps, stationed at Doune.

The friendships formed between the visitors, during those short leave periods, continued long after the war ended. One Australian

visitor, Stephen H Rieck, when his son was born in 1950, named him
Malcolm Durward, the middle name of Robert. It would be delightful
to record all the comments made about the kindness and hospitality that
the young men so far from home had received from the Clarkson family,
but that is impossible. However, one comment cannot be allowed to go
unrecorded, a New Zealand lad wrote 'Scottish hospitality certainly does
show up England. The most enjoyable leave since coming to the British
Isles.'²

Robert and Emily were not the only civilian family members involved
in helping the war effort. Agnes Maude worked tirelessly throughout the
war, helping to alleviate the plight of victims of the ceaseless bombing
raids. Between 1939 and 1941 she was a member of the First Aid Nursing
Yeomanry, a territorial unit of the ATS. In 1942 she was Welfare Supervi-
sor for Blackie's Munitions Factory. As well as this, Agnes Maude was the
Area Organiser of the WVS -- a unique voluntary service established by
Lady Stella Reading -- the wife of George Alfred Isaacs. The green and
mauve uniforms worn by the WVS ladies gave thousands of evacuated
children a feeling of reassurance and comfort.

Stella Reading was, as befitted someone in her position, an inde-
pendently minded person -- although not a rebel, she was certainly not a
shrinking violet in the Victorian mould. She believed in individual initia-
tive on the part of her ladies -- and the term is used loosely for she had
no time for class distinctions, nor did she have any truck with regimenta-
tion. Stella allowed her ladies to wear their hats at any angle that suited
them. Winston Churchill strongly disapproved, he believed that as a uni-
formed organisation, hats should be worn at the same angle.

By the beginning of autumn 1943, the Allied troops had begun to feel
that the German enemy was not, after all, invincible. In January, Tripoli
had fallen to Field Marshal Montgomery's 8th Army; in May, German
and Italian forces in North Africa surrendered. In the same month, the
RAF Dambuster's Squadron, destroyed the Ruhr dams, using Barnes
Wallace's bouncing bombs. In September the Allies invaded the Italian
mainland, and on 8 October Italy surrendered.

FHY was very pleased at the progress of the war. Returning to his home at 21 Kirklee Road, after a day spent at the factory, he may have thought that peace would soon be in the grasp of the Allies. A peace that would ensure he and Iris could, after all, look forward to a pleasant trouble-free old age. It was not to be. He died on Saturday 9 October 1943 of a coronary thrombosis: he did not live to see the peace he yearned.

There were many moving tributes to FHY, but none was more appropriate than that which appeared in the *Templeton News-Letter* in December. FHY had devoted his life to the Templeton factories and their workers, and it was only right that they should remember the man they knew and loved:

> [He] possessed intense personal interest in those with whom he came into contact. It was not a case of curiosity, but a very real interest in the doings and welfare of his fellow-men and women. His friendliness, alike to the youngest on the staff and the oldest in the factory, was most marked, and there are many to-day who cherish the memory of the gentle word and the kindly inquiry.[3]

The obituary concluded with an epitaph that few could ever hope to achieve 'we mourn the passing of a fine gentleman who leaves behind him the memory of kindliness and culture, of friendliness and justice. Let us set our steps along the paths of duty and responsibility in which he led us for so many years.'[4]

Iris, who had been in poor health for a number of years, mourned the loss of her generous, thoughtful and considerate husband. But she was heartened in her grief to receive a personal message from His Majesty King George VI and Queen Elizabeth, expressing their sympathy and condolences on her sad loss.

The reading of FHY's Will, which was probated on 18 October, raised a few eye-brows among those who might have expected or hoped to benefit from his considerable fortune. He made a few small bequests to his executors; he asked Iris to make similar small bequests to members of his household staff. He left Iris the bulk of his Estate, including the house used by his chauffeur in Shakespeare Street, Maryhill, a substantial monetary bequest and an annual annuity. He left Iris's sister Minnie a small legacy, but to his many nieces and nephews he left nothing.

The vast bulk of FHY's money he left as a bequest, with the wish, a wish he had often expressed, that the money should be used to build or buy a convalescent home for Templeton workers. It must be remembered that when FHY died in 1943, the National Health Service was still only a suggestion from Sir William Beveridge. It took a further five years before the Report on the modernization of the Welfare Services was implemented, and then not as Beveridge or FHY would have wished.

For those who lived through the Second World War, there was one sight that all feared: the telegraph boy with his dull gold envelopes. Those little envelopes, almost without exception, contained news that no one in the household wanted to receive. Shortly after 28 January 1944, Dorothy Grace Templeton and her husband Doctor Edward Taylor Wright heard the news that their twenty-year-old Royal Marine son, Eric Archibald Templeton Wright, had been killed. Dorothy's grief was unbearable, but so was that of Eric's grandmother Elizabeth Templeton. She had lost two sons in a war that was fought to end all wars. Her youngest son Clement had been badly injured, now she mourned the loss of a grandson.

Peace in Europe finally came on 8 May 1945 and a collective sigh of relief spread rapidly across the nation. The years of austerity and shortages would not immediately end, but people prayed that six years of war would not be followed by decades of depression, as had happened at the end of the Great War.

Alice Young died at her home Freston Lodge, Sevenoaks on 14 May, six days after the end of the war. For a little over a quarter of a century since Dan's death she had lived close to Nancy and Eric Whitcombe: she had been surrounded by people who loved her. Arthur had been a constant companion when his Parliamentary duties allowed.

The war years had been particularly hard for Alice; her younger son, Eric, had died in the Great War, and during the Second War she endured the horror of knowing that her grandson Alastair was a Prisoner of War.

Alastair had just celebrated his twenty-first birthday when war was declared. He had been educated at Rugby and was at Trinity College, Oxford, but as a member of the Territorial Army he was one of the first to enlist. In the early months of 1940 he was taken prisoner at St Varley and spent the next five years as a POW in various German camps.

For the first time since the General Election of 1935, the Churchill-led coalition Government called a General Election in July 1945. In the resignation honours list, Arthur Young was created a baronet. Clement Attlee led the Labour Party to a landslide victory and against a tide of socialism Arthur held his Partick seat for the Conservatives. Arthur was disappointed that his friend and mentor Walter Elliot had lost his Kelvin-grove seat, but he would be back in the House by November 1946 when he won a bi-election for the Scottish Universities.

Elliot summed up Arthur Young's attitude to politics better than any other of his friends:

> He thought politics important -- important enough for him to give up so much that he loved and that he was so well fitted to enjoy -- business, pleasure, his own life. Yet he always retained his own standards of criticism, his own undisturbed inner sanctuary.[5]

It can only be a matter of conjecture whether Arthur considered quitting politics after the death of FHY. He inherited FHY's mantle and could have steered the company through the difficult post-war years. In 1947, Templetons were forced by economic and taxation problems to become a public limited company. Although Arthur remained a director his commitment to politics had the greater call on him, and he chose to serve both his party and his constituents as an active member of the Opposition.

Arthur had good reason to believe that now his son, Alastair, was safely back home, he would bear some of the responsibility for the carpet manufacturing business. Alastair joined the staff in 1946, but before that, in November 1945, he married [Dorothy Constance] Marcella, the widow of Lieutenant John Hollington Grayburn.

Grayburn, attached to the Parachute Regiment, won the Victoria Cross during the disastrous and bloody battle of Arnhem. Wounded twice, Grayburn and his platoon held their positions for four days until they were finally ordered to retreat. Against appalling odds, and fighting to the last, Grayburn was killed as he attempted to get his men to safety.

Alastair's marriage to Grayburn's widow, once again threw up one of those strange coincidences that are so much part of the Stephen/Templeton family saga. Alastair's sister, Barbara, had married John Grayburn's brother, William Echlin Hollington Grayburn, in May 1939.

Alastair had many of the same qualities that had played such an important part in the lives of the Stephen/Templeton family: he was passionate in his commitment to youth welfare. He was for many years connected with the Glasgow County Scout Council, eventually becoming its chairman. It almost goes without saying that he was a keen yachtsman, a member of the Royal Yacht Squadron and the Royal Yachting Association and Commodore of the Royal Northern and Mudhook Yacht Clubs. At Mudhook he was particularly keen to see that young people were given the opportunity to participate in the sport he loved.

He had the same gentle dignity that his father had in abundance, 'it would never have occurred to him that he was important. His concern was not for himself, always for others -- colleagues, employees and friends alike; and his essential kindliness will be remembered.'[6]

With a new Government and the war in the Far East finally over, Iris renewed her desire to see FHY's wish to build a convalescent home realised. She wrote to the Templeton directors, telling them that £25,000 could be made immediately available, if they would proceed with establishing a convalescent home.

John Anderson, managing director of Templetons, was delighted to pass on this news to the workers, that thanks to Iris's generosity, work could commence on finding suitable premises for their convalescent home. The search for the right premises took them until December 1947.

Fight the Good Fight

THERE should have been a sense of optimism in the air at the start of 1946, but expectations rarely measure up to realities. Murray Stephen did have a reason to celebrate: in the New Year's Honours list he was awarded a knighthood. As President of the Shipbuilding Employers Federation, he and his team had played a major and vital role in resolving the problems of organisation and production during WW2. As they had in WW1, the shipbuilders of Clydeside played a pivotal role in both building and repairing warships.

Unhappily, when raw materials again became available, the Yard could not recapture the glory days of shipbuilding that Alexander and Al had witnessed. If the latter part of the 1940s is remembered for anything it is remembered for the beginning of the great industrial and social unrest between employers and employees.

In 1946 Murray was appointed to the committee of the newly constituted Shipbuilding Advisory Committee. Increasingly his duties pushed him further into the realm of government and government initiatives.

John Graeme was still a director, but he was spending more time at his home of Glenlogan, Sorn, Ayrshire. Always a reluctant shipbuilder, he now turned his talents to farming and engineering innovations. He designed and built a machine for cutting and picking up silage, a machine that is still in use today. Even back in the 1930s he had designed a hydraulic cold bending machine for ship frames; before then the frames had required a furnace to heat them before bending, a very time consuming and labour intensive operation. The war years had ruined the International yachting scene, but even so John Graeme maintained his interest and built a test tank for yachts in the grounds of Glenlogan.

There were few homes in the land that did not rejoice that the killing was over, yet the horror of war was not over. The physical and mental condition of prisoners returning from the Burma arena haunted all those who saw them, for years to come.

Nancy and Eric Whitcombe had reason to celebrate that their two sons, John and Hugh, had survived the war. However, the New Year was only eleven days old when they heard that Hugh had been killed in Indonesia. To Nancy, the death of her younger son reopened the despair she had felt at the death of her brother Eric in the Great War.

There was a striking difference between Alice and her daughter Nancy, a difference not of personalities, for they were both alike, but of their ability to show emotion. James Murray had wanted Alice to fling her arms round him and say that she loved him. She could never do that. Nancy, on the other hand, had no problem with showing that she loved her children and her grandchildren.

FHY's Trustees worked hard throughout 1946 to find a suitable house for their convalescent home. In December, the Trustees were able to tell the staff that they had successfully purchased Thinacre in Racecourse Road, Ayr. The house had been the home of Edwin R Boyd, a chartered accountant, and his wife Gertrude Lyford Boyd.

In buying a house in Ayr, the Trustees followed a well trodden path; for decades the Clyde Coastal town had been a haven for holidaymakers and those seeking convalescence or a rest. In those dark post-war days the news excited the workers, as they looked forward to spending a few days 'doon the watter':

> *Thinacre* is a large house which up to now has been used as a private residence and has a very attractive garden of two acres. It is situated within easy reach of the beach and is close to a fine shopping and entertainment centre. The necessary alterations and the equipment of the Home may take some time, but when it is ready we feel sure that many a happy holiday will be spent by Templetonians in need of rest and convalescence.[1]

War-time restrictions on the supply of building materials delayed the project quite considerably; all available materials and tradesmen were being used to repair the thousands of houses that were damaged during the six years of war. Indeed, even the soldiers, particularly the Royal Engineers, who were lucky enough to return from the battlefields of Europe, were recruited as building tradesmen. In December 1947, a year after the purchase of *Thinacre*, things had not advanced very far:

> It is with some disappointment that we have to report that so far we have not yet been able to make a start with the alterations at *Thinacre*. ... Delays have arisen in connection with the granting of licences for the necessary work, but following recent discussions, it is hoped that at an early date some of the work will be proceeded with. It is unfortunate that this very desirable scheme of having a Convalescent Home for our own employees should co-incide with a period of economic national difficulties, and it is impossible to forecast when the work of alterations may be completed.[2]

Iris did not live to see the completion of the project that had been so much apart of FHY's legacy. She died at the age of sixty-three on 21 December 1946, after a long struggle with tuberculosis and Addison's Disease. Her obituary rightly paid a gracious tribute to the fact that FHY had relied upon her 'judgement in all social developments at the factories, and he could always depend on her enthusiastic co-operation and encouragement in new social ventures.'[3]

Iris's death was not the only one that occurred around that time; Elizabeth Helen Templeton died on 9 March, at her home in Crookfur, Newton Mearns. She was in her eighty-seventh year and had been a widow for more than twenty-three years. Her marriage to Revd Archie had given her life stability and direction, but it had been marred by tragedy. If she had been honest on her marriage certificate, citing only her mother's name, then on her death certificate her parents were given as Hugh Aitken, a calico printer and Margaret Hutton. In death she was afforded the respect and admiration she so richly deserved.

Six months after her death, Elizabeth's son, Clement, died. Since being badly injured in the Great War, he lived very simply at Craignure, Kilmore, just a short distance from where Charry and William Sloan had a home. Kenneth was the informant of his brother's death, but there is little to suggest that he was with Clement when he died. The Revd Archie had ensured in his Will that Clement's material needs would be catered for, but there is a feeling that the isolation of rural Argyllshire did much also to help him forget the horrors of the Great War. In returning to Argyllshire he was returning to the land of his forefathers.

Twelve years had passed since Olympic Games were held in Berlin in 1936, the war had prevented the games taking place in 1940 and 1944. Now, The International Olympic Committee decided that, in spite of opposition, the 1948 Games should go ahead and they duly awarded the Games to Great Britain. It was not a decision that was universally welcomed, but there was support for the Games from some quarters:

> ... many people feel that it would be better were they not organised in Britain ... on account of food shortages and other difficulties ... provided we keep the catering and organization of the Games on our own austerity standard, it will help foreigners to appreciate the true state of this country. ... As to whether International contests are a good thing or not, I think that the intense rivalry which sprang up during the last Games as a result of dictatorships was in the wrong spirit.[4]

Arthur Young had every reason to believe the Games were a good idea, as Vice-President of the Yacht Racing Association he was heavily involved in drawing up the rules and classes for the racing. The five classes were finally agreed as six-metre, Dragon, Star, Swallow and Firefly. The chairman of the YRA was John Graeme's old adversary, Sir Ralph Gore.

The races were held off Torquay, between 5 and 12 August; Arthur was chairman of the judges, and he was now able to use *Thendara*, the auxiliary ketch built by the Stephen Yard in 1937 but which had been laid up during the long years of war. The duties of a judge, especially at International level, were never easy but Arthur was delighted with the response he received:

> The spirit in which the racing was carried on, with competition at its fiercest, was in the traditions, not only of the sport, but of the Olympic conception. Protests were comparatively few, and mainly on matters of fact. The decisions of the international jury, under the able and sagacious chairman-

ship of Sir Arthur Young, were never for a second questioned, and in the future Games it is hoped that this spirit of sportsmanship and friendship will increase.[5]

Whatever the pessimists thought, the Games were an outstanding success. They did much to lighten the mood of those who struggled day-after-day to cope with the aftermath of the war. Not even the publication of George Orwell's *Nineteen-Eighty-Four* could dampen the general feeling that things were going to get better.

The Royal Naval sloop, *Amethyst*, was built by Stephen and was launched in 1943. She saw action in WW2, including sinking the German *U-1208* off the south of Iceland. She was in the Far East on 25 August 1945 when she was present at the surrender of Japanese troops off Rabaul, New Guinea. In 1949, during the Berlin blockade and the Communist take-over of the mainland China, she saw action again: she was attacked by an on-shore battery of the People's Liberation Army as she sailed away from a replenishment visit to Nanking. Communist gun batteries opened fire, killing her captain and sixteen of her crew. The ship was then held prisoner by the PLA forces for three months, until a Naval Attaché, Commander John Simon Kerans (1915-1985) went aboard. Negotiations with the Communist Chinese failed to produce a peaceful resolution, and Kerans decided that he had to make a dash for freedom or they would all perish.

In a daring move, *Amethyst*, having been rigged to look like a Chinese cargo boat, slipped past her captors and made for the open sea. The sturdy sloop, built with all the pride of a Stephen's ship had proved her reliability during her months of captivity, but now she would need to prove her invincibility.

Kerans planned to slip away under the cover of darkness without alerting the Communist gunners on the shore. The dash down the Yangtze had about it all the madcap adventure that has thrilled every school-boy for decades. Hit by a shell, which buckled and loosened a few plates, *Amethyst*, nevertheless, managed to make full speed. Shaking off all obstacles, she and her gallant crew finally sailed into the open waters of the estuary of the Yangtze. They were greeted by the delighted captain and crew of HMS *Concord*, with the signal of the immortal words: 'Fancy meeting you here'.

In such exploits, heroes are made. *Amethyst* earned her place in history. Her exploits in China were due as much to the men of the Stephen Yard who built her with such care as they were to the bravery of Kerans and his gallant crew.

Progress in completing the refurbishment of *Thinacre* was unbelievably slow. The lack of raw materials, the constant need to apply for permission from the Government, both local and national, caused endless delays, but in June 1950, the company was able to announce:

> We are pleased to be able to report that considerable progress has been made in the reconstruction of the house in Racecourse Road, Ayr, as a Convalescent Home for the firm's employees. All the structural alterations which have meantime been permitted have been completed and the painting and furnishing will shortly be underway.[6]

The house provided separate accommodation for twelve girls and six men, in two and four-bedded rooms. Accommodation was also provided for the staff. A new kitchen, dining-room, a recreational room and lounges were established on the ground floor, and the whole house was, naturally, carpeted with Templeton carpets.

On Saturday 14 October 1950, the Templeton Convalescent Home was formally declared open by Provost James Smith of Ayr. Included in the opening ceremony were the Directors, factory managers, welfare supervisors and representatives from each of the Templeton factories.

Today, in the spring of 2006, *Thinacre*, now known as *Templeton House*, is run by South Ayrshire Council as a residential home for elderly people, but it also accommodates short stay patients who need convalescent care. The spirit which FHY and Iris strove so hard to achieve is still much in evidence, and for every one who enters the house, they are

instantly reminded of those two farsighted and generous people who
made the project a viable proposition.

Iris's stunningly beautiful portrait by Hugh Somerville still hangs
in the foyer, and to gaze at it is to know her beauty and her quiet dignity. Climb the first flight of stairs and FHY's portrait, painted by the
Royal Academician, Maurice Greiffenhagen, looks down ever watchful.
Greiffenhagen has accurately caught FHY's sense of right over wrong,
and above all his sense of belonging to the greater Templeton family.
Like them, FHY was at first a lowly employee, then, through his abilities
and his dedication, he became a father figure. He and Iris were never
blessed with children but they were unofficial guardians to the young
women who worked for the Firm. A memory that the passing of time
can never diminish.

For the third time since he first entered Parliament, Arthur Young had to
fight a General Election. He had held various government posts since his
election in 1935. He had two years as Scottish whip, a period as a Government Whip, and a Lord Commissioner to the Treasury. The 1950 election, however, caused him problems, there had been boundary changes
and his Partick constituency had been split, forcing him to stand for the
newly created seat of Scotstoun. He had held his seat against a Labour
landslide in 1945, and there was hope that he would again buck the trend.
He did, holding the seat with the slender majority of two hundred and
thirty nine votes.

Walter Elliot, his long time friend, wrote graphically of Arthur as
the results were declared on election night:

> I still remember him coming up to meet us in the Conservative Club late
> on the evening. ... Party fortunes hung in the balance. Arthur Young's own
> constituency was undergoing, I think, its third recount. He was as unruffled
> as a bird on a bough. After all, he had done all that in him lay. If the verdict
> was for him, good. If it were against him, so much the worse. He was the su-
> preme example I have ever known of a good sportsman. He never repined.[7]

Arthur, unfortunately, was not to enjoy another full term as a parliamentarian. During the summer recess he went to France on a sailing holiday aboard *Thendara*. On 14 August, at Bénodent, he suffered a heart attack and died; he was nearly sixty-one-years-old. The world of yacht racing lost one of its great sporting heroes; Parliament lost a great parliamentarian. His family -- his extended family -- lost a devoted husband, father and friend. Obituaries are often over-stated, but in Arthur's case the words of Walter Elliot summed up what most people knew:

> He was in a very special sense an outstanding Scotsman; all the more because he never insisted upon it, often because he did not even notice it. In the tumultuous striving assembly of 600 members of Parliament he remained, without the slightest effort, himself. That is really why he occupied so special a niche. That is why he leaves a gap which will be so difficult to fill.[8]

It was almost inevitable that after WW2 and the devastation caused by Germany bombing, the shipyards on the Clyde would need to be rebuilt and modernized. It was also inevitable that families like Stephen would not have access to the enormous sums of money needed to fund that modernization. In 1946, for the first time in its history, Alexander Stephen & Sons Limited became a public company. In October 1950, Murray Stephen wrote of that decision:

> The Firm is now a public company; it was forced to become one by the present high levels of death duty and other taxation. But the traditions are still strong enough, and it seems probable that members of the family may take in the future as full a part in the management as others have taken in the past. If, by any fell chance, the deadening, soul-destroying and inefficient hand of nationalisation is ever laid on the shipbuilding industry, I, for one, would feel that all the efforts of my family, which have gone to make this Firm, had in the end proved vain.[9]

Murray Stephen's words were prophetic, and an ill-omen. The postwar Labour Government thought the answer to all industry's ills lay in nationalization. But when it came to raising the capital needed for improvements, they balked at the idea. Successive Tory Governments were equally reticent, and the shipyards, along with the nationalized coal mines and railways, starved of money, slowly died, and in dying they destroyed a whole way of life. In the early nineteen-seventies the shipyard workers' on the Clyde, like the miners a decade later, were determined to fight to save their industry.

They fought the good fight, led by a charismatic, fiery trade union leader, Jimmy Reid: they won the battle but lost the war. Strangely, Reid was born exactly a century after Al Stephen, the man who more than any other had built Linthouse. The Clyde is now silent, the few cranes and gantries that do remain are memorials to the past. Lower down the Clyde, Fred Stephen and his sons would be amazed that the mighty river is home to many hundreds of yachts. On any Saturday during the sailing season their multi-coloured sails bring the river alive.

Leiper's façade on the Templeton building remains as garish and as eye-catching as it was on the day it was finally completed in 1891. The future of that magnificent building is still to be decided. The looms are silent, the chatter and laughter of the girls has gone. Who now looks at that façade and remembers the family who commissioned it, or the twenty-nine young girls who died when it collapsed? Memories fade but the men and women of the Templeton family should not be forgotten, they gave the carpet world beauty and quality, and to the thousands of Glaswegians who worked for them they gave them dignity.

A part of the Stephen Yard has survived. The great Linthouse Engine Shop now houses the Scottish Maritime Museum at the Harbourside, in Irvine. The Engine Shop was taken down brick by brick in 1988 and rebuilt on the Irvine site in 1991. A little road close to the Museum now containing refurbished houses was named Linthouse Vennel. The Museum also houses a recreated Shipyard Workers' Tenement Flat, all tangible reminders of a world long forgotten.

For now the story ends. There were so many stories, so many lives not covered. What happened to James's two sons James and Robert? To Margaret Mary Dundas? Did she marry and have children? Did she tell them of their Stephen heritage? And what of William Stephen's second family? Perhaps one day, it will be possible to continue the story of their lives from where it ends here. Will the lives of future generations be as interesting as their ancestors? They will certainly be different. One of James Stewart's descendants, Hugh Grant, is an actor; Arthur Young's grandson is a lawyer; The Revd Archie's descendants are doctors, lawyers and stockbrokers. No one in the family now builds ships or weaves carpets, yet the legacy of their forebears is still there, and who knows what the future will hold for the next generation and for the one after that.

SOURCE NOTES

PART ONE 1795-1866

In the Beginning

1. The unpublished *Memoir of John Stewart Templeton*, in the Personal Archives of Sir Stephen Young [SSTY Archives]
2. *Dundee Advertiser*, 28 April 1875
3-5. *Memoir of JST*
6. *Stewart of Lovedale, the life of James Stewart*, DD, MD, Hon FRGS, by James Wells, DD, p.2, Hodder & Stoughton, London

Expanded Horizons

1. *Modern Britain 1783-1964*, Dennis Richards & J W Hunt, p.123n, Longman's, 1965
2. *Scotland, A New History*, Michael Lynch, pp172, Pimlico, 1991
3. *J Templeton & Co's Magazine*, April 1920
4. SSTY Archives
5-7. Personal Archives of A M M Stephen -- Al Stephen's private diary. [AMMS Archives]

Brothers in Conflict

1-3. *The Glasgow Herald*, 26 Jan 1856 p.4
4-5. *Memoir of JST*
6. AMMS Archives
7. University of Glasgow Archive Services, UGD4/4/1 p.1
8-13. UGD4/4/1 p.9/10
14-15. *Memoir of JST*
16. *The Oxford Dictionary of Quotations*, Revised Edition, p.44 , OUP, 1996, *Marriage & The Single Life*, Francis Bacon, 1561-1626

The Black Sheep

1.   AMMS Archives -- Al's Dairy 1863
2.   UGD4/8/5
3.   AMMS Archives -- Margaret Clark's letter
4.   *St Matthew Gospel*, chXII-v25
5-8.   AMMS Archives -- letter from Samuel
9.   UGD4/8/20
10.   UGD4/8/8
11.   University of Glasgow, Special Collections, *Short Essays*, James Murray Templeton, privately printed, Maclehose, 1887.
12.   UGD4/4/1

An African Adventure

1-2.   UGD4/8/8 AS Scribbling Diary 1866
3-4.   UGD4/4/1
5.   *Livingstone*, Tim Jeal, Yale University Press, 2000

PART TWO 1867-1883

Happy Day

1.   *Stewart of Lovedale*, p.102
2.   AMMS Archives -- Al's diary
3.   *A Century of Carpet Making, 1839-1939*, p.42 Fred H Young, Collins Publishers, Glasgow
4.   UGD4/8/10
5-7.   UGD4/4/2 f.39
8-10.   UGD4/4/2 f.37
11-12.   *Stewart of Lovedale*, p.110

A Death at Sea

1.   John Maggs: Letter from J S Templeton, 17 July 1873
2.   *The Glasgow Encyclopedia*, p.36 Joe Fisher, Mainstream Publishing, 1994
3-4.   John Maggs
5.   UGD4/8/16

6-8.   UGD4/4/2 f.175
9.   *The Glasgow Herald* 15 Jan 1874
10.   UGD4/8/16
11-13.   *Stewart of Lovedale*, p.124
14.   *Kintyre and The Kintyre Club, Historical Sketch of the Peninsular*, Published by the Kintyre Club, 1884

End of an Era

1.   *Dundee Advertiser*, April 1875
2.   AMMS Archives -- Al's Diary
3.   Psalm, XVII v15
4.   UGD4/4/2 f.287
5.   UGD4/4/2 f.247
6-7.   *Daily Mail*, 21 Sept 1875
8.   UGD4/4/2 f.285
9.   UGD4/8/18
10.   *The Oxford Dictionary of Quotations*, OUP, 1996 p.142
            To: - Music, when ... P B Shelley, published 1824
11.   UGD4/4/18
12.   University of Columbia, New York, Thomas Lake Harris Papers, Diary of James Murray Templeton.
13.   *Memoir JST*
14.   UGD4/4/2 f.346
15.   UGD4/4/2 f.291
16.   UGD4/4/2 f.348

Money Worries

1.   UGD4/4/2 f.424
2-3.   James Murray Templeton's Diary
4-5.   UGD4/8/21
6.   UGD4/4/2 f.424
7-10.   AMMS Archives
11.   *Trials of the City of Glasgow Bank Directors*, Edited Wm Wallace, Wm Hodge, 1905
12-13.   *Stewart of Lovedale*, p,213

Duty or Destiny

1-5.	James Murray Templeton's Diary
6.	AMMS Archives -- Al's Diary
7-10.	*Govan Press,* 24 June 1882

Death on the Clyde

1-2.	UGD4/4/3
3.	James Murray Templeton's Diary
4-5.	*The Times,* 4 July 1883
6.	AMMS Archives -- Al's Diary
7.	*North British Daily Mail,* 4 July 1883
8.	*Glasgow News,* 19 September 1883
9-10.	AMMS Archives -- Al's Diary
11.	*Scots Baronial, Mansions & Castle Restorations in the West of Scotland,* Michael C Davis, Spindrift Publishing, Argyll, 1996
12.	*Memoir of JST*

PART THREE 1884-1897

A Clash of Beliefs

1-5.	James Murray Templeton's Diary
6.	*Templetonian,* No 11, July 1926
7-14.	James Murray Templeton's Diary
15.	*The Loretto Register 1825-1964,* T & A Constable, Edinburgh 1966
16.	J Maggs
17-19.	*Memoir of JST*
20.	James Murray Templeton's Diary
21.	*Memoir of JST*
22.	*Short Essays,* J Murray Templeton, privately printed, Maclehose, Glasgow, 1887
23.	*Memoir of JST*
24.	*Short Essays*

Happiness Eludes Him

1.	*Autobiography of a Journalist,* William Stillman, 2 vols.

p.455, The Riverside Co, Cambridge, 1901, Houghton,
Miffin, New York & Boston
2.   *Memoir of JST*
3.   J Maggs
4.   *Templetonian* No:6 Oct 1921
5.   Haddington Local Studies Library, *East Lothian*
            Antiquarian & Field Naturalists' Society, June 1927
6-7.   *The Magazine of Art*, Cassell & Co Ltd, 1891

Death of an Idealist
1.   *Haddington Courier*, 26 Aug 1921
2.   *Haddington Courier*, 6 Jan 1888
3.   Dundee Library, A C Lamb Collection, 218 (46)
4.   *Evening Times*, 27 April 1888
5-6.   *Dundee Advertiser*, 2 May 1888
7.   UGD4/8/30
8.   AMMS Archives -- Al's Diary
9-10.   SSTY Archives

A Terrible Accident
1.   *The Times*, 22 June 1937
2-3.   *The Glasgow Herald*, 2 Nov 1889
4-8.   *The Glasgow Herald*, 4 Nov 1889
9.   *St Matthew's Gospel*, chXXIV, vv42-43
10.   AMMS Archives -- Al's Diary
11.   UGD4/4/7 f.384
12.   UGD4/4/7 f.209

The Loss of a Son
1.   *Memoir of JST*
2-5.   AMMS Archives -- Al's Dairy
6-7.   *Dundee Advertiser*, 8 Sept 1893

Odds and Ends
1-3.   *Templetonian*, No: 39 July 1940
4-5.   *Edinburgh Medical Journal*, Jan-Dec 1952
6.   *Stewart of Lovedale*, p

7.   AMMS Archives -- Al's Diary
8-9.   *Stewart of Lovedale*, p
10.   Odhams Concise English Dictionary

Part Four 1898-1923

A Sad Farewell
1.   AMMS Archives -- Al's Diary
2-3.   AMMS Archives -- Letter
4-7.   *Stewart of Lovedale*, pp.303-306
8.   *Dundee Advertiser*, 20 May 1899
9.   AMMS Archives -- Letter
10.   *Memoir of JST*
11.   *Templetonian*, No 57 1945
12.   *Memoir of JST*

A Church Divided
1-2.   *Glasgow Herald*, 30 August 1904
3.   *Glasgow Herald*, 4 August 1904
4.   Ibid 8 August 1904
5.   *A Layman's Mind on Creed and Church*, pp.7-8, J S
            Templeton, privately printed 1906.
6.   Ibid
7.   SSTY Archives
8.   AMMS Archives
9.   UGD4/3/7
10-11.   AMMS Archives
12.   *Stewart of Lovedale*, p.400
13.   UGD4/3/7
14.   *By God's Grace, A History of Uppingham School*, pp.134-5,
            Bryan Matthew, Whitehall Press Ltd, Maidstone Kent,
            1984

An Uneasy Peace
1.   *Daily Mail*, 9 Jan 1889
2.   Fettes College Year Book
3.   NAS SC36/51/181

The Great War

1-4.	UGD4/3/7
5.	*Glasgow Herald*, 15 July 1914
6.	Glasgow Royal Infirmary,
7-8.	UGD4/3/8
9.	*The Baille*, 2 July 1902
10-11.	The National Archives Kew, WO95/5110
12-13.	NA Kew, WE339/18280
14.	NA Kew, WO339/18280 3a
15-16.	University of Durham, Wingate Papers, 160/1/39
17.	*Memoir of JST*
18.	SSTY Archives

Anglo/American Yachting

1-2.	*J T Co's Magazine*, Feb 1920
3.	UGD4/21/1
4.	*J T & Co's Magazine*, Oct 1921
5-7.	*Haddington Courier*, 2 Sept 1921
8.	*Stirling Journal & Advertiser*, 24 Nov 1921 p.9
9-10.	UGD4/21/1
11.	*Yachting World*, Sept 1922
12-13.	*J T & Co's Magazine*, Oct 1921
14.	*Yachting World*, 1923

PART FIVE 1924-1950

Not the Best of Times

1.	*The Times*, 29 August 1924 p5g
2.	*The Times*, 14 July 1925 p6g
3.	*Templeton Magazine*, July 1925
4.	*Templeton Magazine*, July 1928
5.	*Templetonian*, February 1969
6-10.	*Templetonian*, Autumn 1963

Yachts and Politics

1.	*Yachting World*, May 10 1929
2.	*Glasgow Herald*, 17 June 1931, p.13

3.   *Glasgow Herald*, 19 June 1931, p.11
4.   *Templetonian*, Autumn 1963
5.   *Templetonian*, May 1937
6-7.   Letter to the author from Rev Malcolm Wright, L.Th,
          Minister of Craigrownie Parish Church, 17 Jan 2003
8-11.   Parliamentary Debates, Official Report, Fifth Series,
          Vol 308 (Hansard)

Drift Towards War

1.   James Murray Templeton's Diary
2.   *Malton Messenger*, 19 Feb 1937
3-4.   *The Templetonian*, June 1939
5.   *The Templetonian*, Dec 1939
6.   *The Templetonian*, June 1939
7.   *The Templetonian*, June 1940

Dark Days Again

1.   *The Templetonian*, June 1941
2.   Heather Atkinson Collection
3-5.   *Templeton News-Letter*, Dec 1943
6.   *The Templetonian*, Spring 1964

Fight the Good Fight

1.   *Templeton News-Letter*, Dec 1946
2.   *The Templetonian*, Dec 1947
3.   *The Templetonian*, July 1947
4.   *Yachting World*, April 1948
5.   *Yachting World*, Sept 1948
6.   *The Templetonian*, July 1950
7-8.   *The Templetonian*, Dec 1950
9.   *Stephen of Linthouse*, John L Carvel, printed by
          Robert Maclehose & Co Ltd, Glasgow, 1950

APPENDIX I

s.son; d.daughter; m.married; c. circa

Stephen, Alexander 1795-1875
   s. of William Stephen & Ann Smith
   m. Elspeth, d. of Andrew Murray & Helen Mearns

Issue:
   Elspeth Murray 1824-1916, m. William S Croudace
   William 1826-1893, m. 1st Jane S Henderson
                         m. 2nd Elizabeth Henderson
   Anne Fleming 1827-1909, m. Duncan W Paterson
   James 1828-1864, m. 1st Williamina Grant née Clark
                         m. 2nd Eliza McCorquadale
   Helen 1830-1911, m. Revd John Logan
   Alexander (Al) 1832-1899, m. Mary Templeton
   Andrew 1833-1887, m. Eleanor Stuart
   John 1835-1916, m. Elizabeth Wilson
   Mary 1836-1863, m. John Stewart Templeton
   Elizabeth 1837-1841
   Mary-Ann 1838-1874, m. William Wright
   Hannah 1839-1911, m. William Adams
   Janet 1840-1912
   Marjory Fleming 1841-1863
   Ruth 1842-1843
   Samuel 1844-1874, m. Euphemia M M (Massie) Baxter
   Margaret 1847-1910, m. Robert Mudie
   Williamina 1848-1928, m. Revd Dr James Stewart

Stephen, Andrew 1833-1887
>   s. of Alexander Stephen & Elspeth Murray
>   m. Eleanor Sophia, d. of William Stuart & Ann Maria

Issue:

William Alexander	1869-
Ernest	1872-
Eleanor	1873-
Beatrice	1874-July 1933
Willoughby	1876-1892
Adela	1885-

Stephen, James 1828-1864
>   s. of Alexander Stephen & Elspeth Murray
>   m. 1st Williamina, d. of William Clark & Margaret Stephen
>   2nd Eliza Little, d. of John McCorquadale & Mary Little

Issue:

James Washington	1859-
Robert Little	1861-

APPENDIX II

Adams, Alexander Stephen, 1867-1938
    s. of William Adams & Hannah Stephen
    m.Anne, (Anne) d. of John Chisholm & Isabella Burnett

Issue:
    John Alexander
    Violet

Paterson, Duncan Wilkie 1828-1911
    s. of William Paterson & Stewart Wilkie
    m. Anne Fleming d. of Alexander Stephen & Elspeth Murray

Issue:

    Emily Murray 1855-c1934
    Alexander Stephen 1857-c1898
    Anne Fleming   1859-c1946
    Mary Stuart 1861-c1890
    Jemima Lindsay 1863-c1952
    James Cowan 1965-1943
    Duncan Wilkie 1867-1936

Clarkson, Robert Durward, 1867-1951
    s, of Robert Clarkson & Emily Thomas
    m. Emily Burlton, d. of William Wright & Mary-Ann Stephen

Issue:
    Robert Murray
    Ruth
    Durward
    Emily Mary

APPENDIX III

Stephen, Alexander (Al) 1832-1899
    s. of Alexander Stephen & Elspeth Murray
    m: Mary, d. of James Templeton & Mary Stewart

Issue:

Mary Stuart	1858-1921
Maud [Matilda]	1860-1937
Alexander Edward (Alex)	1861-1942
Frederic John (Fred)	1863-1932
Elspeth Murray	1867-1961
Bernard	1868-1919

Stephen, John 1835-1916
    s. of Alexander Stephen & Elspeth Murray
    m. Elizabeth, d.of John Wilson& Barbara Harvey

Issue:

John Wilson	1867-1869
Elsie Mina	1869-1869
infant son	1870-1870

Stephen, Samuel 1844-1874
    s. of Alexander Stephen & Elspeth Murray
    m. Euphemia Mary Marsley, d. of John Baxter & Frances H
    Gardiner

Issue:

Mabel Alexandra	1874-1945

Davidson, George 1863-
> s. of George Davidson & Mary Birnie Ferguson
> m. 1st Joanna d. of William Black Ferguson & Amelia Smith
> 2nd Mabel Alexandra, d. of Samuel Stephen & Euphemia Baxter

Issue:
> 1stm. Mary Birnie Ferguson   1901-
> 2ndm. Euphemia Mary   1910-

APPENDIX IV

Croudace, William Storey 1821-1894
    s. of John Croudace & Ann Storey
    m.Elspeth Murray, d. of Alexander Stephen & Elspeth Murray

Issue:

John Stephen Croudace	1851-1897
Helen Stephen	c1853-1937
Lawrence	c1855-1886
Blanche	c1857-1953
Elspeth Murray	c1858

Croudace, John Stephen 1851-1897
    s. of William Storey Croudace & Elspeth Murray Stephen
    m. Isabella Jane d. of James Mitchell & Elizabeth Deuchars

Isssue:

    Aime Helen 1883-1924, m.1922 Robert McNaughton
    William Deuchards 1885-
    Patrick Douglas 1889- m. 1918 Georgina Reid
    Gordon Logan 1891-1891
    Dorothy Isobel 1892- m. 1920 Montague J Antel

Luke, David Smith 1849-1908
    s. of James Luke & Mary Laird Smith
    m. Helen Stephen d. of William S Croudace & Elspeth M
    Stephen

Issue:

Elsie Mary	1873-
Hilda	1877-

Moffatt, William Todd 1860-1921
> s. of William Moffat & Margaret Surtees
> m. Elspeth Murray, d. of William S Croudace & Elsepth M
> Stephen

Issue:

Blanche Surtees	1892-
Elsie F	1895-
William M	1896-
Ida H Croudace	1900-

APPENDIX V

Stephen, William 1826-1893
    s. of Alexander Stephen & Elspeth Murray
    m. 1st 1851 Jane Skair, d. of Andrew Henderson & Barbara
    Jarrow
        2nd 1878 Elizabeth, d. of John Henderson & Jane Freer

Issue:

1st m.	Jane	1851-1954
	Anne	1853-1870
	Alice Murray	1854-1916
	Alexander	1859-1860
	Andrew Henderson	1861-1921
	William	1863-1888
	Edith Mary	1865-1891
	Frederick Sommerville	1870-1926
2nd m.	Mary Henderson	c1879-c1960
	Charles John	c1881-1921
	Edward Freer	1882-1954

Thomson, William Gordon 1823-1835
    s. of James Thomson & Mary Gordon
    m. Margaret Catherine, d. of Joseph Milne & Jane Emslie

Issue:

| Alexander Gordon (Alex) | 1854-1899 |

Thomson, Alexander Gordon 1854-1899
    s. of William Gordon Thomson & Margaret C Milne
    m. Alice Murray, d. of William Stephen & Jane Skair
    Henderson

Issue:
>
> Jean Maud Henderson
> William Murray Gordon

Thomson, William Murray Gordon c1877-1913
>
> s. of Alex Gordon Thomson & Alice Murray Stephen
> m. Evelyn Maud, d. of Robert Malcolm & Elizabeth Cuthbert

Grant, Ernest 1977-1956
>
> s. of James Grant & Jane Easton Beatte
> m. Jean Maud Henderson, d. of Alex G Thomson & Alice M Stephen

Issue:

James Alastair Gordon	1904-1933
Alice Maud Gordon	1906-
Edith Easton Gordon	1908-
Ernest Lovat Gordon	1914-

APPENDIX VI

Stephen, Alexander Edward (Alex) 1861-1942
   s. of Al Stephen & Mary Templeton
   m. Daisy, d. of James Young & Agnes Robson

Issue:

Agnes Robson	1893-c1964
Mary Templeton	1895-c1974
Margaret Frew	1896-c1971
Alix Leslie	1970-c1972

Stephen, Frederic John (Fred) 1863-1932
   s. of Al Stephen & Mary Templeton
   m. 1st 1891 Agnes Renton Young, d. of James Young & Agnes Renton
      2nd 1909 Mabel Frew, d. of James Young & Agnes Renton

Issue:
1st m.

Alexander Murray	1892-1974
James Howie Frederic	1894-1917
John Graeme	1894-1974
Agnes Maud	1898-c1989

MacLellan, George Scott 1854-1942
   s. of Walter MacLellan & Margaret Walker
   m. Maud, d. of Al Stephen & Mary Templeton

Issue:

Walter Scott 1885-1959 m. 1914 Cecily C Hicks-Beach
Alexander Stephen 1886-1966 m. 1918 Annie MacKinlay
Elspeth Mary 1887-1930 m. Arthur Lennox Skinner
George Douglas 1890-1917

Gray, Walter Wingate 1856-1931
    s. of Walter Gray & Helen Richardson Wingate
    m. Mary Staurt, d of Al Stephen & Mary Templeton

Issue:

Helen Mary Wingate	1889-
Walter Stuart	1890-
Mary Dorothy	1891-
Alexander George	1894-
Elspeth Maud	1897-

APPENDIX VII

Templeton, Archibald 1765-c1830
 s. of Thomas Templeton & Agnes Colville
 m. Anne, d. of James Harvey (Harvie) & Jean McNair

Issue:
 James 1802-1885, m. Mary Stewart
 Agnes 1804-1894
 Thomas 1806-1871, m. Frances J Lowdes,issue: Elizabeth Mary
 Jean 1809-1864
 Archibald 1811-1896, m. Jane Stewart
 Nathaniel 1812-1896
 Elizabeth 1814-1907
 Ann 1817-1895

Templeton, James, 1802-1885
 s. of Archibald Templeton & Anne Harvey
 m. Mary, d. of John Stewart & Margaret Tod

Issue:
 John Stewart 1832-1918, m.1st Mary Stephen
 Anne 1834-
 Mary 1836-1902, m. Al Stephen
 James 18368-1921
 Agnes Jane 1841-1931
 Archibald 1843-1923, m. Elizabeth H Aitken

Templeton, John Stewart 1832-1918
 s. of James Templeton & Mary Stewart
 1st m.1859 Mary, d. of Alexander Stephen & Elspeth Murray
 2nd m.1877 Emily Jane Fraser, d. of William Campbell &
 Emelia Beach
 3rd m.1885 Maria Zelinda, d. of Charles A Glennie & Leonora F
 Aguiar Andrada

Issue:

     1st m.   James Murray 1860-1892

            Elizabeth Alice 1861-1945, m. D H L Young

            Mary 1862-1863

     3nd m. Mary Caroline Ada (Charry), m. W N Sloan

Daniel Henderson Lusk Young, 1861-1921

     s. of Robert Young & Ann Henderson Lusk

     m. Elspeth Alice, d. of J S Templeton & Mary Stephen

Issue:

     Arthur Stewart 1889-1950, m. Dorothy Spencer

     Eric Templeton 1892-1915

     Anne (Nancy) Templeton 1895-1977, m. E A H Whitcombe

APPENDIX VIII

Templeton, Archibald (Revd Archie) 1843-1923
    s. of James Templeton & Mary Stewart
    m. Elizabeth Helen, d. of Hugh Aitken & Margaret Hutton

Issue:
    Archibald Douglas 1889-1915
    Dorothy Grace 1891 - m. Dr Edward T Wright
    Joanna Marjorie 1894-
    Godfrey Allan 1897-1918
    Kenneth Griffiths 1899-1976 m. Isabella M P Younger
    Anthony Godard 1901- m. Mary Gibson Anderson
    Clement Bennet 1893-1947
    Isabel Nora 1896-
    Constance Hope 1902-

1901 Census, Huntley Terrace, Shettleston, Glasgow.

Edward Wright Head m.	33 Registered Practitioner Medical Missionary	b.Ireland
Annie E [Taylor] wife	38	Ireland
Edward [Taylor]T	8 Scholar	Ireland
Evaline J	6 Scholar	Ireland
Arthur D	4	Ireland*
Edith E	2	Ireland
Herbert S	1	Ireland

* Arthur Dickson Wright 1897-1976, father of Clarissa Dickson Wright

APPENDIX IX

Reid, Peter 1801-1881
    s. of Hugh Reid & Janet Langwill
    m. Margaret, d. of John Stewart & Margaret Tod

Issue:
    Hugh 1833-
    Margaret 1835-
    Jessie 1837-
    John Stewart 1839- Immigrated to New Zealand
    James Robert 1843 m. 1874 Alexanriana Thomson Orr
    Patrick 1841-c1875
    Mary 1845-
    Harry 1847-

Reid, Patrick 1841-c1875
    s. of Robert Reid & Margaret Stewart
    m. 1868 Anna Aenea Rogers, of Hampstead

Issue:
Margaret Anna	1869-
Edith Aenea	1870-
Ernest Stewart	1871-
Francis Patrick	1872-
Frederick James	1874-

NOTE: These Appendices are not meant to be full family trees, but are given only as a guide to who are the main characters. In some cases I do have more information but space dictates how much I can include in this book. If any readers wants to know more they can contact me and I will try to answer their queries.

Maureen Borland.